Call the Midlife

Call the Midlife

TFI Friday vs *Top Gear*
and Other Middle-Aged Dilemmas

• • •

CHRIS EVANS

WEIDENFELD & NICOLSON

791.45092
EVA

First published in Great Britain in 2015
by Weidenfeld & Nicolson

5 7 9 10 8 6 4

A CIP catalogue record for this book
is available from the British Library.

ISBN HB 978 0 297 60982 7
ISBN TPB 978 0 297 60983 4

Printed and bound by CPI Group (UK) Ltd, Croydon, CR0 4YY

Weidenfeld & Nicolson
The Orion Publishing Group Ltd
Carmelite House, 50 Victoria Embankment,
London EC4Y 0DZ
An Hachette UK Company
www.orionbooks.co.uk

The Orion Publishing Group's policy is to use papers that
are natural, renewable and recyclable products and made
from wood grown in sustainable forests. The logging and
manufacturing processes are expected to conform to the
environmental regulations of the country of origin.

To all the mums in the world –
but especially my own,
and Eli's, Noah's and Jade's.

Contents

The Chinese word for crisis
is the same as their word for opportunity.
There is no better example of positive thinking
than this.

Prologue

Bollocks. Bollocks. Bollocks.

I've always wanted to write one of those crystal ball works of fiction that ends up coming true. You know, the ones that make the author look like some kind of prophetic supernatural genius.

And you know what? I was almost there with this book. But then the something I was going to predict might happen after it was published, happened two weeks before I was due to hand in the final manuscript.

Basically I decided I wanted to write a book about turning fifty and the twelve months leading up to whatever that's like and whatever that ends up meaning. This would involve me taking the time to assess where I was at the beginning of that twelve-month period, where I would like to be in, say, ten, fifteen or even twenty years' time, and how I might go about setting off in the right direction to give myself the best chance of succeeding.

It would also have to include detailed and brutally honest self-analysis in certain aspects of my life, training for and competing in the London Marathon IN SECRET, resurrecting my cult Nineties television show *TFI Friday* for a ninety-minute one-off special, plus one other thing that I always swore I would never do.

However, in the final week of preparation for *TFI Friday*, in fact only the day before the show was due to be broadcast live, I received a text that may have changed my life for ever. Certainly for the next three years. It was a text, completely out of the blue, from the Head of Entertainment at BBC Television asking me if I would like to take over *Top Gear*.

That's *Top Gear*, my favourite television show of all time.

The text pinged up on the screen of my battered old BlackBerry at 4.07 p.m. on a Thursday afternoon. It was a question I never even dreamt I would be asked. After Jeremy's shock departure, I honestly thought 'the slow one' and 'the short one' would carry on without him. That's what I wanted to happen. That's what everyone I knew who was a a fan of *Top Gear* wanted to happen. And that's what seemed like the most likely scenario right up until the death. When at the last minute James and Richard informed the BBC that they had decided to take their chances instead and stick with Jeremy. The Three Amigos off in search of a mega-bucks deal with a rival television network.

What followed was the most unpredictable 72 hours that I've ever experienced.

Never in a million years contemplating what the heck would come next did I think *TFI Friday*'s revival would have, could have, been the triumph it turned out to be. And never in a trillion years did I imagine I would end up sitting outside a pub three days later as the news of my *Top Gear* appointment was posted to an unsuspecting world on Twitter.

Nor did I imagine that I would end up in a legal tug-of-war between Channel Four and the BBC which resulted in me writing, producing and presenting both *TFI Friday* and *Top Gear* as well as hosting my daily radio show on Radio 2.

None of the above was in any of my reckoning.

There is no doubt in my mind that writing this book focused me like I have never been focused before. Subconsciously I was gradually positioning myself to be ready for what I sincerely believed was the beginning of the most exciting decade of my life so far. Albeit not quite as immediately as it turned out to be.

But out of everything I did, it's the marathon that had most effect. Training to shuffle around the streets of the capital on that damp, overcast Sunday morning at the end of April 2015 made me realize that huge undertakings are all about preparation, preparation, preparation.

To free up the time and space required for such commitment meant I had no choice but to declutter my life of the distractions and nonsense that I'd allowed to build up around me. Training for a marathon, especially if you've never done it before, is the definitive SuperSorter. The ultimate masterclass in how to formulate a strategy, employ the right tactics and execute the plan to achieve one's goal.

The rules are simple: if you commit to the weekly regime – you will make it round; if you commit to most of the weekly regime but not all – you will make it round; if you commit to half the weekly regime – you will still probably make it round . . . but anything less and you might as well not bother.

As well as the basic training involving a variety of runs – long, short, recovery, hills, fast, marathon pace, tempo and gentle slow jogs – proper consideration to sleep, complementary cross-training, the right gear and, most important of all, the correct nutrition and hydration is also mandatory. All of which being vital on the day taught me a lesson I will never forget.

When you stack the cards so much in your favour off the field, it's almost impossible not to pull off a victory on the field. This is how battles are won.

Completing a marathon also changes other people's perception of you way beyond anything you might allow yourself to imagine. Everyone instinctively knows that running 26.2 miles from never having really run at all requires immense dedication and determination. They can see that you look and feel different, that you've become much stronger, both physically and mentally; they can sense that your capacity to cope with and therefore enjoy life has become probably more infectious.

I ended up feeling more like the person I hoped I always was but feared I may have lost touch with forever.

If you have never run a marathon you really absolutely, definitely must. Walk one, or hop one, or wheelchair one; whatever way you can, just do it. The whole experience will leave you no choice but to prioritize what is important in your life. It will give you a reason and a deadline, the two things all human beings need to do ANYTHING.

PART 1

My Early Stab at
the Male Menopause

Top Ten Buckets List:

10 Wooden milk-maid's bucket.
 9 Builder's bucket.
 8 Sandcastle bucket.
 7 JCB bucket.
 6 Bronze ceremonial situla.
 5 Plastic wheelie mop bucket with wringer.
 4 Galvanized round bucket with rope handles.
 3 Galvanized pail.
 2 Galvanized mop bucket.
 1 Ice bucket.

I was an early developer when it came to the symptoms of a midlife crisis, displaying some of the more obvious clichés at least ten years earlier than might usually be expected. At around the age of thirty-two my very public male menopausal hyperactivity was plain for all to see. Especially when it came to girls and cars and the vicarious paranoia of not knowing who I really was and where I was really at.

I was also suffering from the masochistic self-doubt and over-analysis that can send a person nuts. Perhaps this is why I was able to recognize the gathering clouds of similar happenings so clearly second time around. Perhaps that's why I found myself whispering under my breath – oh no you don't, not this time – we've been here before and we're not going through all that nonsense again.

That said, my own initial experience of the insane desire to rip my life apart amidst the backdrop of wandering around a daily hinterland of confusion and self-loathing was more of a mid-career crisis than anything else. Or to put it even more accurately, a mid-success crisis, the don't-look-down-whatever-you do-syndrome.

I often ask my six-year-old son Noah how his day has been during the homeward school run each night, a question he frequently struggles to provide an answer to. I used to think this was because he was being lazy when it came to recalling the events of a few hours earlier. Over time, however, I could see it was something he really had an issue with, like I was suddenly asking him to speak a foreign language. This is because kids never 'look down'. They live totally in the now, with perhaps a light dusting of the future, but as for the past – recent or otherwise – forget it.

My God, how is it then, as we get older, we become increasingly prone to tying ourselves up in the kind of knots that render us incapable of seeing the world for what it is and what it always has been: a plethora of joy and opportunity out there for us to enjoy and make the most of every day? How do we become so deaf, dumb and blind to what a gift this all is? How do we see it instead as some kind of troublesome chore that's stopping us from doing whatever it is we're really here for?

Obviously life gradually sends you mad, that much we know. What we have to do is try to recognize this and not be tempted to rail against it. Our biggest mistake is to assume we have a divine right to be better at the tough stuff the more tough stuff we experience. The reality is nothing of the sort. Kids don't try to tame life because they don't see the need, just as our elders no longer try because they know there is no point. The impasse we find ourselves in is the rite of passage from one state of mind to the next. So transparent on either side, so fuzzy in the middle.

That's how come we turn into some kind of befuddled, insane Looney Tune for several years. An ill-thought-through cartoon character everyone around us is forced to put up with until we finally come out, battered and bruised, barely able to remember why and how all this self-doubt started in the first place.

If we make it through in one piece, that is.

This period of turmoil is simply too much for some poor souls to endure; the experience changes them beyond the point of no return, rendering re-entry to their old lives impossible. It is their destiny to be lost forever in a new world order of their own design: a new partner that's younger and firmer but little else, a new wardrobe that is too tight and bright for them but no one likes to say, a new fitness regime that sucks all the personality out of them, leaving them looking more saggy than sexy.

Sure, taking time to regroup for the betterment of one's future is a very wise use of one's time, but it has to start from the point of self-congratulation as opposed to self-flagellation. Before we set about worrying what we haven't got and how to go get it, we need to take a beat and reflect on what we have got and how to keep it.

In order to do this, maintenance is the key. Beginning with as high and wide a vantage point as possible from which to have a good look around and make some decent notes. Trying to skip this maintenance stage and move on is like abandoning a risotto and expecting it to stir itself: it just ain't going to happen.

This 'steady as she goes' approach will help head off midlife clichés like the dreaded bucket list. The separated-at-birth, long-lost twin of the midlife crisis, said to have first appeared in the book *Unfair & Unbalanced: The Lunatic Magniloquence of Henry E. Panky* by Patrick M. Carlisle. Text reads thus:

> So, anyway, a Great Man, in his querulous twilight years, who doesn't *want* to go gently into that blacky black night. He wants to cut loose, dance on the razor's edge, pry off the lid of his bucket list!

Since then the phrase has enjoyed an exponentially stratospheric rise to fame and universal annoyance in equal measure. There are now millions of bucket lists that have been published in print and online to terrorize the world into various frenzies of tail-chasing 'before it's too late'.

Ride a Harley across America. Yawn.

Sky dive. Double yawn.

Get a tattoo. Triple yawn.

Have a threesome. All right, fair enough.

The thing about bucket lists *per se* is not what's on them. Indeed, any of the above is perfectly acceptable and enjoyable as 'a thing to do'. Just not as part of some synthetic emotional rollercoaster ride drawn up as an admission of what you might so far have missed out on.

I recently appeared on a TV show where they were discussing the ultimate Brit's bucket list. I was one of several guests who was asked to add up how many experiences on the list they could already tick off.

One guest claimed not to have done any, which I found plain weird. Another said she'd done three. And someone else said they'd done seven. When it came to me, my answer was twenty-seven. Not that I am particularly adventurous. Perhaps it's the opposite, perhaps I'm entirely predictable and have already been overcompensating in a major midlife way. But I'd like to think I'd come across them more as a matter of course.

I don't know why I have a beef about things like this. I think it's the same apathetic insincerity I hate about beach holidays. I mean it's OK to lie in the sun, fading in and out of consciousness while listening to the waves gently lap against the shore for an hour or maybe two – but for a whole day, week or fortnight? What are they slipping into these guys' mojitos – benzodiazepine and Night Nurse?

And as or fulfilling our lifelong dreams and ambitions in our midlife years, careful and respectful attention must be paid to what we really yearn for in the first place. For years, I 'thought' I'd like to move to Italy one day. But proper Italy, far away from the madding crowd, where they only spoke Italian, the days were long and the sun was high. Until myself and my girlfriend visited Brindisi in Puglia, which was exactly that. After three days, not only was I as red as a beetroot but we were desperate for our creature comforts, except the locals didn't speak a word of English. This meant they became more humpy with us the more we tried to explain ourselves, and we became more grumpy with them the less they understood anything we were saying. A simple lesson in the reality of fantasy that taught me it wasn't Italy we liked, it was Italian restaurants in London that we could walk to.

Ergo, far more fulfilling than an ill-thought-through and embarrassingly predictable bucket list is an all guns-blazing, blood-and-thunder, fuck-it list. A list of brilliant things already in the bag. The mere thought of which should be enough to keep us smiling from ear to ear for the rest of our lives, regardless of what else society attempts to brainwash us into thinking might be a good idea.

I'm forty-nine years old. My thirties rocked, my forties were a mixed bag of calming down, realizing the magnificence of parenthood and becoming a safe pair of hands at the BBC. As far as I can figure I'll be pretty much spent at seventy-five. I will probably be able to do most of the things I can now and still want to do until at least sixty-five.

And so it was with this in mind that I decided to embark upon the notion of giving myself one hundred straight days to set up the rest of this party called life. One hundred days dedicated to the planning of the next six thousand or so. That seems like a worthwhile thing to do, don't you think?

Hence *Call the Midlife*.

Notwithstanding gross misfortune, our fifties should be our golden age. When we can still physically do pretty much whatever takes our fancy. Mentally we are streets ahead of where we've ever been. We also have more influence, more sway; we know more people who are useful to us and us to them. Even the odd tinge of wisdom begins to creep in. Oh, what joy there is with each new slice of self-realization. Self-acceptance. Self-awareness. Self-understanding.

We have finally begun to be able to discern what's important and what's a waste of time. With every passing day, time itself nudges its way closer to the top of the 'most wanted' list. We know who the friends we should be making more of are, and those we should be cutting loose – both for their sake and ours.

But of course there is an issue. Even though I am fully aware of all of the above, as we all are, none of us have the first clue as to how to go about delivering the half-time team-talk to ourselves that we could so crucially benefit from. The right combination of words and encouragement that will have us bouncing out back on to the pitch, gagging for more.

We almost certainly have fewer summers and Christmases left than those we've already seen but we have the wherewithall to make them fuller, more rewarding and more memorable than any that have gone before.

Add so began my quest for received wisdom. First, by knocking on the doors of a group of life's illuminati I believed could tell us midlifers some of the more high-priority things we need to know. Anyone who might be able to help us improve our chances of identifying the most advantageous course to follow in this most priceless quarter of a century or so we have left.

We are the children of the technological revolution whose mums and dads stood up to the Nazis so we could be free to listen to The Beatles, get stoned in the company of *Dark Side of the Moon* and watch Noel Edmonds on *Deal or No Deal* every day.

Therefore we owe it to them at least to show we are not going to allow our middle-age optimism and enthusiasm to be thwarted by that infuriating phrase, MIDLIFE CRISIS, every time we tinker and make a change for the better.

Comrades, it is our duty – indeed it is our calling – to declare to the world that our proactive decisions are ours and ours alone. And that we do not need to shag our secretary, our boss, or our best mate's missus to feel better about ourselves.

'Midlife Crisis' is a phrase we've been lumbered with long enough. Ever since its appearance in a magazine article published in New York one weekend back in 1967, penned by a journalist who I can only imagine was stuck for an idea. I can hear him now: 'What are they thinking, what are they doing? Why are they so pathetic as to feel they so desperately and embarrassiningly need to try to reignite the cold and sad ashes of their youth to make up for the fact they can't deal with thinking they are now OLD?'

This wasn't *our* midlife crisis he was talking about. It was his. Before this article, no one had ever suffered a 'Midlife Crisis' because the term didn't exist. I shall write it, therefore it shall be. Just two words, but two words that forty-eight years on continue to blight perfectly reasonable and justifiable aspirations of hundreds of millions of wholly decent, energetic, forward-thinking, forward-looking, thirtysomethings, fortysomethings, fiftysomethings and beyond.

Generation after generation, we have been tarnished by his apathetic excuse for his own lack of brio, and hoodwinked into asking ourselves 'Why should we?' instead of 'Why shouldn't we?'

Except, I suppose, without his monochrome negativity, lethargy, pessimism and all-round gloomy funk I would never have had reason to write this book.

And you know, that's the thing with losers, if we listen to what they're really saying, they push us to a better place.

Always.

Panic Attack

A midlife moment of reflection can be sparked off by anything. The death of a friend. A change in work circumstances. The breakdown of a long-term relationship. Going to see a band we used to like when we were younger but haven't seen for ages. A particular film. Becoming a grandparent. Taking a long drive alone. Looking in the mirror. Standing on the scales. Having an accident. Even peeking through the curtains one morning in a particularly vulnerable state of mind and seeing the grass only as something that's going to need cutting as opposed to something alive, lush and beautiful.

All of the above are tremours of panic. But good panic. Panic that is there to help us. Our internal alarm clock telling us it's time to take stock and make a gravy.

Panic therefore in many ways instantly means – DON'T PANIC!

Panic having already done its job.

Thank you, Panic.

We owe you.

If we continue to panic thereafter, this is merely our choice. Breathing is by far the preferred option. To continue to panic will lead to haste that will in turn lead to the great myth that doing anything but nothing is the way forward. Because nothing is the one thing we don't have time for.

Wrong!

Unnecessary panic is born out of time claustrophobia. To stop panicking, here's what I do.

Think about what's past. Anything. You as a kid being brilliant or happy or sad. Your eighteenth birthday. Passing your driving test. Remind yourself who you are and that the past is forever calm.

Allow it to bring you back to today. On your own terms.

The future loves to take us hostage. But if we don't unlock the door and allow it in, it's stuffed. We NEVER have to succumb to the future because it will NEVER arrive.

Breathe, listen, relax.

We are HERE, it is NOW. That is our greatest gift. Add to this all you have seen and learnt and consider yourself to be the go-to expert on you.

As we grow older but not old, never old, we have the great advantage of no longer having to think – about anything. We know so much already, all we have to do from now on is to give ourselves the chance to listen. All the problems the universe likes to throw at us are no match for the experience we now possess. They are random and disorganized whereas we are sophisticated ultra-intelligent super computers. We are ready for anything. We are International Rescue.

Midlife – the chance to understand who we are and what we are truly capable of.

We are the Harlem Globetrotters. We take on all-comers knowing we can run rings around them just for fun. We are better than we ever have been. It's time to show the world and ourselves just what we can do.

Health

Top Ten Near-Death Issues
I've Experienced so Far in Life:

10 Broken finger.
 9 Broken nose.
 8 Broken wrist.
 7 Broken ankle.
 6 Broken ribs.
 5 Stitches to left elbow.
 4 Stitches to forehead.
 3 Rhinitis.
 2 Getting shot at.
 1 Polyps in colon.

It was only when I wrote this Top Ten that I realized just how lucky I've been with regard to serious illness.

With the exception of number one and number two, it seems I've never really been in mortal danger, which is quite something considering the way I've abused my body and brain over the last few decades.

Like most blokes, I have been an acute sufferer of white-coat-phobia most of my life, until my unforgettable bright-red-paint-poo moment. Since which I have become a changed man.

Now, if it's a medical issue and I can be tested for it, count me in: bring on those syringes, I'm your guy. And the more likely it is to kill me, the keener I am to find out about it sooner rather than later. There isn't an examination in the world I wouldn't sign up for today if I thought it might do me some lasting good.

So when was the epiphany?

As I've already alluded to, mine came not so much out of the blue, as out of the loo.

T'was a Monday afternoon and the only person home was me. There I was, having a relaxing afternoon flicking through car magazines in the front room of our crumbling old ruin of a house. A house which local folklore claimed had originally been commissioned as a hunting lodge by King Charles II. A regal base from which to enjoy the sport of his newly constructed game reserve at Virginia Water, as well as, it is rumoured, doubling up as a love nest for His Majesty to enjoy some secret tiffin. And general pleasures of the flesh with his long-term mistress, Nell Gwyn.

Easy now, Sire!

All very clandestine and cloak-and-dagger, but whatever had or had not happened there in the past, I was about to experience my own dramatic chapter written within its legendary walls.

The call of nature having beckoned, I thought I was in for an entirely run-of-the-mill five to ten minutes of throne time. Off I scooted from the kitchen, through the hallway, first on the right, just beyond the large framed black-and-white photographs of John McEnroe, Michael Caine and James Hunt. My three wise men of cool and inspiration.

Once ensconced in our downstairs lavatory, I sat a while, as one does, a little longer than necessary perhaps. Thanks this time to a particularly compelling back issue of *Auto Italia*, featuring a rather lovely piece of artisan Carrozzeria on the front cover. All's well that ends well, however – or at least that's what I thought. Ten or fifteen minutes later, with the inevitable sense that haemorrhoids were becoming an ever more likely side effect of my ill-advised straining, I reluctantly began to finish up.

It was while completing this process that I glanced down into the pan, only to wonder exactly what the rather beautiful rich cloud of ruby red liquid floating in the water was all about.

That couldn't be blood, could it?

And then, after a few seconds of initial shock and continued examination. I had to admit to myself, it was indeed blood, undoubtedly blood. And what's more, undoubtedly my blood.

But there was almost too much to comprehend, like someone was trying to play a joke but had blown it by going over the top with the density and colour.

What was this? What was going on? Sure, I'd experienced spits and spots of blood before, many people have, even the odd wisp of thin red cloud, but nothing compared to this. This was too much, surely?

Plus, it wasn't as if I'd experienced any such spits or spots recently, to serve as some kind of warning that a more serious issue may be afoot. But yes, it was definitely blood. And the closer and longer I looked, the more of it there seemed to be. As if it was intent of leaving me in no doubt.

There was obviously something wrong. How wrong, I had no idea. But easily wrong enough to shock me into action.

What I did next still surprises me to this day.

I calmly finished up, flushed the toilet, and walked purposefully back into the kitchen. I then picked up the house phone and proceeded to dial my assistant's number, one of only six I can remember by heart. I never use the house phone as a rule, but I wanted to make the call as quickly and as clearly as possible.

'Hi, Hiten.'

This was the moment I'd been dreading all my life, and now it had arrived. Finally – thirty-four years finally to be precise. Thirty-four years, the length of time that had elapsed since my dad died of bowel cancer.

'Hi, what's up?' We usually text, email or chat face to face. We hardly ever call and talk. 'I need an appointment with Dr Ed as soon as possible. Any time at all from now, whenever she can see me soonest.'

Getting the same thing and dying the same horrible death as he did had been scaring the shit out of me for most of my adult life. And now here I was, facing the weird irony that the very shit in question may well have just saved my life.

Not only did bowel cancer see off my dad, it claimed both his brothers too. Ronnie went first, Dad second and my lovely Uncle

Bill third. They died in order of their age, picked off one by one by a ruthless assassin at the top of his game. Infuriating, to say the least, especially as now I am aware that bowel cancer is one of the most curable cancers currently known to mankind.

EARLY DETECTION IS EVERYTHING.

You could therefore be forgiven for thinking that those of us in the high-risk categories would have to be raving lunatics not to take heed of this. Surprisingly, millions of allegedly entirely sane people do exactly that. They are of course considered moronic idiots by the medical profession and quite rightly, even though for years I was one of them. I had never yet been tested for any cancer in any way.

But when I saw all that blood, it was as if a switch had flicked inside of me. A switch I didn't even know existed. A switch that had evolved over all those years of worry and woe 'in case of emergency'. A switch that had secretly been on permanent standby to launch me to battle stations should there be even the faintest whiff of a genuine red alert.

Well, it didn't get any redder than this.

It was spooky and bizarre at the same time, but the most unexpected sensation was that of relief. Relief that I could finally confront this spectre, deal with it, hopefully get rid of it and move on with the rest of my friggin' life. A life I can now see one aspect of which had been on permanent hold ever since I was thirteen.

It was a genuine 'thank God' moment.

My nightmare scenario at last, thrust upon me to HAVE TO DEAL WITH. All those sleepless nights asking myself, 'Would I want to know if the worst came to the worst?'

Well, now here I was, my answer a deafening:

'YES I BLOODY WELL WOULD!!!'

In fact I'd never been more certain of anything in my life.

A few rings later and my doc was on the line: she instructed me to come see her at the first available opportunity. She would make time whenever.

I knew a few hours wouldn't make any difference, regardless of what might be lurking in my backside, so I made an appointment to see her first thing the following morning after my radio show. I told her what had happened, whereupon without even examining me she referred me to undergo a colonoscopy.

'It's the best way to see what's going on and what might need to be done. Go this afternoon, I've already called my oncologist consultant friend who says he can see you at 1 p.m.'

A couple of hours later it was time to lube up, close my eyes and welcome a camera probe up my rectum and on to wherever it needed to go. And yet again, there I was, feeling more liberated than agitated, more prepared than scared, more intrigued than squeamish. The beginning of a new me.

The new me that had finally discovered the kahunas to tell the school bully where to shove it, while receiving a rapturous round of applause from myself to myself. In stark contrast to a few years before when I would have more likely been a shaking, quaking mess of pathetic self-pity, running to the pub, sobbing in my drink for a miracle, rather than embracing reality, sobriety and a perfectly sensible solution.

Somewhere inside me, deep in my psyche perhaps, a quantum shift had obviously taken place, clearly for the better. Whether it was to do with having my young sons Noah and Eli and making up with my daughter Jade, and them – instead of me – now shouldering the shared responsibility of our lineage, I don't know. Or maybe it was the opposite, maybe it was more to do with the fact that, because of their existence, I now had something more tangible than my nebulous self to stick around for. Or maybe it was simply because I was a lot happier than I used to be and I would dearly like a bit more of the same please.

And all this 'heroism' without telling anyone other than my assistant.

No fuss, no playing the victim and soaking up as much sympathy as I could elicit. I just got on with it. For the first time in my life I felt totally in control of a situation – grown-up almost.

Choosing to go to have a test which might tell me I was no longer for this earth, instead of just doing nothing and hoping everything was going to be OK, had opened a box inside me that had been closed for a very long time. A box that held the answer to my own big personal 'why?', a box I had always known existed but which was too scary to contemplate, let alone take a peek inside.

The same box that I greatly suspected of being the drive behind my intermittent yet never-ending carousel of must do, must get on, must everything, nonsense. Heart attack material.

Since getting back in contact with my daughter Jade and having two new young sons, the lead weight of a lifetime of 'why?' had begun to lighten. But it hadn't vanished completely, still weighing heavy enough to cause the permanent dull ache and distant nagging from the demon of unfinished business.

Until now. Until my own mortality challenged me to a staring competition. So far, so good, there was no way I was going to blink first.

My appointment with my own thirty-odd years of lost property had popped up out of nowhere for me to confront. And though I realize this may all sound very wise and convenient 'after the fact', I cannot put into words how much of an awakening it became.

'OK, what we're going to do is go in with our camera,' announced the consultant, a cross between James Bond and Indiana Jones's older, more intelligent brother.

'Then once we're in, we'll have a thorough look around and if we find any nasties we'll snip 'em out there and then and send the little buggers off for a biopsy. OK?'

Already lying on my side with my bare bum exposed to two nurses, an anaesthetist who was standing by to put me under and this besuited superman, it's not as if I was about to say no.

'Sure,' I squeaked unconvincingly, 'go ahead.'

Which is exactly what they proceeded to do.

Fast-forward no more than ten or fifteen seconds later and off I was floating somewhere up in the sky between Central London and the ionosphere. Unable to give two shakes of a donkey's tail what they were about to find or not find.

As I came to with no idea whatsoever of how long I'd been out – although I've since been told it was no more than twenty-five minutes – there was the same handsomely lined, tanned face of the consultant looming over me once more. If this friendly smiling gentleman was about to tell me I was going to croak, at least it would be with exemplary bedside manners and a reassuring British tone.

Again I felt strangely calm with regards to any potentially unwelcome news. What was bothering me much more was the throbbing erection I seemed to have acquired at sometime during the 'procedure'.

'Ah, Mr Evans, don't worry about what's going on down there. It happens all the time – as does the fruity banter you were entering into with the nurses.'

What?

'All you need concern yourself with is the fact that you did the right thing in coming to see us because we located two polyps. One quite large and the other one not so. Anyway, we've snipped them out and that usually does the job. But we're duty bound to send them off for a biopsy so that's what we've done. We'll see what happens from there. So far, however, so good.'

Don't you just love medical professionals when they tell you everything's all right? Even if it's only 'for now'.

I was on a golf course a few days later when Indiana Bond rang me with the biopsy results.

As his number came up I excused myself from the order of play, again my cancer-mode calm surprising myself. This isn't exactly what he said but it's exactly what I heard.

'I'm delighted to say your polyps biopsy came back ALL CLEAR.'

Wow, what a message! People who have experienced this will tell anyone who hasn't that hearing those words CHANGES YOUR LIFE ON THE SPOT.

By far the best message I have ever received.

I discovered subsequently that polyps are the chandeliers which cancer needs to hang on to so it can then set about growing in your colon and killing you. Without the polyps, cancer is a monkey with no arms, it has nowhere to cling to and nothing to cling on with. Get rid of these little polyp fuckers and cancer's party is yours to ruin.

The saddest and maddest thing is that if my dad and both my uncles had been able to benefit from this same procedure circa 1980, there's copious evidence to suggest they would still be around today.

And there I was, that was me done, completely cured. And not only of troublesome polyp syndrome but also, as an added bonus, no longer hostage to my thus far self-imposed life sentence of 'don't tell me, I'd rather not know' syndrome.

Completely hypocritically, the phrase 'I'd rather not know' now makes my blood boil and causes me to spontaneously spit bullets of ire. 'I'd rather not know' is one of life's great non-phrases. Because not knowing is NOT AN OPTION.

Eventually you will know one way or another, come what may, whether you want to or not. It's just a question of whether you will know *in time*. Whether you will still have a chance of doing *anything to save your own life*. Or whether you will have no choice but to succumb to a HORRIBLE, shitty, DEGRADING, long, SLOW and utterly miserable DEATH.

Like my poor old dad did. HIDEOUS and HUMILIATING.

He withered and wilted and disappeared in front of our constantly crying eyes: day by day, inch by inch, breath by breath.

Martin Joseph Evans – once a stout and sturdy jocular man who wanted little else but to survive the war, marry his childhood sweetheart and then give his family everything he possibly could. A man who ended his days ebbing, wasting, and fading away until there was nothing left of him. Eaten away from the inside out, a hale and hearty fifteen-stone force of nature eventually reduced to a pitiful six-and-a-half stone of dead and decaying skin and bone.

And of course death to one brings pain to many. The way Dad died devastated me and still does to this day. It also completely fucked me up for years to come, much more than I realized for a long time.

So please allow me to reiterate: when it comes to detecting any potentially fatal disease, the phrase 'I'd rather not know' should not be anywhere on your radar. You will get to know eventually and you will definitely wish you'd done something to get to know sooner.

There are thousands of people, millions of hours and billions of pounds of research, development, equipment and treatments, waiting to save you from yourself.

The very least you can do is what little it takes to help them work their magic.

As you have probably gathered by now, I have become an annoying and committed don't-fear-the-check-up convert. An evangelical reborn pain in the arse, following my own very real and bloody message from the arse – and I offer no apologies for being so.

But here's the thing: once I had seen the fire of my life light up again in front of me, burning brighter than ever, I became intent on embracing every single second of whatever time I might have left.

I made a promise to myself that I would set aside a serious chunk of time to figure out how to squeeze every single drop of JOY, EXCITEMENT, LOVE and FASCINATION out of anything, everything and anyone whom I come into contact with.

One day life will kill us.

The sooner we accept that the better.

And then suddenly there is so much of life to think about.

How about that phrase we often hear in old movies when a bespectacled crotchety doctor informs a soon-to-be-deceased unfortunate, 'It is with great regret that I must inform you it would be most remiss of me if I did not advise you to get your affairs in order.'

Well, why wait until then?

We're all in the same boat from the moment we're born. Let's stop fannying around, get our affairs in order now, and free ourselves up to roar like never before.

The Doc

Top Ten Bits We Need to Worry About Post-Forty Years:

10 Bladder.
9 Skin.
8 Lungs.
7 Teeth.
6 Cells.
5 Brain.
4 Heart.
3 Muscles.
2 Bones.
1 Joints.

My doc's name is Edwina but she always abbreviates it to Ed, which makes most people that haven't seen her presume she's a man. Because the world's like that. I'm sure it's a gaffe she encourages so she can toy with the consequences.

She also asked me specifically to include how old she was if I were to include her in the book.

'I can't stand any of that "never ask a woman her age" nonsense.'

So, she's fifty-nine and will be sixty a month after I notch up my own half-century on 1 April 2016.

Maybe she wanted me to include her age because she doesn't look anything like fifty-nine. Forty more like. She also happens to be beautiful. In a very Mrs Robinson way, but a bit more aloof and untouchable, like a work of art.

She's tall and strong with a handsome face, big brown eyes, deep and sparkling, a strong nose, her lips almost criminally alluring. Totally hypnotic. Luscious shiny waves of dark brown hair, tinged with vapour trails of grey. Even her fingers are spectacular.

'What can I help you with today, Mr Evans, another steroid shot for your myriad allergies?'

I am the most hysterically allergic person she has ever tested. I suffer from *seven* different pollen allergies alone.

'No thanks, I'm fine on the hay fever front at the moment. I am here instead on behalf of the nation's – who knows, world's – midlifers.'

'Ooh, intriguing. Pray, do tell.'

I explain that I want to know about age-specific health issues for us folks somewhere in the range of forty to seventy. (The more I have researched and thought about this book, the more I have come to the conclusion that the midlife spread is wider than it's ever been – in a very good way.)

'Ahhh, hang on a moment.' She presses a wonderfully clunky button on the vintage grey-and-white intercom machine in front of her. A small red light illuminates. 'Mrs Lewis, see if Dr T can take my eleven o'clock. Mr Evans is here for a bit of digging.'

Right, that's it, I was in.

'As I see it, we are faced with an increasingly worrying, incalculable and unanswerable problem,' says Dr Ed. 'In as much as we are keeping people alive for much longer than is good for either them or the rest of the world. Yet no one has the balls to ask why. Furthermore I suggest we would be much better off letting nature take its course a little more.

'Dinner parties aren't better for going on later, they're better for being more fun, or more engaging or more stimulating. Films can become interminable if they start to drag, as can those dreadful best man's speeches. I find holidays too wretched if they go on too long. Why should life be any different? Surely, ninety is the absolute tops we should be aiming at. After that, unless nature dictates otherwise, everyone but the Queen and the Pope should be put out to grass and have done with it.'

That's why Dr Ed's ten health issues that over-forties should be worrying about (see page 25) has a top three many of us might not have expected.

'The thing about my "top three", as you like to refer to them – your joints, bones and muscles – is that they may not be directly life-threatening but they very much dictate the quality of your life while you are still here. The vast majority of people spend their whole time faffing around worrying about the things that might kill them – none of which matter if you can't have a decent time while you still have oxygen in your lungs and your wits about you.

'If you are able to still move, you'll be amazed how that will continue to help maintain your health. Stretching, exercise, massages, saunas and steams. Lots and lots of water. Greens, fish, meat. And the crossword and reading to keep the old grey matter ticking over.'

What's the *number one* thing we can do to improve our health?

'Oh that's easy. Choose your parents well. Ha ha! Good, strong, healthy parentage is the golden ticket when it comes to the school of preventative medicine.' She's now guffawing.

'Good genes are second only to luck in the superhuman stakes. Some people do everything wrong and nothing right, yet still manage to outlive the rest of us. Entirely unfair, but then again like so much in life. Bad luck makes good people better. Good luck makes bad people even more of a pain in the backside.'

Thirty to fifty are our golden years in health terms, according to Ed. The time when time itself and our maturing years have least influence on our aches, pains and unmentionables.

'Thirty-five can be a bit iffy on the gout and testicles front, but other than that you're pretty much clear. Approaching your half-century, beware of shingles and dreaded blood pressure – that's a killer waiting to happen. Stress is a huge factor, although exactly why, nobody really knows.

'Also, do anything and everything you can not to get fat. Imagine you're a Morris Minor and then one day someone comes along and sticks the body of a double-decker bus on your chassis. That's what happens when we start to pile on the pounds. Same engine, same fuel tank, same suspension and yet somehow we're surprised when we begin to break down. Sometimes we humans and our lack of logic completely bamboozles me.'

Dr Ed doesn't do fat.

'Fatness leads to lethargy which leads to immobility, which leads to more fat, more lethargy and eventually seizure, which is the beginning of the end. Not to mention diabetes, which can be horrible and costs the Treasury billions every year in health care.

'Use it or lose it is the key thing to remember as we get older with all things physical and mental. This is so important. Especially when it comes to your muscles and your brain, which of course is a muscle anyway. As you get older you need to keep moving, which means you need to move more in the first place. Your whole life in fact. Just don't ever stop. It's much easier to stay fit than get fit, to maintain rather than rebuild.'

Dr Ed pauses for a moment and plucks at her bottom lip with one of those long fingers of hers.

'What else is really important?' she muses.

And then she *screams*:

'Oh yes: DON'T BLOODY RETIRE! Whatever you do – DO NOT RETIRE! Unless you absolutely have to or absolutely want to – and you have to be so sure that you want to. Certainly don't retire because you think you should. So many of my friends in the medical profession have retired and literally fallen off their perch a few months later.'

She cackles and then checks herself.

'Well, actually it is OK to retire as long as one doesn't stop being interested and engaged in oneself, the people around and the world in general. But we must always retain a getting-up-and-going-to-bed schedule. This is vital for keeping a shape to our lives. Decide on a healthy regime and make a promise to yourself to stick to it. Do not let it become a choice. And if you do miss an alarm, or press the snooze button once too often, fine yourself in some way. There has to be a consequence to everything we do. When that stops being the case, things begin to go seriously off track.'

What about all the dreaded cancers?

'Catching cancer early is the absolute name of the game. More people now survive cancer than don't, but I cannot over-emphasize how important early diagnosis is. You are crazy if you don't get checked for any cancers you may be particularly vulnerable to. On a regular basis. Or, should you suspect anything in the slightest untoward. The only fear one need have is the fear of doing nothing.'

Pause.

And the cue:

Another glorious outburst.

'And don't accept ANYTHING that leaves you feeling unsure or uneasy in the slightest.'

What does she mean exactly?

'What I mean is when things start to creak and threaten to drop off or break down or show signs of wear and tear, if you can, get them fixed immediately. Or at least die trying. DO NOT TAKE NO FOR AN ANSWER from yourself or anyone else unless you absolutely have no choice in the matter. And even then I'm not quite so sure.'

Can we drink?

'A little, yes. More than a little I cannot condone. Not that I don't indulge myself. I do and I love it, one of life's great pleasures as far as I'm concerned. If you want to put a figure on it, I can only officially sanction a glass (or two at absolute most) of wine a day. This has been proven to be good for the heart and head when it comes to reducing levels of stress and anxiety. More than that though and you're on your own.'

Thanks Doc.

'Next!'

Drinking

Top Ten Questions Most Likely to Drive You Mad If You Keep Thinking About Them Too Much:

10 Who am I?

9 Where are am I?

8 How did I get where I am now?

7 Is it where I want to be?

6 Is it where I thought I'd be?

5 What do I have that I really want?

4 How do I get rid of what I don't want?

3 Who do I love?

2 Who do I like?

1 Do I like me?

There are more questions than answers.

Wrong!

There are more answers than questions. Answers are reactive whereas questions are proactive, which means they are more original and therefore more difficult or effortful and burdensome to think up.

That said, I love questions. I wander around all day, every day, wondering out loud what, why, when, where, how, how come. Questioning things makes me feel at peace because it's indirectly telling me I'm giving my life the time and space it needs to breathe. When I'm too busy or too distracted I never question anything.

Constantly questioning things is also the reason I have trouble getting through books. Or even getting through a single paragraph of a book. Sometimes there's little if anything I can do to prevent my mind wandering off to the great thought bubble in the sky. Perhaps this is how come my subconscious master planner has become so adept and efficient over the years.

We really don't need to concern ourselves with the exhausting process of 'coming up' with an answer if we feed in the question thoroughly enough. We are full of answers like a vending machine is full of snacks. What we need is the correct change and item number to access whatever it is we're after.

Again, once we have properly and earnestly worked on feeding in the question, quiet, breathing and relaxation is all we need to 'hear' the answer.

As a result of affording myself fair old slabs of all three of those prerequisites over the years, three subsequent 'answers' have made themselves known to me:

1 My father's death and the way my mum covered up his illness made me very grateful for my life on the one hand but also very distrustful of people on the other.
2. My constant energy comes from not wanting to miss out on anything while I'm still around to witness it.
3. Most of my habits, tastes, dreams and aspirations come from the movies I escaped to when I didn't have anyone around and available for friendship, confiding and conversation.

What does all this mean?

I am yet to have my heart broken in adulthood, having had it smashed to pieces as a kid.

I am very happy in my own company but ideally like to be on my own while still around other people. That is to say I am happy alone but preferably not on my own.

For years, my favourite three things in life were women, cars and alcohol.

Which is fine where women and cars are concerned but when alcohol is thrown into the mix – that's when the situation can get a little sticky.

The problem with waking up when the 'beer buzz' is still in full effect is its endless optimism. The false hope that gives rise to a thousand new beginnings, not a single one of which has even the slightest suggestion of how it might end.

The beer buzz is one of the world's most uncelebrated catalysts. All the possibility with not a whiff of sustainability or exit strategy.

My own casebook of evidence includes the morning I bought a massive house in Chelsea, which I never moved into, before selling it to George Michael, who also never moved into it, before selling it to Puff Daddy, who never moved into it either. Were we all beer buzzing at the time?

Add to that various major car purchases, like the time Tash and I were particularly buzzing one morning in Italy and decided to go to bid on James Coburn's old Ferrari California Spyder. The day before I had no intention of going anywhere near the car. It was tatty and scratched and I hadn't researched it AT ALL. But waking up with the beer buzz negated all that and . . . two hours later, there I was sitting at the front with my hand in the air as the hammer went down.

My beer-buzz scenario often involves the presence of a female. A Bonnie to my Clyde, if you like. Almost literally, as my love for and fascination with the opposite sex is down to the likes of the great and glamorous actresses of the world: Julie Christie, Joanna Lumley, Anne Bancroft, Beatrice Dalle. As my love of cars is down to *Magnum, P.I.*, *The New Avengers* (Ms Lumley again!), *The Professionals*, *Chitty Chitty Bang Bang* and of course 007. But it was only in writing this book that I realized my love of alcohol is also down to love of the silver screen, i.e. the first 18-rated movie I ever went to see: *Arthur*.

We need to talk about Arthur.

Until I 'heard' the answer one day, all I could recall when it came to analysing my history with booze was that for as long as I could remember I had wanted to 'take the edge off'. At the end of the day, at the beginning of a night out, after a particularly good day at work. Whether it was a cold tinny of contentment from the fridge after a bathtime full of giggles with the kids, a glass of fine ruby-red wine to accompany a robust steak at a fancy restaurant, or a volley of shots to kickstart a bout of rebel rousing, having a drink was for years the home straight around which every twenty-four hours has revolved.

And even though I have undoubtedly managed to rein in my alcohol intake considerably during the last few years, there have still been times when it has become more of a necessary crutch than an exercise of free will.

Last year I lost my voice. No big deal usually, I know. Except for a couple of reasons where I'm concerned.

1 I make my living using my voice and if anything serious should ever happen to it I would have to completely reorganize my life.
2 This was not a couple of days we're talking about. I actually lost my voice for four weeks and it didn't come back properly for almost a year.

So why the concern with what alcohol might have to do with any of this?

Alcohol dries out your throat, especially at night. It causes snoring, which again is bad for the throat. As it's a stimulant it interrupts sleep, leading to tiredness, one of the first symptoms of which is . . . ? Yup, you've guessed it – losing your voice. Alcohol affects energy levels, which means we are less likely to want to exercise, which in turn leads to tiredness and a weakened immune system. Which means we'll be more vulnerable to infections and allergies. None of which is good news in life in general but especially if you have been gifted the responsibility of hosting the biggest radio show this side of the Atlantic.

After being plunged into a well of melancholy, by what I would subsequently be informed was a super virus from which it could easily have taken me up to two years to fully recover, my subconscious question machine began to scream at me in a new language. The likes and volume of which I had never heard before:

Why was I continuing, however tentatively, to risk sabotaging everything I cherished on a daily basis so I could have a drink? Why was I happy to repeatedly dim the chances of prolonging the various aspects of this wonderful life I had been blessed with? What was that about? Surely no one in their right mind would voluntarily indulge in such ill-advised, self-destructive behaviour?

Back to the movies then.

Trading Places enlightened me as to the existence of the stock market, as well as how grand houses can be and how cool it might be to have a big, fat, cheery chauffeur driving an even bigger and fatter car. *Ferris Bueller's Day Off* gave me my first trouser movement with regards to the sublime Ferrari 250 Short Wheel Base California Spyder that then ended up in my garage (until I lost my mind one day and sold the bloody thing).

Could it be that my lifelong fascination with alcohol began with watching Dudley Moore in *Arthur* when I was fourteen?

Arthur is such an amazing film on so many levels. It's so escapist, hedonistic, clever and packed full of pathos. Not that I fully appreciated the pathos of Steve Gordon's brilliant script at the time perhaps as much as would have been good for me.

'Not everyone who drinks is a poet. Some of us drink because we're not poets.'

One of the greatest lines in movie history as Arthur sits at the bar having ducked out of his own wedding.

Arthur's right up there with my other favourite films on permanent rotation: *The Graduate, Pretty Woman, Betty Blue, American Beauty, Midnight Run, Citizen Kane, It's a Wonderful Life* and *The Godfather Trilogy*.

And the thing is I've always watched *Arthur* with a drink by my side, drinking along with him, laughing along with him and most of all crying along with him. The parts of the movie where Arthur's ever-faithful butler Hobson begins to get ill and the roles become reversed have me in bits.

No sooner does the habitually mischievous and profligate Arthur finally find a purpose and realize what life's all about than Hobson passes away, leaving Arthur enlightened one moment and devastated and alone the next.

It's the gentlest, most telling, perfect articulation of what it's like to lose someone you love and not be able to do a damn thing about it. I know because I was Arthur and my dad was Hobson. I was little and young and confused and my dad was old, soft-spoken and wise. My dad slipped away gradually, day by day; in my old bedroom where I would sit on the floor and talk to him for hours about anything and nothing. Smiling up at him on the outside, while falling apart with grief on the inside, until one day I came home and he was no longer there.

He'd just gone, exactly like the scene in *Arthur* where we see Sir John Gielgud lying peacefully, before the visceral stab in our guts hits us the next time we see the bed, perfectly made but with Hobson nowhere to be seen. So subtle, yet so powerful at the same time. A moment of concise cinematic genius.

Even more ironic when I remembered the only reason I could afford to go to watch *Arthur* in the first place was because I'd been allowed to get a part-time job following Dad dying.

'I never want you to be alone,' purrs the ever stoic and fiercely protective Hobson from his deathbed.

'I know you don't, Hobson,' replies Arthur.

Shit, shit, fucking shit. It has me sobbing every time.

But the thing is I've thought all this before. Something that immediately caused my heart to quicken on this occasion – simultaneously causing tiny droplets of sweat to form on my forehead, the only sound I could hear was that of my blood circulating in my ears – was the realization that after going to see *Arthur* that first time, I never went to the movies again without sneaking in some form of alcohol.

'My God,' I thought to myself.

Almost exclusively half a can of Seven-Up topped up with a couple of whisky miniatures, as I recalled. How could I have forgotten this? My relationship with alcohol didn't begin when I was seventeen at the pub with those godawful, ghastly flat pints of brown over mild, served by way-out-of-my-depth gorgeous, nubile bar staff. It began a full two years before with each secret sip of sweet-tasting whisky and lemonade every time I escaped into the darkness of the movie theatre.

Blimey.

I've always convinced myself that I actually really enjoy the taste, the refreshment of an ice-cold beer, along with the separation it brings via an evening of calm after another hectic day full of madness, deadlines and needless self-imposed pressure. The effortless and often dreamless (which means nightmareless in my case) sleep that ensues as a result. Alcohol's ability to anaesthetize the mind, keep worry on the doorstep, hope on the horizon.

But the truth of the situation is, as soon as the first drop of booze passes my lips, I ever so gradually disengage from myself, the world around me and everything and everyone in it. Sip by sip as the evening (drinking) develops, I begin to float away behind an invisible curtain of comfort and security. Or at least, that's how it seems.

Wherever it is I end up feels so nice; so restful, so tranquil. It does, however, have its own Achilles' heel. Everything is fine in Boozyland until one thing is reintroduced into the scenario. It really cannot cope with anything to do with real life. As one's tendency to worry and care about the more nonsense aspects of being a human being is diminished, so too are all the things we need to excel or sustain or survive.

My tolerance and patience levels, for example, go out of the window, to the extent I order multiple rounds of drinks so I don't have to wait between rounds. Likewise if there is any sign we might be moving on soon to another venue or calling it a night, I order the bill way ahead of time, as I do the taxi. Other victims include my ability to remember anything from the night that might be useful the next day, or names or facts that might be useful on the night itself.

Now obviously I'm not a man of science, but even I am aware that while this cacophony of emotional and intellectual conflict is taking place inside me, I am almost certainly pickling several of my internal organs beyond what is perhaps good for them. Which is not what a sensible person would voluntarily do to themselves, is it?

Yet I persist. Along with millions of others.

So why do we continue en masse to do something we intrinsically know is detrimental to our general well-being?

And when should we be concerned that perhaps we might have a genuine problem? Are we already there and have been for years? Or is drinking part of the new 'us' generation? Civilizations long before ours have drugged themselves into happy oblivion. Is it all right? All wrong? Are we hamstrung somewhere in between the two?

I decided I wanted to go and find out for sure.

In my wilderness years, little of what I had meant anything. But now the opposite was true. And yet here I was still with my finger hovering over the trigger of a gun pointing at my own head. Why on earth would I do that?

I've worked so hard to get the cake. Why would I now willingly and intentionally stick two fingers up to the icing?

We have the rest of our lives to change our minds but we need all of our minds to change the rest of our lives.

The effect alcohol had on my decision-making has been the single biggest and most constant threat to my happiness and well-being. Therefore I decided I needed to go and investigate how far towards the point of no return I may or may not be when it comes to the demon drink.

The Wounded Healer

Top Ten Negative Effects Drinking Has on Human Beings:

10 Loss of perspective.
 9 Loss of communication skills.
 8 Loss of choice.
 7 Loss of energy.
 6 Detrimental effect on the body.
 5 Emotional anaesthesia.
 4 Financial ruin.
 3 Imprisonment.
 2 Wet brain.
 1 Death.

I went to see an old friend of mine. Her name is Amanda and for the last ten years she's been part of an organization that helps people try to help themselves where alcohol is concerned.

Amanda is more than qualified to know what she's talking about, as she's been to the darkest side of what alcohol can do to a person. It's not for me to divulge exactly how dark her night became, but suffice to say it was black enough for her to realize it would be best for everyone concerned if she tried to abstain from drinking ever again.

Seventeen years later – so far so good.

'What exactly is an alcoholic?' I ask her to begin with.

'Well, there's no simple answer to that. I mean, there are various tests and questionnaires one can partake in, but they're more of a rough guide than anything approaching a definitive diagnosis. In my experience, alcoholism is different for everyone. It's very cunning in as much as it's very adept at becoming bespoke to the individual.'

All right, let me put it differently then, because, in the past, I successfully set myself a challenge to not drink for a hundred days and found it infinitely more manageable than I ever imagined it might be. Does this mean I'm not an alcoholic?

'Again, I don't know. This is all too simplistic. What immediately is more interesting to me is why you thought you needed to stop at all?'

I did it because I wanted to know what it felt like to be totally sober for three months. (This was a lie, I did it to prove to myself that I could. Not that it mattered; Amanda was already on to me.)

'Ah, now, there you see, that's not a thought that just appears from nowhere. It's a premise that suggests to me you've been thinking about your relationship with alcohol for some time, perhaps longer than you care to admit, or at least feel comfortable admitting. Now, for one reason or another you felt like you wanted to do something about it.'

Talk about cutting to the chase! But of course she is absolutely right. Bang on the money. I have increasingly thought alcohol was becoming the puppet master rather than the puppet. Certainly more of an issue than I would like it to be. And certainly more than it has ever been before, even though I did successfully complete a hundred-day booze fast and am now drinking far less than I have done for years.

But I suppose that's part of the reason in many ways. During my three months and eight days of total sobriety, my life was so much more liveable. I smiled more, I thought more, I achieved more, I had more extra capacity, awareness and energy to do more of all the things I liked.

Not only that but I didn't miss 'the taste' of beer, wine and spirits at all – the main reason I cited for liking them. In fact, during my self-imposed period of abstinence I often smelt friends' wine and brandy and found it almost repulsive.

This reminded me of when I was little and my dad offered me a sip of his pale ale one Christmas; I thought it was utterly disgusting. I truly believe learning to enjoy alcohol is a three-stage process: firstly we close our eyes, hold our nose and try merely to bear its disgusting taste, then we become used to how horrible it tastes, before convincing ourselves that we've actually come to love it.

'I stopped because I was no longer sure I could or wanted to handle what alcohol was doing to me,' continued Amanda. 'It began to make me feel paranoid as soon as the first drop passed my lips, or even the thought of it. Like I'd walked into another room, but one I wasn't used to. Almost like I knew it was the beginning of the end of whatever it was I'd been doing as another state was about to ensue. A definite line between before and after I am drinking seems to have emerged. A line that, once the line is crossed, brought in a whole new set of terms and conditions.

'Where this had once felt like a place I couldn't wait to get to, it had somehow become a place I began to dread and eventually fear.'

So can drinking ever be a good thing?

'Absolutely, yes, but it's very much a one-hit wonder rather than a whole back catalogue of timeless classics. One of the things alcohol does is gradually and systematically shut down every part of your conscious brain, including the ability to control one's behaviour or inhibitions.

'This is why it can be so useful at parties to help break the ice. But taken to its extreme (which begins to happen startlingly quickly), this is also how come otherwise perfectly reasonable people go on to do dreadful things. When they're said to be "under the influence".'

Oh dear, this was all sounding a bit too close to home. Meanwhile Amanda had yet more home truths up her sleeve . . .

'Alcohol is often perceived to be liberating, but it's really only a one-trick pony. Sure it can maybe take away the fear and awkwardness of a situation but it also simultaneously blinkers you as to where you might end up as a result.

'Ultimately I found alcohol did for me exactly the opposite of what I wanted it to do. Instead of facilitating my freedom, what it actually ended up doing was reducing my ability to be free at all. When I thought I was escaping, what I was in fact doing was wilfully jumping into a rowing boat already floating off downstream without any means of getting back to dry land.

'What alcohol does is dull everything in its path and put all the useful bits of our personality into lockdown. We may think we are being more interesting or profound or funny or cheeky, but only if we're surrounded by people who are also drinking; anyone who isn't will be able to run rings around the lot of you.

'Once I'd had a drink the treasure chest of my natural strengths and abilities was slammed firmly shut until I either went home or passed out – usually the latter.

'And it didn't end there. The next day, or days, even if I went a week or two without drinking, which I did a lot, I would still be picking up the pieces from the fall-out of my last few drinking sessions.'

Oh my goodness, so you were (are) an alcoholic even though you didn't (don't) drink every day?

'Well, of course, Christopher!' she laughed. 'Some people are alcoholics who barely drink at all. There's myriad differences between drunks and alcoholics. Neither are pretty, both have issues, but everyone who drinks suffers in their own unique way as a result.'

Is there not a single trait therefore that you can identify that all alcoholics have in common?

'Well, I used to have all sorts of theories along those lines. But eventually I realized there are always exceptions to any rule – and times that by a thousand where alcohol is concerned.

'One of my favourite theories used to be that, generally, alcoholics are consumed by low self-esteem and all that other unfortunate nonsense where such fragile personalities are involved.

'I classified them via a phrase I really rather liked for a while – here it is:

'*A lot of alcoholics are egomaniacs with huge inferiority complexes.* No wonder they struggle with life and themselves if that truly is the case.'

How do you feel about the claim that sometimes, when grieving for example, alcohol is a helpful catalyst to get things going?

'I've heard this countless times and I'm afraid I'm just not an advocate of such thinking. It's the booze that's doing the crying, not the person. Whatever sorrow it appears to alleviate on the day is still in residence and will come back to bite you on the behind unless you deal with it properly, i.e. soberly.

'By all means, if you feel it may help and if you can cope with it, apply alcohol as a temporary sticking plaster. But bear in mind that's all it is. You must be prepared for the mess and gunk to ooze out again the instant you rip it off.'

Amanda is almost convinced that for her and her fellow recovering alcoholics there is no such thing as healthy drinking. Furthermore, in a bizarre twist of the tale, she also believes that she and people like her need alcohol less in the first place than those who end up being able to cope with its more destructive effects better.

What an entirely positive force for good she has become. She's gorgeous and sparkling and full of life. Like champagne without the side effects.

● ●˙ ●

Why don't we not drink?

That's one way of saving a shitload of money.

I don't know about you, but for the brief period I arrive somewhere before drink is in play, regardless of how little or how much, I am fairly flying. I'm funnier (not difficult), I'm more thoughtful, I'm more tolerant, I'm more of everything that's good for me and everyone else.

If I continued to 'not drink' as the night went on my options would remain open whereas everyone else's would begin to narrow. I would leave when I intended to, largely because I would still be able to drive home – bliss, driving at night is one of life's underrated pleasures. And, like my son, the next morning I would be good to go straight off the bat without having to write off at least the first half of the day to recover.

Not drinking increases our chances of becoming more successful.

Here's some proof.

I have a pal who started working for a record company around the same time as I started working on the radio, back at the beginning of the Nineties. He is now the global head of a huge media empire. He couldn't be any more successful in the corporate world if he tried. There's nowhere else left for him to go.

He has also never drunk in his life. Has he missed out? Not for a moment. He has led one of the most exciting, stimulating and rock-and-roll existences imaginable.

'How did you do all this?' I once asked him.

'Chris, it really wasn't that difficult. A) I'm good at my job. B) I love what I do. C) It doesn't do any harm when most of your competitors have spent the vast majority of the last thirty years partying and not being able to function properly anytime this side of three in the afternoon.'

Mmm. I want to be in his gang.

We shall see.

Marriage

The Marriage Guru

Top Ten Reasons Not to Get Married:

10 How do we know we know?

9 How do we know we know, we know?

8 How do we know we know, we know, we know?

7 How do we know we know, we know, we know, we know?

6 How do we know we know, we know, we know, we know, we know?

5 How do we know we know, we know, we know, we know, we know, we know?

4 How do we know we know, we know, we know, we know, we know, we know, we know?

3 How do we know we know, we know, we know, we know, we know, we know, we know, we know?

2 How do we know we know, we know, we know, we know, we know, we know, we know, we know, we know!

1 It's a really stupid and outdated idea that for some reason billions of us are still drawn to, even though we don't subscribe in any way to the foundations, deeply questionable morals or outdated religiousness that it's based on.

Marriage is the ultimate proof that we human beings are the nuttiest bunch of idealistic romantics in the universe.

Why, for example, do we not feel compelled to marry our cats or our dogs or our cars or our shoes?

There's no point because there's no need. Most of us marry, I'm guessing, because it makes us feel more secure. But I fear the truth is few of us truly know the answer.

The same goes for why some of us stay married and some of us don't. The odds suggest it's a crap shoot at best.

I've been married three times now. So what does that make me? Really bad at marriage, or an expert? Does it make me a liar for going back on my vows? Or does it make me the epitome of honesty because I had the courage to admit when the vows I had undertaken no longer felt genuine?

A recent survey put a series of questions to people who had been told they were going to die. Some had reached their life expectancy, some were a long way short of it, some had outlived their own predicted mortality. Assured of anonymity, each individual was asked to disclose the biggest lie of their life. A staggering 76 per cent of those questioned revealed that they regarded their marriage as the biggest lie; they were no longer in love with the person they were married to. Furthermore, 85 per cent of those who gave that response conceded that this had been the case for many years.

It seems incredible, doesn't it? At first, that is. But, realistically, what are the chances of meeting someone – purely coincidentally – and then successfully forging a partnership until death do you part?

So when did the concept of marriage begin and why?

Marriage has been around for thousands of years. Its original purpose was to confirm ownership of a woman by a man. Where genuine affection was involved, a wife might enjoy the protection of her husband and no longer need to worry about predatory males, be they rapists, drunkards, murderers or braggarts. In many cases, however, it was more a matter of, 'She's my personal slave now, so go sling your hook and find your own.'

Times have changed in the thousands of years since the legal contract of marriage was first introduced, and society has changed beyond recognition. Marriage needs to be readdressed accordingly. In many ways, it's the relationship equivalent of global warming, a situation in which we have tacitly and collectively agreed that apathy is the way forward and one day we'll wake up and everything will suddenly be all right.

Most men and women I know who are happily married – and for 'happily' read 'still' – remain so purely because they have made the decision that that's how it's going to be. No more, no less.

Put another way, they have come to the conclusion via whatever means or reasoning available to them, that life will be infinitely more enjoyable, sustainable and economically sound if they face it as part of a double act rather than as a free-spirited but potentially lonely old solo artist.

There was a time when most couples met at work – not ideal for cultural parity but undoubtedly an advantage when it comes to sharing common ground and references within a common parlance. These days, many couples meet via the Internet – which used to be a bit embarrassing, though not any more, and quite right too. Far better for the world, in my opinion, to have more diverse characters swimming in a much deeper and more interesting pool. Not to mention the advantage of being able to check one another out before committing to so much as half a shandy and a bag of crisps in each other's company.

The other thing I like about this approach is that it marks a return to the original ethos of marriage as a workable deal based on what each party can bring to the table. From day one there is a gritty honesty about what the relationship is based on. Far better that than all the *Romeo and Juliet* nonsense. Hollywood has a lot to answer for, as does Prince Charming, *Swan Lake* and all that other mush and slop.

So, how do we go about evaluating marriages/relationships we might already be in without giving the game away?

Comparison between our own relationship and those of others is one way to go, I suppose. We none of us really know what makes other people's relationships tick unless one or both parties invite us in for a look (such an insight can never be requested). To truly find out what works and doesn't work for other couples, one must wait, silently, like a patient angler perched on a riverbank.

And then boom, there it is, a huge bite that's almost impossible to miss.

What I'm talking about here is the moment when someone trusts us enough to bring up the subject of their marriage and tell us how they feel about it. The key then is to listen to what they have to say and see if any of it can help us fathom out our own. And believe me, they won't stop talking unless you interrupt them. And the longer we can resist butting in, the more they'll open up.

They'll probably claim to be seeking your advice, but of course they're doing nothing of the sort. They are merely downloading all their shit on to you. And it will get heavier and heavier the longer they continue. So heavy perhaps that you may reach breaking point and want to step aside to avoid suffocating under the weight and stench of it all. In which case, fear not for their fragility or the risk you might upset them – the chances are they won't even notice you've moved. They're on a roll, they've come to talk and there's nothing and no one that's going to stop the flow.

After a good listening session we should have plenty to work with when it comes to comparing and contrasting our own relationships – their strengths, weaknesses, foibles and idiosyncrasies – with theirs. A rare moment of context in the mysterious, non-sensical world of a man and woman committing to decades of unwarranted, unworkable togetherness, and trying to make the impossible possible, or at worst bearable.

After ten or so good listens to ten or so good mates or colleagues (the latter tend to be even keener to open up/download due to the lack of intimacy and therefore reduced risk of their partner finding out), we should have a useful and usable swatch of what constitutes a sustainable modern-day relationship.

Be mindful, however, of placing too much stock in what people say about their marriage/relationship when they are away from their partner. Partners together in public often interact very differently to the way they do in private. Those that are not getting on well often put on a brave face, while those who get on reasonably well can end up inexplicably bickering for no apparent reason.

You always hurt the one you love. Ain't that the truth?

As individuals, the best we can do is go through life with the aim of creating and preserving as much joy and laughter as possible without hurting anything or anyone en route. But what's the point of all that joy and laughter if we don't share it? That's the reason many of us form relationships and decide to get married. But marriage is a legal contract involving practicality and pragmatism – and we all know what a shitstorm of complications that combination can lead to.

'It's no good sweeping problems under the carpet,' goes the age-old phrase.

Well, why not? If the carpet's big enough and no one's going to be around to discover what might be under there long after the main protagonists have departed this mortal coil, what harm can it do?

I have one pal whose marriage is an intermittent 'nightmare', her husband doesn't understand her, blah, blah, blah. She's had one affair and is contemplating another, yet you've never seen a happier, more caring couple when things are going well. Surely it's OK to be like that, providing everyone's happy in the final mix?

Conversely I know lots of couples who never row, never call each other names but are utterly miserable. Surely that's worse?

Then there's a guy I've known for years who unapologetically states that he and his wife are like a pair of inseparable attack dogs, trained to rip apart anyone or anything that gets in their way, front, back and all over. They don't get invited out much, but it really doesn't seem to bother them.

Another friend of mine worships the ground his wife walks on yet he never tells her. Never has done. As far as I'm aware she has no idea how much he adores her.

'Why don't you tell her?' I ask him every now and again when I can be bothered.

'Well, it's obvious, it would ruin everything.' So sad. Or is it? What if he did let her and it did ruin everything?

Each of these couples is as crazy and illogical as the next, each locked in their own unique bubble of togetherness. Living by their own rules of coupledom. But how about this: SHOCK HORROR, I recently discovered all three couples have something huge in common. They've all undergone marriage counselling in one form or another.

In my experience, relationship therapy is like a lot of things in life: once you start talking to people about it, you realize it's far more prevalent than you ever imagined. I remember the same sense of revelation when it came to discussing miscarriages and latterly IVF treatment.

So many couples have been through so much of the same crap, but it's only when you bring up the topic that you find out. And you also find out that talking about it, this deep dark secret you've been carrying, makes everyone feel instantly better.

Talking, sleep, exercise, good food and plenty of water: the famous five of healing.

Anyway, the marriage guidance fact got me to thinking: why don't we all go preventive as opposed to reactive? Why wait to be stuck in a mire of depression with poisonous doubts and dark thoughts when all the help we need is out there? As a famous sportsman once told me, 'It's easier to stay warm than get warm'.

The Relationship Counsellor

Determined to seek some sage advice for all our sakes, I popped off one morning after my radio show to spend a fascinating few hours in the company of someone I will refer to only as Dr H. Having worked with couples for over forty years, Dr H is considered by many to be the über-guru of relationship counselling.

Dr H works from home, the top floor of her beautiful grand old Victorian house. She considers her job something she was born to do, a lifelong vocation of trying to help couples help themselves. Dr H tells me she is as fascinated and compelled by what she sees and hears today as she was the day she started.

My mission is to gather as many tips as possible for the future. Plain and simple. To find out what we might want to bear in mind in order to safeguard what we have. Or point us in the direction of what we might need. Even though I have been reliably informed that tips and quick fixes are not Dr H's style, but no matter: I'll take what I can get.

It is a Tuesday morning in early June, but more like autumn, blowy and rainy like the opening scene in a Woody Allen film. Dr H answers the door with what may have been a brief half-smile, but so brief I can't be sure. Whatever it was, eye contact was not part of it; her eyes were looking down at the floor before mine had any chance of engaging. Was this nerves? Reluctance? Or was it perhaps her way of letting me know any exchange between us was of no importance until we were upstairs in the room where the couples' 'work' took place.

The situation was already a lot more serious than I expected. But then what was I expecting? This was not a lady desperate to become part of television's roster of so-called experts on all matters of the head, heart and spleen. It had taken weeks of persuasion for this woman to even consider seeing me.

As I clambered up a never-ending spiral of marvellously creaking stairs, becoming ever more breathless, I couldn't help wondering if this is why she looked so fit, healthy and sparkling for her age. By the time we arrived at the top floor I was fairly wheezing whereas Dr H was flat calm and breathing normally.

Her counselling room set in the eaves is small but light with white-painted walls – reassuringly secure and private. Dr H instructs me to sit in the single chair, which will position me to her left as she settles in her usual spot with her back to the window. I can't help noticing how her mass of thick, snow-white hair blends into the fluffy white clouds behind. Eerily, there's an empty couples' sofa to my right, a world away from the champagne and roses of a first date.

I'm nervous. I need to be on my game. I can sense that this is perhaps the most no-nonsense person I've ever interviewed staring back at me. For sure there's eye contact now. For sure we're now working. For sure I'd better not waste a word and get on with this.

First, I ask her about marriage as a concept.

'What a load of old stuff and nonsense. What a remarkably unworkable idea. No wonder so many of us struggle with it at various times in our lives,' she begins.

Immediately I'm gripped.

'You may have already worked out that none of us are at all sure why we get married in the first place. All one has to do to come to that conclusion is ask yourself that very question and see what you come up with. Then go and ask some of your friends. And after that, if you're feeling super brave, I dare you to actually ask the person you're married to. Marriage is weird, plain and simple, but people continue to go through with it every day, somewhere in the world.

'The most popular, which also happens to be the least convincing answer I repeatedly hear is, "We just wanted to make a statement to ourselves and the rest of the world." Not at all insincere but flimsy at best, entirely unconvincing if I'm being less kind.

'To me this smacks of an after-the-fact attempt at mitigation. Have you ever heard of someone proposing to someone else and qualifying it with, "Please, will you consider marrying me as I think it's time we made an official statement to ourselves and the rest of the world"? That sounds more like an emergency meeting of the G8 than love personified.

'The harsh reality is: many of us don't know why we get married, we just do. There's invariably a moment when it suddenly seems like a good idea. Or, "it's time". In the same way it might be a good idea to retile the bathroom or time to have a ham sandwich. There's a lot more hit and hope going on than we might think. Should we not discuss what game it is we're playing in the first case?'

Before going to see Dr H, I checked with my mum and asked her if people's reasons for getting married were any different in her day. Her answer surprised me:

'Not really, to be honest. I mean, marriage did have more of a function back then in as much as it made a relationship more respectable in the eyes of society at large. A young couple being very much frowned upon if they had been together any length of time and not considered tying the knot. They might even be deemed "suspicious", which sounds hilarious today. But other than that, no. People met someone and if they got on with each other marriage was just the next step.

'Now, as for having a child out of wedlock, that was regarded as most unacceptable. I remember thinking at the time: Well, what on earth did they think Adam and Eve were up to?'

But the pressure back then must have been unbearable, with phrases like, 'It's time you made an honest woman of that young lady', constantly doing the rounds. And young men going off to war, desperate to know they had a sweetheart to keep the home fires burning.

Then there was the pressure coming from older generations. A pressure that still exists in certain cultures today, and in my experience is usually nothing but destructive. This reminds me of a wizened, stale ash-tray of a 'journalist' who once took me to task over embarking on my third marriage, the previous two having ended in divorce.

'It's your job to stay married', she huffed disapprovingly, and as animatedly as her lolloping old black-coffee-soaked bones would allow. The worst advert for 'hanging on in there' you could imagine. I couldn't wait to get her out of my house. It was like having death in the room.

The polar opposite of what it feels like to be in the company of Dr H.

'In the eyes of many, marriage is simply an old behavioural habit that seems to have slipped through the net of prejudice to swim another day. Bye-bye beheading. Bye-bye hanging. Bye-bye lynch mobs. And witch hunts. And all manner of barbaric goings on. But marriage – NO! You stay, dear. Pull up a chair, old girl. I'll put the kettle on. Let's have a cup of tea. You're all right.'

And I suppose that might be the long and the short of it. While marriage is around, at least we all get a nice day out, a free meal and the bride, her mates and her mum get to look nice in the pictures.

So where does marriage come from?

'Ah, that's a good one. Did you know marriage as an idea was originally conceived over five thousand years ago? It was primarily a legal and binding agreement to proclaim ownership of a woman by a man. A far clearer, albeit outrageously immoral, reason for a contract than any we have today. Marriage often didn't change the man's life at all, as there was no commitment required from him whatsoever. All it meant was that he could stick a "keep off my grass" notice outside his new wife's door. As for the poor wretched woman in question, she had little or no say in the matter.'

So marriage, how and why does it happen? Or perhaps now let's drop the marriage question and simply talk about relationships. Why on earth do we think, how dare we think, that the random encounters of this modern age could/should/would lead to anything more than a brief fling?

For example: I met my first wife at a radio station. My second when she came on my TV show as a guest. And my third on a golf course in the middle of Buckinghamshire.

According to Dr H: 'The causality of meeting, the random ways in which almost all of us get together, is wholly irrelevant in the grand scheme of things. One person's piercing arrow across a crowded dance-floor is another person's methodical study of countless Internet dating sites. The virtual dance hall of its day minus Glenn Miller and the need for a spare pair of flats for the walk home.'

Dr H is a big fan of the Internet.

'More diverse characters getting together from more diverse walks of life can only be good for the sustainability of this ever-simmering melting pot of humankind! Plus, Internet dating can be much safer and more efficient, usually carried out with the added bonus of a sober state of mind.'

More efficient, Dr H? Isn't that a little too unromantic?

'I'll tell you what's unromantic: domestic violence, a life of depression – sometimes leading to suicide – or losing all you've ever worked for when it wasn't even you who had the illicit liaison with the builder, or the yummy mummy next door. Perpetual romance is for fantasists, who frankly have a lot to answer for. Science fiction has nothing on "romcoms". Just that phrase makes me want to scream.'

Excellent point, well made.

'Except for *Sliding Doors*. That film is a perfect representation of how random all this relationship stuff is. Or at least how random it is when it first begins. All coupling up is born out of millions of sliding-doors moments. So we don't need to concern ourselves with "how we met", just what's happened "since we met".

'You met your wife on a golf course. You probably thought about not going that day. And had you not, those two amazing little boys that you dote upon every single waking moment wouldn't exist. But you can't think like that, it's a recipe for insanity.'

I'm struggling to write all this gold down quick enough, and frankly in a bit of a flap, when Dr H stops me in my tracks.

'May I ask you a question now please?'

Eek.

'I'm getting a little paranoid answering all yours, it's usually the other way round in this room.'

'Of course, go ahead.'

'Do you think some people prefer to be with someone rather than on their own?'

'Yes, I do.'

'Well, there you are, that's really all that matters. It's when they stop feeling like that they come to see me.'

So how and why does that happen? This was what I'd come to find out.

'Almost without exception,' Dr H says, 'there are two things that come to light when couples have a problem with their relationship. The first is that a gradual and almost invisible breakdown in basic day-to-day communication has occurred somewhere along the line. If it goes unchecked this can culminate in a permanent disconnect. The second is that as a result of this breakdown in communication, one or both parties begin to suffer from some sort of trauma (long- or short-term) that they or their partner are not aware of. It's actually all so frustratingly simple.'

I'd heard that some experienced relationship counsellors can tell immediately if a couple are not destined to be together. Is that possible?

'I try to avoid doing that, but it is sometimes more evident than not. In such cases there are usually two predominant defining factors. The first is the refusal of one party to respect the things the other party considers important in life, regardless of whether the rest of the world agrees or not. And the second is a terminal decline in any shared commonality. In other words, reasons to enjoy and feel fulfilled about being together.'

Again, Dr H reiterates it doesn't matter how or why people get together in the first place, a theme she returns to again and again, as if to hammer it home. Like when she explains that even many of the most perfectly matched couples she sees end up going their separate ways for the sake of everyone concerned.

'What a lot of people don't realize is that often my job is the successful management of couples who have decided to part. Sometimes it's better to agree to dance in the rain instead of sticking together, being miserable in the sun.'

'Should more couples seek help than actually do?' I ask.

'People have to realize first that they need help and second that they want help, it's counterproductive otherwise. So the direct answer to your question is no, but if you were to ask me would more couples benefit from counselling then the answer would undoubtedly be yes.'

'So why don't they?'

'Because unlike a bleeding wound that's spilling out on to the floor, feelings and emotions are not visible to the naked eye. And if something's not visible, people think they can hide it, even from themselves. They say seeing is believing, but I've found often in life it's the opposite.

'Some people see counselling as an admission of defeat or a sign of weakness, especially if they're successful in other aspects of their life. Though this attitude is entirely understandable, it's about as logical as saying you're never going to brush your teeth again because that would mean having to admit they might be dirty.

'The simplest thing about anything breaking down, especially relationships, is to try not to let things get out of hand in the first place. Get to know the danger signs and look out for them on a daily/weekly basis. If you keep watering the flowers, they stand a better chance of living longer than if you forget.

'This is the best approach. For example, I am a huge fan of dedicated and regular date days for couples. Never be afraid of it just being the two of you – you have nothing to lose and everything to gain. Remember that's how you started, for heaven's sake. A daily half-hour catch up, or dinner sitting opposite each other without the kids, phones off – all the obvious stuff. But sometimes so obvious people we mistake thinking about doing it for actually doing it.'

How about not having enough time?

'Quite frankly, make time. You would if the Queen suddenly turned up unannounced. Well, just imagine she has. Half an hour every day out of twenty-four is nothing compared to how much it will benefit you.

'In essence, treat your relationship with your partner, and the whole of your life for that matter, like you would a car. Regular maintenance is the key to it running smoothly and sustainably. The topping-up of levels and the checking of temperatures and pressures, plus a ten-thousand-mile major service at least once a year is vital.

'If you can't be bothered to look after something, then don't be surprised when that something eventually gives up on you. Especially when the road gets rocky.'

And with that I sensed my time was up. She'd given me the look. My cue to chance my arm with the question I'd decided days before would be my last:

If she could suggest a cheat sheet of handy hints for a healthy marriage, what might be on it? Reluctantly she turned around, reached into her desk drawer and handed me a printed sheet.

'Now, whatever might be on there, there's no guarantees to any of it, that's the most important thing I ask you to remember. Don't read it now, save it for later.'

Back downstairs, the descent far more manageable than the climb up, Dr H smiles as she shakes my hand, this time much happier to hold my gaze.

In the car all I can think of is getting home to read the magic recipe, resting in the crisp white envelope on the passenger seat next to me. Several times during my journey I glance across, desperate to take a look. But no, this is too important to speed-read every time I hit a red light.

Eventually I arrive home, the world outside Dr H's inner sanctum already filtering its way back into my consciousness. Immediately through the door, I put the kettle on, make a cup of tea and bounce upstairs. I plonk myself on the bed and unfold the three sheets of A4.

The highlights of which were:

Top Ten Golden Nuggets to Keep a Relationship on Track:

10 More compliments.
 9 More showing that you care.
 8 More helping out.
 7 More listening.
 6 More replying.
 5 More date days/weekends.
 4 More proper kisses hello.
 3 More proper hugs goodbye.
 2 More proper night nights.
 1 More of You for more of Them to enjoy.

Who would have thought?

'Not everyone needs therapy,' Dr H told me. In fact she fairly rails against the idea of serial therapy, 'just for the sake of it'.

She thinks it's a nonsense and a waste of everybody's time. She considers therapy addicts a nuisance, a drain on her surgery and on the world in general. She is also highly respectful of the fact that different people have different ways of working through their problems and some never need to go to see anyone and figure things out for themselves. It's very much a case of whatever works for the individuals concerned.

But the key is, fixes don't just happen. Things don't just 'sort them-selves out'. Issues need to be addressed, understood and worked through. If that means going fishing once a week or never going fishing again, so be it.

That said, I don't believe there's anyone in the world who wouldn't benefit from spending an hour with Dr H. Relationships are notori-ously fragile for a whole host of reasons, but most of all because they consist of two sources of free will instead of one. When we contemplate how much trouble we have managing and under-standing ourselves, it's no wonder things become mind-numbingly complicated when we attempt to try to include and understand someone else as well.

So why do we bother?

Truckloads of conflict with only pipettes of resolution, that's about the size of it.

The meaning of life is to get life to mean what you want it to mean. Being with someone is not dissimilar. Things don't have to be justifiable or logical to work. And sometimes things don't work simply because they're justifiable or logical.

I think all the best things in life are like miniature versions of the Big Bang. We may not have the first clue of how they came about, but that doesn't mean we can't enjoy every fragment of the fact that they did.

And talking of Big Bangs . . .

Sex

Top Ten Passion Killers:

10 Insecurity.
 9 Menopause.
 8 Smell.
 7 Weight.
 6 Food.
 5 Alcohol.
 4 Tiredness.
 3 Worry.
 2 Children.
 1 Work.

In the locker room of the posh gym I attend there is a daily soap opera of who's got what wrong with them, why and how. It's like a competition. One maturing man listening reluctantly and faux-sympathetically to another man's woes, biding his time till he can retaliate with his own ailment, or attempt to trump all comers. Derek's floating kneecap took some beating for a while.

But what is it that drives us to go to the gym in the first place? Simple.

We want to do all we can to remain attractive and feel sexy. Just in case.

Anyone who claims otherwise is lying, pure and simple. Sure, it makes us feel good. Sure, it gets all our endorphins racing around. But it's actually because somewhere in the deepest recesses of our dormant libido there's a voice whispering, 'Psst, come on, don't give up – there's life in the old dog yet.'

But the thing is, sex in midlife needs a preservation order

slapping on it. They say that one of the many traits we humans share with monkeys is that we are the only two species who have sex primarily for pleasure. I'm not so sure: I suspect monkeys may be on their own. As the years tick by, I'm only ever more convinced that we humans have agenda-fuelled intercourse.

By our age, we've all had sex when we're not really in the mood, just as we've all been denied sex when we are in the mood. That's what cups of tea and crosswords are for.

But the overarching issue, for the vast majority of us, is that sex is an ever-diminishing factor in our lives the older, saggier, baggier, and generally LESS BOTHERED we become.

The problem is that sometimes, as we become less bothered about something, we become more conscious of the fact it never existed in the first place.

Whereas when we first have sex with someone new, it just flows, it just happens, it just is. And isn't it wonderful? New sex is scary and exciting and naughty. New sex is like magic, it can make us feel older when we're young and younger when we're older. It liberates us from many of our inhibitions.

As our relationships develop, sex evolves into serving different purposes. To procreate, to help us tell each other we're still in love where words aren't enough, to heal wounds or to build bridges, or as a naughty treat. Sex also informs trust. But whichever way we look at it, all the time sex begins to take on all these different meanings, one thing is constantly happening – the sex brakes are gently being squeezed more and more.

The biggest brake for women being childbirth. And who can blame them? Their bodies have just created another human being. The shutters on the shop window are battened down, the factory's in full swing: why are we whimpering males at all surprised when whispers of 'Any chance of a quickie?' are met with the death stare to end all death stares? Considering what their bodies and psyches have just been through, frankly, I'm surprised women ever let us near them again.

Here's my dilemma, though.

Why do a lot of us blokes carp on when our partners put up the 'closed for business' sign? This is the thing that befuddles me. We live in a perfectly full world, too full to even begin to tap the potential of opportunities and possibilities out there. Yet we obsess and fret about something as temporarily irrelevant, unreasonable and unavailable as sex when it's no longer on the menu, at least for the time being.

Basic human need?

No, I'm not having that.

I think the real reason a lot of men get hot under the collar about a sudden or gradual dearth of skin-on-skin with their partner is because it represents a sea-change in the domestic world order.

Similar to when our mums and partners used to think we were hilarious, the kings of comedy and now just say things like,

'Oh don't be so stupid.'

'Take no notice of him, he's trying to be funny.'

We haven't changed our act but the audience has moved on.

Our craving for sex isn't a genuine physical need, it's a cry for help, for attention and recognition that we might still be part of the scenario in some small but significant way. Nothing at all to do with Dr Saveloy's meat injection. Yet still we delude ourselves, some poor souls to the extent that they risk everything by going in search of a shag elsewhere.

BIG mistake of course.

To paraphrase Paul Newman: why sneak out for a cheeseburger when there's a prime rib waiting at home?

Having an affair is another example of perfectly sane human beings going perfectly insane of their own accord.

Even if you can cope with the stress of spinning all the plates and remembering in which order each one might come crashing to the ground, what if you get found out? You stand to lose everything: your house, your life, your family, your wife, everything you've ever worked for and everything that IS YOU.

This is numpty behaviour on a colossal scale, yet people convince themselves it's their only viable option. What about the guy who has completely given up on any intimacy with his wife but can't bear to confront the situation and goes for the permanent mistress route instead? Thus perpetuating constant unhappiness at home masked by serial infidelity playing away.

He spends every waking moment deluding himself that he's having his cake and eating it, while so conflicted inside that he's only ever one misdial away from a coronary. I've seen trapped flies with more sensible strategies.

Sure, there will be fleeting moments where he feels safe and warm and secure. But only like a heroin addict, hoping the initial hit's going to last forever and no one's going to get hurt in the crossfire.

And what about the guy I know whose wife came out of the other side of mummydom to triumphantly reclaim her womanhood, hitting the gym and ending up hotter than the devil's griddle pan. But STILL denying access all areas in the bedroom department? She'd never looked more alluring but this time she was doing it all just for her, or for the world in general, but definitely not for her old man at home.

Not that she imposed a complete ban; the odd intimate moments were permissible. But that's almost worse. Sometimes it's more bearable to leave the switch in the off position than flick it on every now and again to give you a flash of what you're missing.

This is how he eventually handled the situation. Once he and his ego had gotten over the sex desert hurdle, his life changed dramatically for the better. He stopped worrying about it, reclaimed the erstwhile contaminated and obsessed head space, and applied himself instead to passions other than those of the flesh.

One of which was a quest to physically identify each one of Britain's fifty-nine species of butterfly. At the last count he'd been and tracked down at least twenty-three.

In the meantime the company he owns has doubled in size and value, he's the fittest he's ever been, and he now assures me that whenever he and his wife do get it on, she couldn't be any more accommodating.

Once again the Chinese have it.

LESS IS MORE.

Top Ten Positive Things Men Do
in Place of Having to Deal with
the Meaning of Life:

10 Sail.

9 DIY.

8 Grow vegetables.

7 Tinker in shed.

6 Tinker in garage.

5 Run.

4 Golf.

3 Fish.

2 Cycle.

1 Watch all of the above on television.

The Sex Therapist

Off I skipped off on my merry way to Harley Street to spend a very pleasant and enlightening afternoon in the company of a relationship and sex therapist by the name of Michelle Bassam.

'Oh no,' I thought immediately. 'Please God, don't let me say bosom instead of Bassam.'

We were meeting to talk turkey about sex. Bosoms are big when it comes to sex. Big bouncing bosoms were suddenly all I could think about. Don't mention the war! What war?

Aaarrrggghhh.

Michelle's surgery is located in one of the huge period terraces that line the most famous physician's street in the world. Only Britain has such streets, something we should be forever proud of.

I am asked to wait in reception until the smiling sun that is Michelle fairly bowls out to meet me. I've never talked to a stranger about sex before, not sober at least. I won't deny I am more than a little excited – in fact I can't wait.

Michelle is tanned and glowing, a blonde bundle that exudes 'So tell me, what would you like to know?' Dressed head to toe in white, trousers and a vest, she invites me to sit opposite her, but at a slight angle, her left to my right, all for a reason I'm not sure of. The pair of soft, welcoming, sumptuous, brown leather armchairs perfect for the candid conversation we were about to embark upon.

So who comes to see her?

Actually more men than women, although it's quite close and getting closer since *Fifty Shades of Grey.*

'Oh yes, *Fifty Shades* has had a marked effect on awaking a previously sexually dormant section of female demographic. Masses of women have suddenly woken up to what they might be missing out on or forgotten was possible. It doesn't take much. All that fun and the naughtiness.'

Michelle tells me that this is not a new phenomenon.

'The kind of stuff Jackie Collins used to spoon-feed previous generations was fantastic for people's sex lives. Once we know something's there, we're all keen to tune in. As a result of *Fifty Shades* thousands of UK women are now crying out for sex like never before.'

Is it the same for men?

'Sadly no, not really. Most men I see are caught in a ménage à trois – but a counter-sexual one, the trois being themselves, their partner and their work. As a result they often end up physically and mentally alienated from their spouse. What used to be a joyous joint hobby has now become an awkward taboo. Sex, that is.'

My goodness, there's a whole book here, let alone a chapter.

Being a man, I am of course aware that we are mad and silly and self-centred and needy. Furthermore, I know it's because we have a deep-down quandary as to why we're here at all. Which is why millions of us sit for hours, sometimes days, on the banks of rivers trying to catch fish that we'll never eat. Or take up golf. Who in their right mind would walk around a big plot of land for four hours trying to get a 1.68 inch-diameter white orb into a hole for no reason in particular?

And if that's not sad enough, when we're not doing this, or perhaps when we return home from doing exactly this, we plonk ourselves in front of the telly to watch other men do the same (only better) for another four or five hours. During which time we might leaf through the sports section of a newspaper or car magazine for good measure.

It doesn't take a doctor of philosophy to realize this is probably not what we were put on the planet for.

'It's for the same reason lots of men throw themselves into their work. And as they do so, everything else can get left behind. It's the "he's there, but he's not there" thing. Physical presence misrepresenting mindful presence more and more in many households.'

There is a direct link between this modernity and what leads to affairs.

'Sex at home or with a partner often needs to be managed because of everything else that's going on, whereas sex within affairs is a much more automatic and less demanding prospect.'

And do we actually need sex?

'I think we do, or at least some form of it. Sex is so much more than just the physical action of a man being with a woman. It's about experiencing regular intimacy between two people that have been together for a long time and what that means.

'It makes us feel wanted and loved and special and free. It can take the pressure of doubt away. Almost like the clouds parting after a rapturous thunderstorm when the sun bursts out, to reassure us that everything's going to be all right.'

Release and relief is another way of putting it.

'Things happen between two people during sex that don't happen at any other time in any other way. Things that are uniquely powerful and meaningful. It's like being recharged with the surety and peace of mind that your partner still loves you and desires you but more than ever. The very elixir most of us pine for and thrive on, a tacit truckload of love that can make a man feel like he can conquer the world and woman dance for the rest of her life.'

But isn't that the problem? Short-term high, long-term low?

'It's only a short-term high if you don't keep it up. But look at it like going to the gym. If you don't stick to your regime, things are going to go pear-shaped – and much quicker than you'd like.

'Sex should not have to wait until you climb into bed. It should be waiting in the wings, on call 24/7. This serves as a useful tool to help couples feel closer and less alone as they battle the trials and tribulations of everyday life.

'The odd cheeky text here of what might be on offer later. Or even a postscript to what might have already taken place the night before. Any little sparkle can lighten the heaviest mood. "Our little secret, no one knows apart from us", things like that.'

And the best thing?

'It's totally legal and entirely free. Usually. What's not to like?'

All right, Michelle, how about protecting the sex life we may already have or reigniting what we used to have – give us some tips please.

'Ooh, a mission statement, I love it, let's go.' She's beaming like a Cheshire cat.

'Partner's timetables are hugely important. You want your man or woman, you need to book a time. Not clinically, so as to take away any spontaneity, but it's an important and obvious factor that many people forget or don't want to admit.

'Date days are excellent for this. Weekends away without the kids. Silencing the bloomin' mobile. Make some time, ditch the distractions and give yourself a chance to feel what it is each other is in need of. And there is absolutely nothing to be ashamed of when it comes to packing something saucy for the suitcase. It's not rocket science, but there is a recipe so you do have to have at least some of the right ingredients.'

'A problem shared is a problem halved, we know, but a plan shared to ring-fence some "you" time is foreplay personified. Even by merely logging on to the Internet over a glass of wine, you'll find yourselves giggling like teenagers planning a clandestine rendez-vous.'

Michelle says couples are never better together than when they're on a joint mission to have fun together.

'To plan, we have to communicate, and communication, communication, communication is the key to couples remembering what they love and like about each other.'

Once a couple begin holding hands they should never stop.

'Show me a couple holding hands and I'll show you a couple together for a good while yet to come. Whether it's walking into the sunset on a beach in paradise, or dawdling down the frozen foods aisle of the local supermarket.'

Is there a joint, low-key, unofficial mantra couples can adopt?

'Absolutely. A good general rule is, always have a shared something going on. Whatever it may be and even if it's a good while away, start talking about it now. Bring it to life on a regular basis. Chart its progress from field to fork and then catalogue the memory of it once it's been and gone.'

And so we effortlessly segue into one of Michelle's absolute favourite topics: the bedroom.

'It's very simple. Bedrooms should be designed for sleep first and sex second: everything else can go whistle. And as for computers and telephones, a blanket ban I'm afraid. Forgive the pun but no, not at all. These are just excuses to avoid intimacy masquerading as essential technology and importance. Nothing should take priority over us letting our partner know how much we still love, cherish, respect and most of all enjoy them. The outside world should cease to exist the moment the bedroom door opens and the bedcovers are thrown back. Or even before that, when your foot first steps on the bottom stair of your staircase. LEAVE IT ALL BEHIND, all the nonsense. I implore you!'

Michelle is adamant that none of the nonsense we insist on surrounding ourselves with nowadays is of any use compared to what we can give and do for each other simply by offering physical love, affection and attention.

'Every night going to bed should feel like chucking the suitcases in the back of the car and sneaking off for a couple of days away without anyone else knowing. Why the hell not? We become geniuses at forgetting how bloomin' simple and inexpensive it is to enjoy what we've got right in front of us. We're all gorgeous and marvellous and sexy, if we allow ourselves to be. It's actually what we're all best at.'

Michelle is on fire. 'Jump in bed and shout, "Phew, thank God that's over. We made it through another mad day. Now come here you . . ." Why would anyone in their right mind pass that up in favour of, "Right, I really must check on those emails."'

She has a parting message for us all.

'Go to bed TONIGHT after purposefully leaving your phone on charge downstairs and see what difference it makes.'

However, Michelle does go on to point out that all the symptoms of space abuse our bedrooms suffer from are abundant in every room in the house: the living room is for living, the kitchen is for cooking, eating, drinking and socializing, the garden is for relaxing and yet THAT BLOODY PHONE comes everywhere with us.

'Treat any electronic device as the unwelcome lodger who you wished you'd never said yes to but has unexpectedly given you a get-out clause. Get rid while you still can.'

Michelle my belle, does sex have all the answers?

'Well, I'm not so sure about that, but it's certainly a useful metaphor and counsellor to help identify what might be wrong.'

'And for SEX see also stroking the back of your partner's neck at a dinner party, or a spontaneous kiss on the cheek as he or she is concentrating on driving. Just LET THEM KNOW. It's all about the constant hovering cloud of I LOVE YOU, I CARE ABOUT YOU, I want you and I want you to want me.'

And the single most important thing?

'The now-ness of now. For some reason business, the government, education and medicine have all forsaken the now for the future. Future goals, future targets, future everything. While planning and organization are important and can be fun, as we've talked about, it has become too much of an excuse for avoiding the now.

'You can't be wrong in the future because it never comes. Living in the future therefore has become the new safe haven for the avoidance of fear and failure. But it's hijacking everything we have fought for over centuries. If we were imprisoned, we would do all we could to imagine and taste what it would feel like to be free. Yet here we are, already free, in constant peril of doing the opposite.

Make love not phone calls?

'Absolutely,' enthuses Michelle.

Michelle, we LOVE you.

Love

Top Ten Best Things
Love Makes Us Feel:

10 Energized.

9 Fearless.

8 Courageous.

7 Protective.

6 Inspired.

5 Needed.

4 Never alone.

3 Alive.

2 Safe.

1 Human.

When I was in the final stages of writing this book I went to stay on a friend's sailing boat in Lymington. During my second morning on board, another yacht silently slid into the mooring alongside.

She was a lovely young thing, navy-blue hull and as sleek as could be. Turns out she and her crew had just taken part in a race all the way from New York.

Bloody NEW YORK!!!

Pulling up to the pontoon were the last few feet of her epic journey. Incredible to think no one would know unless they were told. No crowds, no banners, just Arnie from Lymington Yacht Charter grabbing a line as she made her last turn of thousands gently to starboard.

After a couple of hours, six of the seven crew on board had departed to go home, or have a drink. Only one soul remained, a lady by the name of Basia, a resident New Yorker who'd been enlisted as local crew a few weeks beforehand, happy to sign on the dotted line for this her latest adventure of many.

Super intelligent, super fit, slim but not at all skinny, with tousled, shoulder-length, slightly wavy brown hair, dark skin and dark eyes; not beautiful but certainly attractive.

We got chatting. Born in Poland, she had moved to New York to go to university and had since forged a successful career in the pharmaceutical industry. As well as being a fascinating human being, she was an experienced yachtswoman with a deep-seated will to win.

But I was more than a little surprised to learn that sailing was not her number one passion.

'Ah so it's your work then, sailing being the release for that. Your escape. Your solace?'

'Actually no, what I really love to do is dance. I originally trained as a ballerina.'

Wow? She really was Superwoman.

By now it was mid afternoon. Since she didn't appear to have any plans or any idea about the local area, I could only conclude that she was planning to spend the evening on board, on her own, with a takeaway and perhaps a well deserved cold beverage. But surely that would never do. How could a woman who had just crossed the Atlantic spend the evening alone, not celebrating?

After mulling it over for a while and considering whether or not it might be appropriate to invite her for dinner, I concluded it was the decent and proper thing to do, especially as I was not going alone but with a couple of pals. Besides, selfishly, I wanted to hear everything about what she had experienced over the last sixteen days. What was it like to successfully navigate over three thousand miles in fewer than three weeks in a boat a little over fifty feet? We would be keen listeners if Basia would be keen to talk.

I asked the guys first and with their approval extended a friendly invitation to my new pontoon pal, the Polish Lady. She accepted in a heartbeat, with a smile. A couple of hours later Arnie was ribbing us over to the Isle of Wight at 40 knots-plus to a brilliant beachside restaurant called The Hut. The Hut is an old pre-fab building that used to be a café and has since been transformed into a supercool half-in/half-out brunch, lunch and dinner venue by a couple of young dudes from Chelsea. If you ever get the chance, go, it's idyllic.

After casting the anchor, and cadging a lift ashore, Arnie, Hugh and I sat spellbound for three hours as Basia had us misty-eyed one moment and gasping with wonder the next via her salty tales of transatlantic hell and high water. Of course, by the end of the night we were all a little bit in love with her. The thing that captivated us most was how extraordinarily matter-of-fact and modest she was about her adventure.

After toasting her success more times than I care to remember with white wine and red wine, champagne and even tequila (which I never normally touch nowadays) it was time to settle up, jump back in the rib and head for the mainland.

A truly great night.

The next day we met up for coffee at The Haven, the bar I have an interest in that looks over the marina.

'So what are your plans today?' I asked.

'I would like to see something typical of the area. I have two days before I have to go home and I would love to see as much as I can.'

The way I write is in three two-hour sessions with a break and mini celebration after each. As the day goes on, the celebrations become ever more extravagant. The rhythm goes like this:

Write
Break
Write
Break
Write
Cake

Cake, eh? Crazy, I know. It might not sound all that celebratory but the thought of a slice of Francis's home-made Victoria Sponge with a robust cup of tea is more than enough to keep me going with the home straight of a day of writing ahoy.

As I can write anywhere, my schedule allowed me to offer to taxi my new friend to various locations that I thought she might like. I suggested she could go off and do her own thing while I holed up at various nearby cafés and car parks doing mine. Then when she was done I could drop her off at the next port of call.

Over the ensuing thirty-six hours this arrangement worked a treat. Basia got to do what she wanted to while I got to do what I needed to. Enjoying a bit of fresh air and several changes of scenery into the bargain, and getting to know each other a little bit more with every mile, one of the things she told me was that she had now been divorced for longer than she was originally married.

'I walked down the aisle at twenty. Mum told me I was too young.'

Not wanting to admit defeat, she'd hung in there for ten years, until she was thirty. Now forty-five, she'd had several boyfriends but none of them was 'The One'. None of them were able to accept or understand her ambition to dance or sail her way around the world.

We also discovered we'd read a lot of the same philosophy books, which then became a recurring theme of conversation. As did this book, the book I was currently writing.

The more I explained what it was about, the more her interest piqued. She was dealing with a lot of the issues I'd been researching and thinking about. Immediately I wanted to record everything she was saying, heartfelt, intensely thought through, intelligent, some of it brilliant.

She even wrote me a recommended reading list before she left for the airport.

During our last 'taxi' ride together after a rare silence, which could have been a few seconds or ten or fifteen minutes, I really have no idea, she turned to me and said softly,

'Is there a chapter in your book about love?'

To which I replied:

'Actually, no.'

'Why not?'

'Because it fries my brain.'

It always has and it always will.

Ten Things Love Can Be:

10 Amazing.
 9 Frustrating.
 8 Fantastic.
 7 Heartbreaking.
 6 Devastating.
 5 Fleeting.
 4 Caring.
 3 Passionate.
 2 Infuriating.
 1 An allotment.

Love equals four innocent letters so permanently open to convenience and misleading interpretation that they cannot possibly cope with the task with which they have been charged.

Love is: whatever you want it to be, bearing in mind it is as volatile as an unexploded bomb.

Death

Top Ten Certainties About Life:

10 The world is mad.
 9 We are mad.
 8 Not enough people vote.
 7 Too few companies have too much power.
 6 A handful of dull people rule the world.
 5 Everyone will lie to you at some point.
 4 We will all lie to everyone at some point.
 3 We can always be better.
 2 Things can always be worse.
 1 We are going to die.

We are all going to die yet it's the one thing most of us like to think about least.

What's going on here?

Straight off the bat, we make least sense of all when it comes to our relationship with death. If we put half as much effort into understanding and embracing death as we do into trying to put it off, most of our lives would be immeasurably better.

If you want your wife or husband or lover or mum or dad or kids, nephews and nieces to start Christmas Day with a smile, there's a good chance you will put a decent amount of thought into what to buy them as a present. If you want to host a half-decent dinner party, then you're more likely than not to put some effort into thinking about who to invite, where everyone should sit and what might be nice to eat. Similarly, if you want the holiday of a lifetime, there's a fair chance it will turn out better if you bother to do a bit of research and planning, as opposed to leaving everything until your first day off work and hoping to get somewhere decent sorted to go in the next few hours.

So why do the vast majority of us fail to apply such common sense and clear thinking to the most important moment in our lives, i.e. the moment our lives cease to be and we return to the non-being from whence we came?

As a family, we recently enjoyed the rollercoaster ride that was organizing my daughter Jade's wedding. It was a hoot for the most part, but the best thing of all was the family meetings it necessitated. Over dinner, down the pub, the girls out on a weekend choosing all their outfits, the lads booking the venue, the church, the restaurants and the tents. Eventually we opted for glamping in our garden and the church over the road, as opposed to remote hotels and an endless fleet of taxis elsewhere and back.

So how come we can't bring ourselves to engender that same *joie de vivre* when it comes to the prospect of our demise – why not approach it with a little *joie de morte*? After having thought about this chapter long and hard, that's exactly what I have now decided to do.

It's our last opportunity to let people know how much we loved them, what they meant to us and what we ended up believing we stood for and what life is all about.

Perhaps the main reason we have learnt so little about being human from one generation to the next is because we are so reluctant to admit and acknowledge the passing of one before another.

Sure it's great to have a load of people stand up and declare what the deceased meant to them, but let's face it, he or she can't exactly hear what's being said. Far more useful and inspiring is to allow the deceased to have their say to everyone still alive.

Our final chance to tell it like it is without fear of reprehension.

• • •

Forget making a will, our top priority should be making our funeral video. What a business that is just waiting to happen. I went to a funeral last year where a letter from the deceased was enough to render the congregation spellbound. Read out by his best mate, it was the bridegroom's speech none of us ever get to make. Assured, funny, wise and, most of all, totally honest.

What a marvellous moment to relish and anticipate if letters, videos and even holograms became the norm at funerals.

Have you written your funeral speech yet?

Am I in it?

Who's not in it?

Are there any jokes?

What are you going to wear for your death video?

Brilliant. It would be like our own personal Academy Awards speech. Who would you like to thank? Who's worthy of a mention and who's not?

Can you imagine the trepidation of the gathered mourners, wondering who the deceased has it in for and who he/she doesn't. I can foresee people ducking out of attending funerals just in case they are the one that 'gets both barrels'.

'Nudge, nudge, wink, wink, buckle up, here we go. I reckon Auntie Edna's gonna get torn off a strip.'

Funerals that people can't wait to go to, or are too scared to go to, that's what we want. With the same sense of revelation and anticipation you get waiting to see if your lottery numbers have come up.

Of course, funerals that have been pre-planned by the deceased have been around for a while. In most cases by people who know they're going to die and have had time to acquire the necessary wisdom, calm and frame of mind to come to terms with what's going to happen.

'They know they're going to die' – there's a phrase that makes me chuckle the more I think about it.

I don't mean to be insensitive, but we *all* know we're going to die. Why are we in such massive denial about the chaos that's bound to ensue unless we put a bit of pre-planning in place over a pie and a pint in a pub for a couple of hours?

I have been to two pre-planned funerals, both of which, I can honestly say, were miles better than any of the loads of others I've attended.

Apart from the funeral that I've already mentioned, the one where the deceased's best mate read out his letter, the other was that of a young girl called Debbie who had been ill most of her life with cystic fibrosis. She'd had months, if not years, to think about her funeral and had it planned down to the very last detail. As a result it was just the most perfect day. Terrifically sad, as the death of a teenager unquestionably will always be. But incredibly beautiful and inspiring at the same time.

Unlike Debbie's funeral, most funerals are missed opportunities in my experience. Some religions are way ahead in this regard. But when it comes to the vast majority of the Western world's non-religious individuals, we are crazy not to give it more thought.

We need to urgently adopt a policy of honesty, admission, straightforwardness and transparency through the whole process of our death and dispatch.

To thine own self be true, if not in life, at least in death. Who do you want to be there? Who do you not want to be there? Do you want a seating plan to reflect who meant what to you?

There's a whole funeral revolution waiting to happen. Bring it on, I say.

Cue one of the most illuminating, refreshing, encouraging and engaging conversations I've ever had. A conversation that pretty much wrote itself into this book.

The Greatest Funeral Director Alive Today

Top Ten Certainties About Death:

10 It's generally far too long and drawn out.
 9 There's too much staring at ceilings involved.
 8 It's getting ever more long and drawn out, almost sadistically so.
 7 Yet more ceilings.

6 There's too much fear of death.
5 Death is the ultimate elephant in the room.
4 Death is the definitive magical mystery tour.
3 Death is vastly underrated.
2 Death is why we feel alive.
1 Being dead doesn't hurt.

David Collingwood is the operations director for Co-op Funeral Care. Dave – or the Funeral King, as he will forever be known in my mind – has been working in the funeral industry since he was ten.

'It's all I ever wanted to do. My dad was a doctor and his surgery was next to a funeral parlour. Like you, I always loved cars and the biggest and best ones I'd ever seen up close were the big black Daimlers of the funeral directors.

'I was fascinated by their sheer size and majesty and was thrilled to inveigle my way into getting a Saturday job washing and polishing them. While generally hanging around I began to learn more about the bigger picture they were involved in. Gradually I became fascinated, obsessed almost, by the art of funeral directing. It was only a question of time before I moved inside, away from my valeting duties, to take up my first post in the business, accessorizing coffins. After that, I was hooked.'

I'm not sure I've ever come across anyone quite as passionate about what they do for a living as Dave.

His voice is a unique blend of enthusiasm, energy, warmth, gentleness and sensitivity. Like a librarian dying to tell a colleague they've won the lottery but not wanting to disturb anyone in the process.

'We funeral directors are available to our customers 24/7, 365 days a year. We have to be, it's our duty. If I get a call on Christmas Day at three o'clock in the morning then either I, or one of my staff, will be there within the hour. That's what happens when you are responsible for dealing with approximately a hundred thousand funerals a year, as my team and I are now. That's roughly a fifth of all deaths annually in Britain.'

A figure I later discovered is down on recent years, as we are beginning to die later and later. This means funerals are currently experiencing a lag until we catch up with ourselves, circa 2018.

'I say to all my team, being a funeral director is a privileged and highly regarded position. Whether you're suited and booted and ready for someone's final send-off, or you're in jeans and a T-shirt down the pub, you are always representing what we do.

'And I have to say – to a man and to a woman, they all totally get it. We funeral directors are a breed unto ourselves; it is a vocation and a calling much more than it will ever be an occupation. We are born to serve and wouldn't want it any other way.'

There is no doubt in my mind. Dave's the perfect person to be our nation's go-to funeral man.

But he's so obviously sincere and genuine that suddenly I feel I don't want to unleash my disapproval and frustration at the general wincing and cowering mindset we have surrounding dying and funerals in the UK. It's not Dave's fault. Though I need not worry: Dave's thought about little else all his life.

'Make no mistake, funeral directors are on hand to help people organize an event that nobody wants. Most people will only organize one or two funerals in their life, if that. We are constantly dealing with bereaved individuals who haven't the faintest idea what to do. And then there are complications when natural causes may not necessarily be the cause of death and legal implications have to be taken into consideration – surrounding cases of murder, for example, or suicide and the like. Add to that the fact that our clients are not exactly in the best frame of mind to make balanced retail and consumer decisions and it's not difficult to see the fragility of many of the situations we encounter on a daily basis.'

Of course. In many ways it's a salesman's dream – but not for Dave, no way.

'It's very important that we ask the newly bereaved what they would like, as opposed to telling them what they should have, or what will make us most money. Every initial meeting is a crash course in funeral planning. We are professionals dealing with the rawest of amateurs in the most extreme emotional circumstances imaginable.'

This response gives me an opportunity to ease into a mildly confrontational line of questioning.

I suggest to Dave that we need to start talking about funerals pre-death. This last-minute-dot-com approach is surely no good for all parties concerned. How come it has been thus, and for far too long?

'I couldn't agree more. Not knowing for certain what the deceased would like presents their loved ones with the ultimate, unwelcome guessing game. It would be fabulous to have a concrete steer on their preferences while they are still here to tell us.

'This is beginning to happen via pre-paid funerals, which are becoming more and more popular. Especially in our "either/or" category. This is where a couple will pre-pay for a single funeral and then whoever goes first is the beneficiary of that package. It can get quite competitive,' he giggles.

Dave is simply brilliant, a living and breathing advert for why none of us should fear the inevitable. How we should all seriously think about what type of send-off we would like.

'Whenever people talk about funerals, before any illness is around or any sad or unfortunate circumstances have evolved, it always ends up with laughter. Which is when people make the best and most positive decisions. And there is so much more funereal fun to be had nowadays.

'For example, the choice of hearses has greatly improved since my Saturday job all those years ago cleaning the cars in Bradford Funeral Directors' yard. There are motorbike side-car hearses, we have a Buddhist pick-up truck that is acquiring a growing reputation, and there's even a tank hearse, if you fancy a bit of that.

'Plus, we are trying to spread the word ourselves. We attend twelve county shows a year where our Land Rover hearse receives a lot of interest. Hugely popular with the rural and farming community. That's the one I would want to go in.

'There's also all the different coffin options we offer: oak, willow, bamboo, banana leaf, and biodegradable cardboard, which is very popular nowadays. Then there's the more pioneering options concerning different methods of disposal.

'In the old days, everyone was buried, and I mean everyone. But with less space increasingly becoming an issue, cremations very quickly became more popular. Once, that is, British society had overcome the taboo of burning bodies – which for decades was extremely controversial.'

The more I listen to Dave eulogize and explain the intricate vagaries surrounding the history of funerals, the more I realize they are very much a subject of glacial evolution as opposed to much needed revolution. Indeed, much of the development of the way we say goodbye to our loved ones has been born out of necessity, like funeral directing itself, as Dave explains:

'Funeral directing can actually be traced back to the Co-op joinery industry. Carpenters were asked to make coffins but then no one knew what to do next, hence the joinery profession saw a business opportunity and thus became the founders of our profession as we know it today.'

Well I'll be, it's as simple as that. I don't know why I'm surprised – necessity the mother of invention yet again, as it so often is. And bearing in mind that last year the Co-op's funeral division turned over £347 million, some business it's become. So does Dave have a crystal ball as to where funerals can go from here?

'Well, yes, I travel the world looking at how other countries and cultures are developing their burial methods and ceremonies. One advancement in particular that interests me is the disposal process, known as resumation or alkaline hydrolysis, to give it its technical name.

'That's how I think I'd like my remains to be dealt with. Far more efficient and environmentally friendly. It's a process different from cremation but one that also results in the creation of ashes. Ashes as we know being very important to loved ones who then take them and spread them somewhere significant to the deceased. This is such a huge boon when it comes to helping people achieve closure.

I've no idea why specifically, but that's not the point. All that matters is they feel better for having achieved a more palpable goodbye.'

How good at his job is this guy?

As we continue to talk I feel like I can ask Dave anything and he won't be offended as he is sure to have already considered it. Besides which it's not my intention to be offensive, I just want to know more.

And so what about children and their exposure or, maybe more importantly, their lack of exposure to funerals and the scar that it can have on them for life, as I sense it has with me?

This is a subject that really sets Dave alight:

'What adults don't understand is that children are brilliant at learning and dealing with change – far more than we are. And far, far more than we give them credit for. I always say to people, if they think their kiddies can cope with a funeral and all that goes with it, they should definitely go and see what all the fuss is about.

'Children see things very black and white compared to older people. It's their job to learn and they are experts at it. Adults shouldn't let their own narrow-mindedness infect what in my experience usually turns out to be a hugely positive thing for a child to witness.'

Whoa!

This sentiment doesn't so much resonate with me as chime deafeningly inside my head. My dad was ill for a very long time and basically died at home. The kind of long, slow, miserable, painful and degrading death you might not wish on your worst enemy. My mum thought I'd suffered enough, so suggested I stayed at home when it was time.

Yet here I was remonstrating at how rubbish we are dealing with death and I still hadn't done anything about talking to my mum about how she might like her funeral to be. I asked Dave for his advice where my own situation was concerned.

'Chris, from what you've told me your mum has had more than her fair share of health issues over the last ten years and in many ways you may have left it a bit late. Indeed, it's always going to be awkward to approach someone else about their funeral. What we need to be doing is leading by example for the benefit of future generations. We need to talk about our own funerals first and then perhaps other people might feel more comfortable about bringing up the prospect of their own.'

Again what Dave says makes complete and utter sense. I have missed the suitable window of opportunity for a creative and light-hearted funereal discussion with my mum by about, oh let's see – a good *fifteen to twenty-five years*.

If I were to suddenly bring up the subject with her now, who could blame her for thinking it sounded like I had concluded her existence was dragging on a bit and it was time to call last orders.

'Sometimes you just have to accept that the moment has passed, even if the person in question has not,' says Dave.

Hilarious. He is so brilliantly pragmatic about everything.

'Like most problems, it's never about what you initially think. If we track the source of the issue right back to where it all starts to unravel, it's down to all of us to take the bull by the horns and bring up the subject of our own demise and departing so no one else has to.'

Our kids and grandkids need to be taught to do this by the generations who are going to die before they are; teaching from behind it's sometimes referred to as, or leading by example if you'd rather. So that means, ladies and gentlemen, that the next quantum shift in how to make dying easier is wholeheartedly and unreservedly down to us.

No longer can we justify crouching in the corner in the pathetic hope that death's creeping shadow won't notice we are there and will pass us by. Death is going to come, regardless of how much we quake and quiver and pray for it not to. No matter how many drugs they invent, no matter how many other planets become inhabitable, no matter how much we meditate for it not to.

No longer can we shirk the responsibility of the inevitable by claiming the ignorance of our forefathers. We are the most blessed species ever to have the gift of life bestowed upon us. It's time we

VE Day, live on BBC One from Horse Guards Parade. The only occasion all year that would get me to wear a shirt and tie. (BBC)

TV takes for ever … and ever … and ever. (Hiten Vora)

The 500 Words writing competition for children
under the age of thirteen is so important to me.
The Duchess of Cornwall has been a great supporter. (BBC)

BBC Music Day. Alex, Jamie Cullum and me.
It was much colder than it looks. (BBC)

One of my absolute bestest friends, genius super-vet
Noel Fitzpatrick at the opening day of his new
Pet Cancer Centre. (Natasha Evans)

Above: Jackpot! Joanna Lumley and my *One Show* co-presenter Alex Jones. (Tom Fenner)

Left: Me doing my impression as Fearne Cotton's dad. (BBC / Guy Levy)

Minnie, Mrs Evans Senior, gives a spellbinding and spontaneous speech at CarFest in front of 30,000 people. Her opening line: 'If the world had half as many people as generous as you, everything would be all right.' (Brand Events)

With the London Marathon world-record holder, my secret marathon coach Paula Radcliffe. (Virgin Money London Marathon)

Above: Finishing line with *that* medal. The smile lasted for weeks. (Virgin Money London Marathon)

Left: Celebrating at the finish with Tash, Eli and Noah. Pizza and ice-cream only minutes away.

Spot the real ginge. Prince Harry appears on the show to talk about the Invictus Games. (BBC / Invictus Games)

accepted that life's specialness comes from only one thing: the fact that it is temporary.

We need to talk about dying much more than we do. And much much more than we ever have done.

Just discussing the research and writing of this chapter with friends and family brought about a collective sigh of relief, release, reflection and eventual merciless mickey-taking and rib-tickling.

Within half a bottle of wine it had become abundantly apparent that there was no point whatsoever in living under a cloak of fear with regard to the subject of our own passing. Like learning to swim, it's best not to wait until you're drowning to begin.

Why aren't kids taught about dying at school? Surely it's more relevant to life than improper fractions or the periodic table. Not only would such conversation open their eyes to appreciating and making the most of more elderly folks around them, but it would provide a huge fillip to help them realize what a marvellous thing it is to be alive in the first place.

'That's a lovely idea, Christoff, but in reality it would be cruel and upset them beyond what their little hearts need to experience at such a tender and vulnerable age!' I can hear the protesters whimpering already.

Well, bollocks to anyone who holds that point of view. I fundamentally disagree. My dad died and it broke my heart. But not going to his funeral twisted the knife, a feeling that has stayed with me to this day.

My funeral hero Dave agrees.

When he let slip over dinner one night that one of the new items that's come to market is the novelty coffin wrap, where one can choose to have photos or various images emblazoned on the coffin, his youngest, Kitty, who was nine at the time, couldn't wait to volunteer what she'd go for.

'I'd like the Tardis option, Daddy,' said Kitty, because she loves *Doctor Who*. 'That would be so cool!'

And with that from Kitty, I feel empowered to be able to move on.

You see, funerals can be cool. It's official. Kitty and her fantastic dad say so.

Top Ten Initial Funeral Changes
We Might Want to Think About:

10 Ditch the dull hearse for a more bespoke vehicle.
9 Wheel out the fun bus.
8 Ditch the wreaths.
7 Hand out the garlands.
6 Sack the organist.
5 Sign up the DJ.
4 Ditch the black.
3 Don the Hawaiian shirts and shorts.
2 Ditch the finger buffet.
1 Break out the barbie, especially for cremations.

And seriously, why all the black?

'It's to show respect.'

NO NO NO.

All it does is scare the kids and make them never want to go to a funeral again.

My mum suggested it was far better for me not to go to my dad's funeral because it would be too sad and make me too upset.

MY DAD HAD JUST DIED – I COULDN'T POSSIBLY BE ANY MORE UPSET.

Not that I'm saying my mum did the wrong thing. More that funerals, and the way they have almost always been, brainwashed my mum into thinking she was doing the right thing.

There is no doubt in my mind that this is where a lot of the psychological nonsense and fear of dying begins.

'But, Mummy, everyone was so sad and miserable. Lots of grown-ups were crying, which scares me anyway because when grown-ups cry they must be really scared. And then there was this weird part where after crying for about an hour or maybe more, everyone went quiet for a bit, then had a few drinks before they all started laughing as if it was New Year's Eve all of a sudden. IT WAS REALLY CONFUSING!!!'

You're not kidding, sweetheart.

It's confusing for us adults too, we just don't like to admit it.

• • •

So is there any hope on the horizon? Any light amongst all that dark?

If you google 'wedding planner' the phrases that come up are joyous and celebratory, not so much to do with the weddings they plan but with the services they offer, e.g.: 'Sarah Haywood is a British luxury wedding planner, internationally renowned for her exclusive and prestigious clients.'

Wow!

'An amazing and unforgettable wedding made easy and affordable.'

Phew!

'The greatest day of your lives deserves the greatest service we can offer.'

Bravo!

Now compare this to the searches that come up when you input 'funeral planner':

'Cover the cost of your funeral now.'

Oh joy!

'A pre-paid plan will bring peace of mind to you and your loved ones.'

What a hoot!

'The perfect prayers, poems and service created with sympathy and sensitivity.'

Yawn – but oh, hang on a moment, what's this:

'The Funeral Planner. Bringing life to a dead business.'

Oh no, hold your horses. It's a movie, not an actual company. But the writers of the film should start the business for real. They'd make a mint. In fact, I might just do that. The Funeral Party Planner – Evans on Earth. This could be the big one.

I can hear the voice-over for my TV ad already:

'I didn't like the way funerals were going so I changed mine and now you can change yours.'

I can just see myself being interviewed by Lorraine Kelly.

'And now, please welcome Britain's first-ever billionaire King of the Casket – Chriiiis Evaaaaans!'

I'm dreamin' the funeral dream, baby. People have to die, it's in the rules. It's time we woke up to the fact and someone wrote a *Fifty Shades of Black – Stuff That, I Don't Think So* to show us the way.

There are so many positives to saying goodbye to our loved ones and barely any of them are being realized. There needs to be a mass reassessment of what it means to die, both for the deceased and those 'left behind'.

Phrases like 'left behind' do no one any favours. Getting 'left behind' is what happens to us when we miss the coach after a boozy day at the seaside. I'm actually quite glad I keep getting 'left behind' at funerals, it means I'm still alive. Just when exactly did misleading macabre messages such as this get signed off en masse?

I wonder if Esther Rantzen is available to revive her fabulous smash-hit show of the Seventies and Eighties, *That's Life!* – but for a one-off special called *That's Death*. Similarly, perhaps Michael Aspel is up for a few one-offs of *This Is Your Death* as opposed to *This Is Your Life*.

Anything to help break down the taboo of death being all too . . . deathly.

Religion

Top Ten Favourite Hymns:

10 Dear Lord and Father of Mankind
 9 All Things Bright and Beautiful
 8 Morning Has Broken
 7 Guide Me, O Thou Great Redeemer
 6 We Plough the Fields and Scatter
 5 For All the Saints
 4 The Day Thou Gavest, Lord, Is Ended
 3 Lord of the Dance
 2 Holy, Holy, Holy
 1 Sing Hosanna

To believe or not to believe? That is the question.

I've often wondered – and when I say often, I mean several times a day for as long as I can remember – whether I'm a man of faith or not.

I never feel alone, so that's one thing. I never feel scared, so that's another. But more than anything, for the last twelve months especially, I've felt a seismic change deep within my very being. I'm far less anxious about things than I can ever remember being. I'm far more honest with myself when it comes to people and situations. My whole attitude to material wealth and possessions has come full circle. I'm more accepting of any situation I find myself in. I've stopped chasing the game. In fact I've stopped playing the game and chasing anything, altogether. It's as if I've been given sharper ears and sharper eyes to help improve my ability to differentiate between what's good for me and what's not, a sixth sense if you like.

So what I'm wondering is how has this come about? Why has it happened now? And all the time I keep coming back to a distant awareness that it's probably because I feel like I'm not alone. I want to call it some kind of force but that's not quite what I mean. It's more like I have access to extra capacity permanently available to draw upon, seek counsel from, gain strength and patience from. I'd say it was more of a new conscience. Like a well that has everything I might need, whenever I might need it. Sure, I still encounter problems and sleepless nights, but even they feel like the beginning of the end of a process of cleansing, renewal and starting again.

The Archbishop

I decided to ask my friend John Sentamu, Archbishop of York, for his insight on the matter. We've been pals now for five years or so, ever since he invited me to present a Christmas show from his official residence, Bishopthorpe Palace. Inviting us to broadcast a show was one thing, inviting us to have dinner and stay the night with him and his wife Margaret was entirely another.

'Meet me at the Athenaeum at 3.15 p.m.,' read his text.

I arrived ten minutes early.

'I'm here to see John Sentamu.'

'I'm sorry, we have no one of that name staying here,' replied the hotel receptionist after checking her computer screen once, twice and then a third time. 'Might he be under another name?'

'Er, the Archbishop of York,' I muttered sheepishly.

It was clear from the young lady's expression she had no idea who I was talking about. Surely, a man as renowned and charismatic as John would be known to even the most unaware of hotel staff, were he staying with them. There was clearly something not right with our arrangement.

'Are you sure it's not the Athenaeum Club? We get quite a lot of confusion between us and them.'

God bless this woman, she was of course absolutely bang-on. I'd never heard of the Athenaeum Club and it turned out John had never heard of the Athenaeum Hotel. Fortunately John's location in Pall Mall was only minutes away from my location on Piccadilly, just opposite Green Park.

Problem number two: John was also entirely unaware that there was no way his club was going to allow me entry wearing jeans and my leather motorsport jacket.

'Oh dear, do you know anywhere we could go for "our chat", young Christopher?'

As it happened, I did. Sort of. Christie's auction house was equidistant between our first two unsuccessful venues. Seeing as, over the years, I've spent a good few quid there and got to know a few of the faces quite well, I decided to take a chance. I bundled J.S. into the back of a cab in the hope that the world-famous auction house would take pity on us both, us refuge and perhaps even throw in a cup of coffee and a biccie.

'Wow, this is fantastic, Chris, but how might we find somewhere to talk here?' asked John.

Right on cue, my main contact at Christie's, Will Porter, arrived with his customary smiling zeal.

'Hey, Chris, I'm sure we can get you and the Right Reverend Bishop Sentamu into a private client room for an hour or so.'

A cappuccino, a pot of tea and a few swipes of several security passes later and finally John and I had the sanctuary we'd been seeking.

What a man this was I had sitting in front of me, gifting a couple of hours of his precious time with little or no idea precisely what it was I wanted to talk about.

One of thirteen children, J.S. was born in the tiny village of Masooli, ten miles from Kampala in Uganda. Masooli means maize, which is what the village was famous for growing. He arrived premature at just four and a half pounds and as a result was constantly in and out of hospital up until the age of five.

'Rejoice in your weakness for it is that which makes you strong,' was one of the many pearls of wisdom he would lay at my feet in the next couple of hours.

Can you believe he was only ten years old when he sensed his calling to his Lord Jesus Christ?

'That's incredible,' I exclaimed, finding this quite difficult to believe. Whereupon he recalled the exact moment his vocational light-bulb came on:

'I had done a deal with four boys who had offered me some of their banana pancake if I gave them each a replacement exercise book for the ones they'd lost, for which they would undoubtedly receive the cane. After I had carried out the dirty deed I had a profound sensation that what I had done was wrong but that I would be forgiven if I asked forgiveness. Which I did. Jesus then told me I must tell my parents immediately. The next day I said a prayer offering the rest of my life over to God's work.'

With, however the razor-smart marks of several whips of the cane on his own pre-pubescent behind. The twist in the tail being the fact that the cane-wielding headmaster was his very own father.

'"We have a thief amongst us," Dad declared to the whole school in an afternoon assembly following my confession.'

'That was a bit raw,' I suggested, expecting John to defend his dad to the hilt as the responsible moral barometer, forced to make an example of his own son rather than show any favouritism. But no.

'I thought exactly the same!' he guffawed. 'I couldn't believe he was punishing me for coming clean and telling the truth. However, this only helped me with my relationship with Jesus. The next day when I pledged my allegiance to him, I discovered there is only ever forgiveness where he is concerned, never any retribution. Jesus will never cane you.'

From that moment on John went about preaching the Word of the Lord. 'I'm sure I got on everyone's nerves most of the time,' he chuckled. 'In fact, I remember my classmates declaring, "Here comes the Pope!" in the playground at break times. The biggest insult one could hurl in a Christian's direction, such was the divide between the Anglican and Catholic churches during that period.'

What I most wanted to hear was how John could be so certain, when it came to his unshakeable faith in the Bible and its teachings.

'Chris,' he began, giggling again, 'the thing with you is, you are a man who deals in words every day and so here you are asking me to explain what I believe and why I believe it, which of course I understand. But let me ask you this: how do you know for sure you love your sons?'

It was a simple but profound question.

'Well, I just do, overwhelmingly. I actually don't know specifically how.'

'Of course you don't. And why do you need to? As long as you know you love them, that's all that matters. That's what sets you free. The overwhelming certainty that comes from being a human being and opening yourself up to something so great and so powerful that we will never be able to comprehend exactly what it is and why it makes us feel how it does. Love can never and will never be able to be reduced to formulae. And so it is when it comes to faith. Hope, despair, sadness, joy – they all fall into the same category. No scientist, no physicist, will ever be able to explain them, but that doesn't mean they don't exist. And yet when it comes to people's belief in a higher power, suddenly it's OK to begin to cast aspersions on such notions. I'm sorry, but you can't have it both ways.'

Wow. This was the closest I'd ever come to getting an answer to my 'How do you know you know?' question. And yes, suddenly I felt like one of the hypocrites J.S. was talking about. How come I was happy to accept love and joy and sadness and guilt, and all those other gut-feeling emotions, yet I had a problem when it came to faith?

'People have always tended to reduce the Christian faith to a series of propositions, when actually it's about trust. Although that trust doesn't have to be about belief. In fact, for me, the whole thing is more about what I encounter than what I believe. We all encounter hundreds of people and situations in our lives where trust is of the utmost relevance. You could say to me, how come we know to trust people? But I haven't heard that question forthcoming.

'Think also, for example, how shocked we are when we hear of some terrible murder on the news. Why are we shocked? We are shocked because it's not "human nature" to do such a thing. So again you could ask me to explain "human nature", but you don't because you know about human and nature and you know what it is, yet you have no idea how you know. Do you see what I'm getting at?'

I did indeed.

'Let me give you another example of how frustrated I could get if I really wanted to when it comes to the kind of conflicting points of view we are discussing. When society accepts a whole host of potentially scientifically questionable doctrines yet stops short of doing anything when it comes to faith. I have come across people who claim to *hate* the church, but if you then threaten to close down the very church in their own village, they go crazy. I have even known the same people to hastily write out a cheque for thousands of pounds to prevent any such travesty happening.'

'So what's that mentality about?' I ask the great man.

'It's simple. It's about exactly what's bothering you. Deep down inside, they suspect something is going on which they can't explain, but because they haven't given themselves time to address whatever that might be, it's easier for them to brush it under the carpet than admit it exists. Or at least, that's what they think. The truth of the matter is we can't brush it under the carpet; once we've sensed it, it's always going to be there. It quietly drives some people insane, or to seek fame and fortune, or turn to drink and drugs, or sex and adrenaline sports. It can become the hugest of deals, if we choose not to cope with it.'

This all made perfect sense to me. So how come I was thinking about it now?

'You are thinking about it because I suspect you have been resistant to the idea up until now, but suddenly it's started bothering you on a completely different level. In the past you may have thought you might lose something of yourself by opening up to the idea that faith might be for you. When actually what will happen is the exact reverse. You cannot be truly free unless you choose to allow yourself to wake up. That's what we say: realizing you have faith is recognizing there is an awakening available to you. Actually, more than that: there is an awakening *already going on inside you*. It can be as soft as a whisper or as deafening as thunder, but either way it is equally loud. And once you've heard it, there is no going back. Sure, you can anaesthetize yourself to it, or insulate yourself against it, but what you might want to do is simply open the door and invite it in. You can always ask it to leave if you don't get on. In short, you have everything to gain and absolutely nothing to lose.'

What John was talking about, I concluded, was 'peace of mind'.

I've had fleeting moments of peace of mind more than usual recently, or perhaps I've just begun to recognize it more of late – and I like it. Thanks to this inner consciousness or awareness, my life has somehow become more what I want it to be without my having to really analyze what that is. I've stopped trying as much, yet more of my life seems to be falling into place.

'Jesus, however, does not call us to religion or theology, they are not what I'm about. He invites us to live our lives to the full with God's life, without fear of being judged, without fear of asking for forgiveness, without fear of being chastised for the things we have done wrong, either intentionally or unintentionally. But that does not mean this forgiveness comes without consequences. The mere fact we recognize we are making mistakes on a daily basis is burden enough.

At first, that is.

It is also the beginning of a process of us mending and bettering our ways. Why else would we bother pointing them out to ourselves, articulating them into unignorable notes to self of "must do better"?'

Maybe I am more aware of these things than ever before because I have given myself this time and space in my midlife to really think about what it is that I want, need and enjoy. And now, having realized how short and simple that list is, there is a long-lost voice emerging to help guide me to where my destiny and happiness lies.

'I think the Church should target you guys. You forty-, fifty- and sixty-year-olds. We need lots of you and lots of you need us. It's the perfect inter-departmental fit, don't you think?'

I wonder if John is where he thought he would be as that little ten-year-old lay preacher getting on everyone's nerves.

'I had not the faintest idea. I have never had a plan. I have only ever tried to do my absolute best. That is it. Since I arrived here in the UK in 1974, right up to today sitting here with you, and for every minute of every day in between. I now chair the world committee campaigning for a global living wage. I sat on the Stephen Lawrence Judicial Inquiry for the retrial of his murderers, where we secured an end to the double jeopardy rule after pioneering forensic new evidence was deemed permissible, resulting in his killers finally being sent to jail. And I oversaw the ordaining of the first of Church of England female bishop. Not bad for a little sick boy from an African village most of the world has never heard of.'

He laughs again. John laughs all the time. Thank God for Sentamu. And thank God for sparing him time and time again, even in the last ten years. He has had to survive prostate cancer, a burst appendix and a particularly nasty, almost fatal run-in with salmonella.

There's so much more I want to ask him, but our time together is running out, and he has to catch a train in fifteen minutes to Cambridge where he's giving a lecture to the Cambridge Union, followed by a question-and-answer session. The man never stops.

'John, I worry about the Church in as much as it doesn't seem to be worrying enough about itself and its declining popularity. They say of addicts we can only help them if they first hold out their hand and seek assistance having accepted there is something wrong. I see the Church today as an addict in denial.'

'Chris, once again I hear you. All I can say is I have a psychiatrist member of my congregation in York who is actively lobbying for people who already believe and want to help spread the word officially but without having to give up what they already do and love and is useful to society. In the Minster at York now people have to arrive early if they want to guarantee getting in. The world is waking up to the fact that what's been rammed down our throats since the end of World War II as the path to a better life has been nothing more than an elaborate self-fulfilling web of advertising and pro-paganda to get us to acquire more and more of what's less and less important to us as human beings. You watch, all successful revo-lutions start sincerely before exploding into an unstoppable force for change, especially the unconscious ones. I am more optimistic than ever before.'

I can't say I disagree with him. For a while now I have been of the firm belief that there is a growing trend towards doing as opposed to having. I see it all the time with the various events I'm involved in, having received thousands and thousands of messages following many of them from families wanting me to know how a few days of togetherness has helped them reboot their long-term priorities.

I know exactly what they mean, which is why I need to change. I need to continue this theme of creating yet more time and space in which to see, hear and simply breathe more casily, more freely. In short I need to get rid of a whole load of crap in my life. It's like I no longer have a choice.

'Chris, people have begun listening to you because you have already changed more than you realize. The authenticity of the messenger is just as important as the message. Children know when Dad is fibbing. They know when Dad is listening and not just nodding, which is why they often repeat questions over and over again. They want a response, they want attention. But most of all they want Dad. Because they need to know you love them. Any-thing that takes away from that, anything that distracts you both physically and mentally, you need to get rid of. It's stealing your life from underneath you.'

By now about a million alarm bells were going off in my head. I needed to instigate the Mother of All Clear Outs. And all this while we were sitting in one of the best-known auction houses in the uni-verse. Where clutter is their business. Much of it beautiful clutter, but clutter nevertheless.

'Do you ever desire things, stuff?' I asked John as we headed out the big plate-glass, bronze-framed front doors back into the sunlight.

'Oh sure,' he replied. 'But only for a moment. Then I instantly realize I have everything I need or could reasonably wish for. If it needs dusting it's usually surplus to requirements. That's my rule.'

Great rule, Archbishop.

I'm going to go with that.

Spirituality

The Shaman

Another one of my ever-growing band of magi is Andy, as I shall refer to him here, primarily 'cos that's his name. He comes as one of several hi-ball recommendations from the ebullient force of nature whom I'm delighted to call a friend, Ms Fearne Cotton.

So what does a shaman do?

Anything they want to, it seems. Sounds so cool though, doesn't it? The thing is, according to Andy, a shaman is something he would never refer to himself as. Whereas I would have it stamped on my passport immediately.

The accepted definition of a shaman is one who is connected with a world beyond ours. That is to say beyond what is more traditionally accepted as ours. Which one could further say is only a temporary stage the human race is going through anyway.

In fact, that's the whole basis of a lot of what Andy and his shaman co-workers believe.

They see it as audacious and ridiculous that we in the Western world base so many of our theories and ideas on relatively recent science and discovery, while choosing to ignore thousands of years of ancient Eastern philosophy. Even though so much of it has its roots in good old-fashioned common sense to do with the seasons – what our environment is trying to tell us and how our seasons and their corresponding elements affect our energy and moods.

Shamans are here as testament to the fact that there is magical and omnipotent equilibrium available to us should we wish to recognize it and tap into it. They, along with others, offer bridges to connect us laymen to the ultimate physical and emotional universal via the ethos of yin and yang.

So what exactly does Andy do for a living?

'Oh, I get involved in a huge variety of things – all people-based. Helping them identify, cope with and overcome challenging situations. I help them to develop whatever skills they might need to navigate through whatever troubled or turbulent waters they may be up against at the time.'

Andy, a former manager of pubs, discos and restaurants, began his own journey into becoming enlightened, awakened, call it what you will, via experiencing his own profoundly adverse set of circumstances. After his daughter became seriously ill due to a string of tragic events, to quote his exact words: 'My life turned to shit, basically.'

He gave up almost everything to look after her, and what he didn't, eventually gave up on him. Including, incredibly, his wife, and mother of his daughter.

Already an epileptic, his poor little girl suffered further brain damage as a result of a cumulative series of misfortunes, leaving Andy feeling helpless and heartbroken. Having lost his home and job and ending up in sheltered accommodation, still with his daughter, he felt he had no choice but to scour the world for any shred of possible hope as to what to do next.

This is how he came across Chinese medicine and, as a consequence, Ancient Chinese philosophy. The initial flashing beacon being the belief that the key to solving an issue is often doing the opposite of what might at first seem most obvious. What is one thing at any one time will eventually become its own mirror image; thinking counter-intuitively, therefore, ofter helps to cut to the chase before it's too late.

'I was so stressed one day I attended a t'ai chi class out of sheer desperation, where for the first time in my life I spent two hours looking inside as opposed to outside. It was an enormous revelation to me and one that I knew was there to tell me something.'

After just this one close encounter with himself, Andy simply had to find out more. To the extent he embarked upon a committed period of studying Chinese medicine here at the School of Complementary Medicine.

'What I discovered was mind-blowing to me. The fact that the Ancient Chinese had an entirely different understanding of our anatomy and physiology than that of the Western world today.'

Andy is in absolutely no doubt that this is the only sustainable way forward for the human race.

'It's obvious to me, yet we collectively continue to ignore it, or rubbish it, or make fun of it. And I know why. Eastern philosophy begins and ends with personal responsibility. What we do as individuals has an immediate and direct effect on anything and everything around us. That's it, period. Whereas, in the West, it doesn't suit our culture for that to be the case. We are brainwashed into passing the buck. We are brainwashed into believing that we can buy, steal, beg, borrow or lie our way out of the vast majority of life's sticky situations, personal conflicts or physical and mental dilemmas.'

It's very difficult to argue with such common sense.

'It's always easier to hand responsibility to other people. But personal responsibility is the key to everything.'

So doesn't it drive him mad when he is surrounded by a world full of people with their eyes closed and fingers stuck in their ears refusing to acknowledge a simple truth that will instantly make our world a better place to be?

'Right and wrong are vastly overrated. Being on the "I am right" side of an argument, however true that may be, is naturally bringing yourself into conflict with other human beings. Remember yin will always to turn into yang and vice versa, it always has and it always will. Journeys of self-awareness are spirals of learning that never stop. Instead of confirming how wrong someone is, you've got to ask yourself: "Why am I concerning myself with that? What good is that stance to anyone?" In fact it tells you more about you than it does about the original subject of observation.'

That really got me thinking. And has stayed with me ever since. Nothing in our minds is ever about anyone else unless we choose it to be. Every time we make a judgement about another human being it is the antithesis of compassion. And at the end of everything, compassion is all that matters.

'In order to improve something in your life, you have to first stop how you've been habitually doing that something before. Always do what you've always done and you'll always get what you've always got. And just like the best stories, letting go of anything has a beginning, middle and end. The reason many of us are apprehensive of change or letting go is because we know deep inside that once we have become mindful of that something we think we need or would like to change, it is very difficult for us to become unmindful to it.'

Accepting responsibility is a huge commitment.

What Andy is talking about here is the epiphany of one's own awakening being naturally irreversible. Each small awakening by definition then becomes part of a much bigger awakening. Either gradually, suddenly, or somewhere in between.

The cracks are there to let in the light.

'Self-awareness gives us the opportunity to change, from which point we will forever thus walk with a well of wisdom inside us to draw from. We will be much more able to interpret mistakes as merely essential experiences in how not to do things right at first so we can then go on to do them much better than we ever could have dreamed.'

'With more voluntary responsibility comes more ease with anything and everything we choose to do. By accepting something is difficult, it immediately makes that thing easier than it was a heartbeat ago.'

And so how should he/we spread the word?

'Ah, well. You can only do that in my opinion by subscribing to the idea of "teaching from behind". What that means is: living by example only and never telling anyone what they should do or how they should do it, unless they specifically ask to be told and you specifically believe they really want to know.'

Chinese philosophy is the ultimate in do-it-yourself. It has its foundations in shamanism which in turn can be traced back to Buddhism and Taoism as well as many other religions and belief systems. The shamanic DNA has respecting and living in harmony with the world around us at its very core. And there are as many different shades of shamanism in the universe as there are languages and dialects on our planet.

As the world changes us, so we change the world. In which case everything changes as a result of everything else. It's unavoidable, which is why we need to be aware of our interconnectedness with everything we come into contact with. We are free to think how we want to think but have to be free in the first place.

The key, Andy says, is to simply seek and feel oneself becoming more and more self-aware with every meditation. It's not about relaxing or mind-clearing, which are both useful in their own right, but more a matter of seeing who we really are. When we see who we really are, we automatically become more humble and change will follow. And when we begin to change, hopefully for the better, everyone around us will have to make adjustments because of what we have done.

'Small doubts lead to small enlightenment and great doubt leads to great enlightenment. Be a great doubter – but doubt yourself rather than directing your doubt at someone else. The only way to change the wider world is to start with the world inside ourselves.'

Andy believes that the decentralization of power via the Internet is no accident but merely the next major step in the evolution of how we run ourselves.

'There are many wonderful things about the Internet which cut much deeper than its many obvious negative effects. Change is inevitable, so we need to work with it, we need to have peace with it, we need to embrace it and find a way of using it for good. I find it thrilling, amazing, mind-boggling.'

History informs us that cruel, greedy and murderous dictators thrive on secrecy, separation and propaganda. All of which is the opposite of mass communication. Sure, bad, destructive and manipulative messages can now be spread just as efficiently and rapidly as good, but education beats isolation every time. And that simple truth, combined with our natural human inclination to want to care, nurture and love each other, can ultimately only mean one thing:

Regardless of what certain doom-mongers want us to believe, we are going to be around for a good while longer.

Not only that, let's leave this chapter with the star of the show. Listen to this for an affirmation of how fantastic it is to be us.

'We are fundamentally programmed to *seek joy*. The best way to achieve this is to stay energized and compassionate, which will give us the balance we need to be able to participate in that joy as and when it presents itself.'

And that, my friends, is as good a message as one could ever wish to hear.

Sleep

The Sleep Guru

'The really annoying thing about good sleepers and the key to their sleeping prowess is that they do nothing. They merely go to sleep and that's it,' says Dr Guy Meadows, founder of the Sleep School and holder of a doctorate on the physiology of the sleeping brain.

This guy, Guy, is a genius on the brink of world superstardom. He is the Deepak Chopra of sleep. When the world wakes up – forgive the pun – to what he knows and how he can help us, he will become a household name, he has to. If I were still as commercially minded as I used to be, I would sign him up for life immediately.

We meet at my house in London on a Friday morning. The early spring sun has already taken the chill out of the air, the pink and white April blossom is being toyed with in the breeze outside the window, all is good with the world. A great day to meet a great man. Actually we've met before: Guy came for what was meant to be a brief interview on my radio show but ended up staying on the air for over half an hour, such was the reaction of the listeners. And not only during the show, as he later informed me; following his appearance he very swiftly shifted no less than three and a half thousand copies of his book, *The Sleep Book: How to Sleep Well Every Night*.

Well good for him, and even better for us that he does what he does. In an ever more insane world, we continue to deny ourselves the basics we need to be healthy, happy and successful.

'There's a story I was once told about a Portuguese fisherman who was talking to a friend while playing his guitar on some rocks and enjoying an afternoon glass of rosé wine. His friend suggested that as he was such a good fisherman and able to come home early as a result, he might want to stay out a bit longer, catch even more fish than everyone else and then use the extra money to buy another boat and perhaps employ another fisherman to fish on his behalf. As his new employee would have the best teacher for miles around, surely it wouldn't be long before he too was then bringing home a bumper haul. Then with even more money his friend suggested the fisherman buy another boat and then a third and a fifth and more and more until he had his own fleet and had become the richest fisherman in the whole of Portugal.

"'And then what would I do?" asked the fisherman.

"'Then one day, when the time is right, you could sell your business and do whatever you want to.'"

"'But that's what I'm doing now.' Exactly what he was doing anyway: sitting on the rocks, playing his guitar and enjoying a glass of rosé.'

And so it is with us and sleep. Most of 'civilized' society is clinging more and more to the belief that amassing more stuff will lead to more of what we want, when of course the opposite is really the case. There's an amazing film documentary, *Happy*, that tells us there is a vast difference in the basic quality of life between someone who earns £50,000 a year as opposed to some poor soul who only earns £10,000 a year, but relatively little actual difference in the basic quality of life between someone who earns £50,000 and £50,000,000 a year.

Chasing anything, except perhaps a bus, train or plane, is usually counter-productive, yet still we continue en masse to fritter away what little time we have here on planet Earth doing just that. Sure, it's good to chase our dreams, if they are worthy of both us and the world; the same is true of the desire to find a like-minded, supportive and loving life partner. But other than that, why bother chasing anything that takes away from what we already have? Especially if that chase leaves us dog-tired, bleary-eyed and looking like death for the remainder of our days. People in Japan are now literally dying of exhaustion on a daily basis.

'The problem with being tired is the more tired we become, the less we are able to cope with the demons that keep us awake,' says Guy.

This makes it all the more galling when he tells me about the proven benefits of sleep. A ten-minute power nap in the afternoon does more for performance, mood and general well-being than any energy drink, protein bar or coffee and cigarette break could ever do. Can you believe a nap as brief as this can enhance alertness by 100 per cent and performance by 34 per cent for up to a few hours afterwards? And all for free! Not only money-free but cal-orie-free, guilt-free, packaging-free, environmentally-unfriendly additives-free. And how about the extra two hours of sleep a night that saw an American collegiate basketball team increase their sprint times by 5 per cent and the accuracy of their free throws by 9 per cent? Everything of any use begins to leave us as we grow tired. For our body and mind to rest, repair and regenerate, sleep is vital. Without sleep, we are fighting an uphill battle, every step of which yields only yet more fatigue, yet more frustration and ultimately less and less sleep.

As Guy talks to me about his passion to get the world sleeping better, to remind us all what we have stupidly forgotten, his face wears a permanent smile. Though I suspect it may be a slightly pained smile, born out of frustration at having to watch us lot, for-ever claiming we are desperate to sleep more than we do, but doing bugger-all about it.

Guy himself sleeps extremely well, testament to which is the fact that today he tells me he's ill. So ill in fact, he's just been to his own doctor, something he rarely does, to ask for some medication for a stinking cold he's been unable to shake off. Well, I'm sorry, but he could have fooled me. Despite his sincere claims to be full of catarrh and phlegm, he looks an almost perfect picture of health. No sign of red or watery eyes or that general ear-nose-and-throat malaise so often evident on the visage of someone with a troublesome sniffle. In fact I'd happily go as far as to say that even when I'm well I may never have looked as healthy as Guy looks this morning, claiming to be under the weather.

'I'm lucky, I simply rest my cheek on my pillow, usually my left cheek, and within moments I'm gone.'

Apparently it annoys the hell out of his wife, which in turn leads us nicely on to a couple of more interesting twists in the whole sleeping shooting match.

'The majority of people who contact me are women.'

This is interesting; I've always assumed insomnia was more of a male issue.

'Not at all. More men may well suffer in silence, we can't be sure, but women suffer in anything but silence. It's often their spouse's snoring which drives them to distraction and not being able to get to sleep themselves.'

But it's not only us blokes that cause our unfortunate beloveds to miss out on their beauty sleep. Women are at the mercy of the physical states brought on every twenty-eight days by the menstrual cycle, playing havoc with their body temperatures, brain patterns and internal biorhythms. And as if that's not enough, they tend to worry more (about things that actually matter!), they are more sensitive to nature's night-time alarm signals due to their mothering instinct, and then there's the life-changing female menopause for them to contend with – which we are now hearing can last up to FIFTEEN BLOODY YEARS.

Our girls temporarily kiss goodbye to their bodies while all this is going on, so it's little wonder they have trouble finding the incentive to get back into shape when all that's waiting for them on the other half of the mattress is a snoring, grumbling, fat-necked fart machine.

'Ah, that would be the bed-sharing issue you're referring to there,' interjects Dr Meadows. 'Or, as I like to term it, the sleeping burden of togetherness.'

As Guy calmly and sagely utters this almost poetic phrase with a knowing, reverent nod of the head, I can hear the strained vocal cords of millions of women silently screaming, 'WELL, THAT'S ONE WAY OF PUTTING IT!'

Guy is the mutt's nuts. If anyone from Oprah Winfrey's office ever reads this, they need to book him for a slot every week for the next ten years. He'd be her next Dr Phil, or Paulo Coelho or whoever she's championing at the moment.

The key to cracking the 'sleeping burden of togetherness' is – guess what? The biggest bed you can possibly afford and/or accommodate.

'It's the best way by far.'

'How about separate beds?' I suggest, having secretly hankered after this situation domestically myself in each and every relationship I've enjoyed, even the most fruitful and compatible ones.

'Well, you can if you like, and many people do. Some even go so far as having their own rooms or even own houses, but I would always counsel loving, albeit perhaps sometimes challenging night-time companionship, over the drastic chasm of separation.'

Nicely put. Although I have to say, I secretly believe that Tash and I function much better and are much happier the morning after when we sleep separately, as long as it's under the same roof. Tash tends to lash out at me unconsciously (I hope) while asleep, sometimes resulting in acute physical pain on my part, while I am one of life's great snorers. We also both seem to emit mutual waves of boundless energy. Can there be too much energy in one bed for that bed's incumbents to drop off satisfactorily?

'Yes, absolutely. Energy often equals restlessness and heat. Too much heat is terrible for getting to sleep, as is not enough fresh air in your bedroom. Air flow and the right thickness of duvet for the time of year are vital ingredients. Remember, most people spend more on their televisions and computers than they do on their whole bedroom, including their bed. That's simply insane. We spend a quarter to a third of our life sleeping, or at least trying to. We really should take it more seriously.'

How about sleep as we get older?

'As we get older, our natural energy levels tend to deteriorate, as does, ironically, our ability to achieve consolidated sleep. Unlike in our teenage years, when most of us temporarily become sleep aces, our talent for consolidated sleep, the most essential of sleeps, gradually reduces as our general sleep becomes more fragmented. The glorious solid blocks of better quality sleep in the past become rarer and rarer as we mature.'

Guy goes on to explain that our natural circadian rhythms, which govern our ninety-minute and two-hour cycles of sleep, become more prone to being separated by periods of wakefulness, whereas when we're younger we're more resistant to the grouting that might wake us up in between our sleeping tiles. Consequently, lots of us try to catch up with daytime sleeps, which although we already know are useful and lauded in many parts of the world as a necessary skill to be proud of, nature would much prefer us to sleep at night, as we were designed to.

Our eyes have now been proven to contain light-sensitive cells that send messages back to our body clock, which helps us tell ourselves what we should be doing as well as helping govern our levels of melatonin, the chemical that regulates our sleeping patterns. The book of how to live life has long since been written, it's just that we have forgotten how to read it.

At this point in our conversation Guy flags up the revelation that the main issue with using electronic devices to read from, work on, or play on in bed at night is that the blue light they emit is exactly the same wavelength as blue sky, measuring 465 nanometres. Thus tricking our internal body clock into thinking we should still be awake. This, he says, is a HUGE PROBLEM. Especially when it comes to children, who need their sleep more than anyone else because of the immense physical, emotional and mental changes their bodies are going through. Sleep is both the sun and the rain in the garden of human growth; without the right amount life will never be as fulfilling as it could be.

The other big sleep issue for midlifers is weight gain and all the associated risks like type-2 diabetes and cardiovascular problems:

'Lack of sleep not only leads to the increased production of ghrelin, a chemical which makes us feel hungry, but also a reduction in leptin, one of the chemicals that lets us know when we are full. Therefore, this is a pincer movement attacking our waistline from two opposing fronts. Not good. Not good at all. And spare a thought for those tens of thousands of shift workers, who are constantly being battered by a barrage of illogical signals made up of some or all of the above.'

My mum was a nurse who worked nights for over twenty years. I now feel even worse than I already did for the selfish nonsense my sister, brother and myself put her through when she was obviously dead on her feet.

Sorry, Minnie.

As the years pass by, we also have a tendency to convince ourselves we deserve more treats. And when are we most likely to succumb to such temptations? Yup, you guessed it: at night, when we're tired and relaxed and our natural resistance is at its lowest ebb. Tomorrow suddenly seems a lifetime away and so why the heck not have a cheeky nightcap or two, with the odd choccie biccy, scoop of ice cream or packet of salt and vinegar crisps.

None of which does us any good at all when it comes to getting off to sleep.

'Sugar and alcohol are stimulants and will return to haunt us soon after our heads hit the pillow. Our bodies are left with the task of having to metabolize our various vices while we pass out, thus interrupting that all-important REM sleep, the sleep that really makes the difference when it comes to rest, relaxation and regeneration. Potholes in the road of our own making. See also diuretics, beta blockers and anti-depressants.

By this point I was practically begging Guy for some middle-aged sleeping super-tips.

'The key thing is duration – make time for sleep. Make sleep a priority. Try to go to bed at the same time as much as you can every night. And then, once in bed, stick to a routine that tells you sleep is coming. You are cleared for final approach and landing, the day is giving way to the night, your energy and effort can begin to slow down until they come to a halt.

More nature, less technology, more books and crosswords, less Internet and emails. Actually, to be frank, ZERO Internet and

ZERO emails. Remember the blue light. Also, at weekends don't sleep in for hours more than you would in the week. Likewise, don't feel the need to stay up extra late on a Friday and Saturday night merely to fall asleep in front of the television in an attempt to prove to yourself you have the weekend off. Madness.

GO TO BED!!!

The more energy you have in the day at the weekends, the more fulfilled you'll feel generally and the less you'll feel the need to stay up late anyway. It's an upward spiral once we realize how much we've been swimming against the sleep tide and for how long.

'Work out how much sleep you need by keeping a sleeping diary for a few weeks. It's quite true that some people really do only need four hours a night, whereas others struggle with anything fewer than ten. For the record, the average UK adult requires between seven and eight hours of good sleep per night. But it's both enlightening and interesting to try to figure out your own bespoke required hours.

'When it comes to your sleeping environment, remember it's the one place you will continue to spend more of your life in than any other, so take care when designing and furnishing it. Make it the most beautiful, aesthetically pleasing place to be. It's amazing how much time, money and effort people put into designing and fitting out a kitchen compared to how little of all those three they employ when it comes to the boudoir.'

I mentioned this last point to my wife the following weekend when she asked me how the chat with Guy had gone.

She vehemently disagreed.

'But a kitchen is much more complicated than a bedroom, with lots more unique decisions called for,' she protested. On the face of it, perhaps; but all Guy is saying is that we should take care to notice and do what we can to give ourselves the best possible chance of drifting off peacefully. Good light exclusion, sleep-friendly ambient temperature and humidity, quiet, comfort, a sense of order, a lack of fuss, space. I've even gone as far as to ban bedside cabinets as they merely provide storage for yet more chaos in the form of coins, leaflets, adaptors, pens, pencils and bloody loom bands!

'Clutter is like our past: we may not be able to see it, but we know it exists and that, as many insomniacs will confirm, is one of the chief culprits when it comes to having our precious sleep stolen from underneath us.'

After meeting this genius, sleep became my number one priority, above all else. I changed my diet, eating patterns, everything. I especially focused on making more time to enjoy my sleep, which I now do. I also kept a sleeping diary and realized I am a six- to seven-hours-a-night man. Any less than that and I really do take a hit the next day.

Surprisingly, the better I sleep the more tired I feel when my alarm goes off in the morning, but the more rested I feel as the day unfolds. I definitely concentrate better for longer and I'm far less irritable. I've also started eating breakfast, which has made a massive difference. I still have a long way to go, but I'm on the right road.

What a Guy.

Thank you, Doctor.

Money

Top Ten Things That Money's Good For:

10 Nice house for you.
9 Nice houses for people you love.
8 Nice car/cars.
7 Nice clothes.
6 Decent travel.
5 Good restaurants.
4 Zero hangover i.e. quality wine.
3 Family holidays.
2 Specialist medical cover.
1 Making a difference where a difference matters.

The Bible says, 'The meek shall inherit the earth.' Well, I'm not so sure they're going to want it after we, the not so meek, have fudged it up like we are doing.

Abba on the other hand once famously sang 'It's a rich man's world'. Well, I'm not so sure about that either. And nor were they, once they'd divorced each other and had to begin all over again.

A lot of rich people I know or have met seem to be thoroughly miserable. As if some vital part of them is missing and they don't know where it's gone. Last seen perhaps sometime before the first million was officially on the scorecard, but no sightings thereafter.

What's really mad is that most self-made rich folks have long since forgotten why they started doing whatever it was that led them to amass their fortune in the first place. Now just doing it because it defines who they are to people who don't really matter.

Often at the cost of everything else that's important to them. And most of which can't be bought anyway.

I was caught in this selfsame trap for a while, one of the reasons I went fruit da loop for the best part of ten years.

When I was a kid we never had any money. That's why I always wanted to get my hands on some. No different from why people want to jump out of an aeroplane or climb Mount Everest. I just wanted to know what it felt like.

Fortunately for me, I also discovered early on in life that going out to work was something I enjoyed. Since the by-product of that was money, my financial dilemma began to work itself out pretty much from the moment I became a teenager.

Little did I know back then how big my pile would end up. From a £1.25-a-week paper round to being hunted down by the stock-market wolves to the tune of hundreds of millions of pounds.

Mistakes are merely rehearsals for getting it right next time, so here's what my experience of (not exactly) rags (but not far off) to riches has taught me.

Not only can money not buy you happiness, it can't buy you a good time either, not even for five minutes. You can only *have* a good time, you can't *buy* one. Easy for me to say, I know, and I realize I may be playing with fire here, but all money can really do is buy you an expensive time.

That's it.

That's all.

Just like owning a television can't guarantee there's going to be anything good to watch. Or inheriting a Fender Stratocaster from dear old uncle Sholto means you're suddenly going to turn into the next Mark Knopfler.

Whether we get out of something what we want, regardless of its physical value, is down to what we, and the people around us, do with it. The New Radicals sang, 'You only get what you give', which is true except when it comes to writing out a cheque. 'You get what you pay for' is another grossly inaccurate phrase. The truth is, 'You get what you do with what you pay for.'

Cool people who handle their success best have one thing in common. Those that have a few quid don't worry about it and carry on more or less regardless, while those that don't have much do exactly the same. This is because between them they have realized that, somewhere along the line, money has got too big for its boots and has been overplaying its hand for years.

The world's money is controlled by the few who make lots of it but to little real advantage to themselves or anyone else. The money markets dominate the news, yet few of us can do the first thing to influence them.

The tail is most definitely wagging the dog where this one is concerned.

Following the financial crash of 2008 the stock markets of the world have all seen record increases in between. Yet the aftermath of how they operated before that continues to devastate the pockets of the vast majority of people who had nothing to do with what went wrong.

Quite apart from the well-documented case of Greece, little Cyprus was nearly bankrupted last year because she couldn't come up with a €6 billion downpayment to secure another bailout from the EU, yet this is the same amount our own national debt here in the UK increases by every two days. This is hypocrisy of the most audacious kind. Yet we're all happy to collectively bury our heads in the sand as if somehow this makes sense and what we're experiencing is merely a blip in an otherwise well-oiled financial machine.

Money is not working. At the time this book went to print, 'The markets' were down again to a new three-year low.

Who cares?

It's all a massive con, as simple as that, and the sooner someone stands up and says as much, the better.

Yet still we live in denial. Govern-'mental' institutions have taken to applying knee-jerk reaction austerity fiscal policies as some sort of answer.

The habitually laissez-faire French now have a president who thinks emergency taxes of 75 per cent on anyone in France with more than half a baguette and an ounce of Boursin in their basket is the way forward. The eternally profligate Italian government has brought in a new duty on anyone who owns a nice old car, let alone a nice shiny new one. And as for the poor Portuguese, whom I know a lot of, they now pay more VAT than anyone else in the history of the world.

And all this because of the stock exchanges, a system which began with the simple ethos of doing precisely what it said over the shop. You want some of my beans, you gotta give me some of your potatoes, or some wool, or some chickens or your granny, whatever – but you gotta give me something. That's how this is going to work, that's how we're going to do business here.

What could possibly go wrong?

Answer: pretty much everything.

Because one day, out of nowhere, along wanders someone with a piece of paper bearing these words: 'I promise to pay the bearer of this note whatever I need to for him to give me some of his parsnips, just not any time soon if that's OK.'

A promise from a stranger to a stranger. Ooh, that's gonna work.

Two people who have never met before, one with actual goods, one with only a piece of paper and a few cobbled-together words on it. And for some unholy and terrible reason the farmer with the booty agreed to take the worthless promissory note from the charlatan.

That, my friends, was the birth of the whole sorry fiasco, the beginning of the end. Why oh why oh why did the farmer ever say yes? And why have we all been saying, almost orgasmically, yes yes yes ever since?

The dreaded, awful, evil, fraudulent, terrible promissory note. And as if that wasn't stupid enough, we then took the same bait by signing up for the credit-card system. The credit-card holder does not even have the old promissory notes so favoured by his forefathers; but if he is willing to commit to at least trying to get his hands on some any time this side of Armageddon, and passing them straight over, then now – even that's OK!!!

INSANITY.

'Always do what you've always done and you'll always get what you've always got.'

More and more credit means more and more financial crashes and more mopping up the spoils, by the ever more elite, who always make sure they have enough ready cash and buying power for when the world's going cheap.

CREDIT CREDIT CREDIT EQUALS CRASH CRASH CRASH.

It doesn't matter that credit doesn't work for the simple reason that most people who can't pay today still won't be able to pay tomorrow. If they could, they would, but they can't so they won't. And what's even more soul-destroying is that the vast majority of those people will now be in debt UNTIL THEY DIE, having spent money they usually don't have on things they will never be able to afford and clearly don't need.

Mrs Thatcher may have been a crazy old dingbat, but one thing she was right about was 'NEVER SPEND MORE THAN YOU EARN with the exception of a mortgage and perhaps a motor car'. Easy for her to say, married to a millionaire businessman, I know, but I always got the feeling she would abide by that rule of hers regardless.

Money is a worry to all but the wisest of people. People who haven't got it invariably want it; people who have it are worried they might lose it. And then there are those who somehow have squared the whole money circle for what it really is: an unworkable nonsense, probably hatched by two winos in a tavern to see if they could get the barman to give them their next drink without having to part with an actual shilling.

Well, whoever it was, it worked then and it's still working now, but money's days are numbered. Like us when it comes to climate change: if we don't come up with a new twist soon, we'll both be toast this side of 2030.

• • •

I believe we may be the generation to witness the death of money. We talk about the birth of the virtual age with the Internet and cyberspace, and so on, but money beat them all to it. Money was the first virtual egg to hatch in the incubator.

Virtual wealth.

Virtual value.

Virtual madness.

Not that money isn't useful full stop, of course it is. Apart from the essentials in life, there is no doubt that me having a bit more of it than I used to has kept my mum alive. When she was diagnosed with breast cancer almost seven years ago, I was fortunate enough to be able to pay for a drug she would not have been entitled to on the NHS. It almost definitely saved her life.

Same goes for when my wife was expecting for the second time and was diagnosed with an ectopic pregnancy. Had she not been seen late one night by a private consultant, she would not be here today. She was suffering from internal bleeding which, had it not been spotted and dealt with, would have seen her off before the morning.

I know this financial advantage is unfair in the grand scheme of things and am aware it will make some people apoplectic with rage, but I seriously doubt those same people wouldn't have done the same thing if they were in my shoes.

Money also makes worries about day-to-day bills less of an issue and I can't say I miss the fear and trepidation I used to experience when approaching the hole in the wall towards the end of the month. Will it or won't it? To dispense or not to dispense, that is the question.

I've also learnt, the hard way, it pays to get hold of your dough before it gets a hold of you, as is so often the case with self-made new money. I'm not talking so much about people trying to relieve you of your hard-earned cash, as people relieving you of days and weeks of your life you'll never get back.

I remember having to attend meeting after meeting when I was 'flying high', while all the time wondering, hang on a minute, when

I was skint I never had to involve myself in any of this nonsense. Sitting at white and shiny tables which did little except remind me of how much I hated school and my O-levels.

I swear, as long as I live I will never sit in a board meeting again. I don't care what the financial benefits might be. I'm not interested, it's not for me. I've been there and done it. Consider me permanently unavailable.

Aside from the bother of looking after whatever cash you might have made, the actual process of making money is rarely glamorous. And not only that, but the fact remains that those who take up an inordinate amount of time and energy trying to amass a great life from outside in have less and less time and energy to live life from the inside out.

That's where the real goldmine lies.

Top Ten Modern-Day Snappy Business Maxims:

10 The first generation makes it.
 9 The second generation spends it.
 8 The third generation loses it.
 7 The best way to a small fortune is to start with a big one.
 6 Every no gets you closer to a yes.
 5 Never name your price whether buying or selling.
 4 Just get in the deal.
 3 First profit, best profit.
 2 First loss, best loss.
 1 Fake it till you make it.

'Fake it till you make it' – this is my favourite of the countless mantras I've heard the big boys of business utter in my encounters with the good, bad, the sad, the permatanned, the cool, the affable and the ugly of the best of them. This, I've heard, has long been their battle cry, even though it's fatally flawed. 'Faking it till you make it' suggests that you are going to make it anyway, in which case you're not actually faking it at all. You are merely faking it as part of making it.

As for first profit, best profit and first loss, best loss – well yes, that can also be true. And my goodness, how my bank account would have benefited from such a philosophy if only I'd taken it on board. But, hey, we are where we are and there's no place I'd rather be.

The thing about all these theories is they are all too often spouted by individuals, usually blokes, who have already become success-ful. These guys then somehow backdate an intellectual framework and narrative as to how they were always a genius and it was only a matter of time before they hit the jackpot.

I see it a lot in the entertainment business. People who have had hit shows standing up in front of packed audiences of eager eyes and ears desperate to know their secret. And then out it comes, the reconstructed ethos of how they always knew exactly what they were doing and why. Total bollocks, most of it.

How do I know?

Because I've even heard myself doing it.

My retrogressive thesis on how I made Terry Wogan's old show my own is a work of utter fiction, frankly. But as long as I keep tell-ing myself it's true then I, along with everyone else, will probably start believing it.

Some 'rules', however, do turn out to be true. Like the really suc-cessful hedge-fund managers, for example.

One such dude came to me to buy a couple of cars from me, their combined cost well over a million pounds. The cars were water-tight with regards to their provenance, condition and investment potential, but because he'd never done anything like this before, he was petrified. Even though this guy was worth bundles – and I mean absolutely loaded. But to say he was nervous would be like saying Osama Bin Laden didn't much fancy his chances when the US military popped up at the bottom of his bed.

I cannot tell you the number of phone calls and hours of my life I will never get back, I spent reassuring him that it was going to be OK, that he was doing the right thing. In the end I guaranteed him a buy-back clause to put his mind at rest. And what happened? Both cars doubled in value within eighteen months before he sold them and bought the ultimate car of his dreams.

The two cars I sold him were a Ferrari 288GTO and a Ferrari 275 GTS. The car he effectively swapped them for was a Ferrari 275 GTB. The fact that the 288GTO alone is now almost worth the same as the 275 is neither here nor there to him, because he got what he wanted with the minimum amount of risk. I would look at the lost profit in the original deal, whereas he is from the little-and-often school of thought. And that's the point. The billionaires of this world never bet the ranch.

While I was getting to 'know' Mr Safe, he told me that hedge funds have been around since the Sixties, a lot earlier than I'd realized. He then went on to explain that most successful hedge-fund dealers deal within a profit/loss window of 55–45 per cent, but the most successful managers, i.e. those who are still around, deal in only a 1 or 2 per cent swing.

'That is the absolute difference between sustainability and success, or ending up on the front page of the *Daily Mail*,' he told me.

Like pilots, there are old hedge-fund managers and there are bold hedge-fund managers, but there are no old, bold hedge-fund managers.

Big, long-lasting and secure fortunes are built on the bedrock of conservatism and considered speculation, with the utmost attention always being paid to the finer detail. This is the true calling card of what makes big business tick. It's grey and unexciting, it's highly repetitive. It's a life I wouldn't want in a million years.

Some of the most dynamic, pioneering and cutting-edge companies in the world, and certainly those I have had personal dealings with, are run by the human embodiment of binary, predictable pragmatism. It's baby steps all the way, water and edamame beans for lunch and black coffee in the boardroom to stop them falling asleep, collapsing on to their Mont Blanc and puncturing a lung.

Risk aversion is the air they breathe.

The bottom line beats a headline every day of the week.

So how come they amass such unthinkable wealth with such a glacial attitude towards growth? Simple. Because they hardly ever sleep, they have few if any passions, they never see their family and most importantly they operate within a world chiefly populated by comparative idiots, shirkers and chancers.

I know five billionaires, two of whom I consider friends, the others I have had personal dealings with but no more. And they all, without exception, work harder for longer than anyone else I've ever met. They are 100 per cent focused 100 per cent of the time. And they will argue every dime, every dollar, every minute of the day – and night. It's not in their nature to ever let anything go, leave any i undotted or t uncrossed.

They cannot risk the slightest crack in the armour of their absolute certainty that no one is going to get one over on them if they can do anything within their control to stop that from happening. Money is their violin and they will only ever draw their bow across it; plucking is not for them.

I remember thinking exactly the same when Lee Westwood once crept up on me from behind when I was hitting balls on a driving range in Portugal.

After he'd well and truly scared the granny out of me, I persuaded him to indulge the now small but not unsubstantial crowd that had gathered to a display of his sublime ball striking. Westy, being the affable guy he is, duly obliged, but not before he had taken the exact same number of practice swings he would have taken had he been playing an approach shot to the eighteenth green while leading the Open in the final round. He simply couldn't. He knows no other way. Or if he does, he knows not to let it creep in the back door in case it affects what he does for a living at a make-or-break moment.

Fascinating and obvious all at the same time.

If you're good at something – and I mean really good – allowing yourself to be just OK, even for a moment, is not the key to sustainability. Perhaps this is why Ian Botham has never once picked up a cricket bat since he called it a day. Be the best or don't bother, and once it's over don't go back.

I've always suspected I could be a serious player, but I don't see the point. This isn't me falling on a faux sword of hedonistic apathy to disguise my fear of failure but the outcome of a life of near-fatal research. I used to 'make things happen', and they do for the most part. The thing is, though, I have subsequently realized that you can hammer a square peg into a round hole if you're hell bent enough in doing so but eventually, if you wait long enough, it will always pop back out again.

Almost everything we try to cajole and manipulate into doing what we want will inevitably end up outlasting us, our energy, or both. Which is exactly what happens to billionaires, their companies, their power and their mountains of cash when they run out of steam.

I honestly believe almost anyone can become stinking rich if they are prepared to burn the midnight oil, lead an extraordinarily dull existence, have barely any friends and end up either divorced or in a marriage that's as dead as a doornail.

Having said all that, I know one guy who seems to have the billionaire thing sussed. Though I suspect he might have special powers – or at least a cape and a mask at the back of his wardrobe.

He is officially the most successful all-rounder I know.

Success

Top Ten Traits of Successful People:

10 Inquisitiveness.
9 Single-mindedness.
8 Vision.
7 Determination.
6 Strategy.
5 Tactics.
4 Attention to detail.
3 Commitment.
2 Energy.
1 They are blessed with the work gene.

Anyone born with a God-given talent is truly blessed, already half-way to having a fabulous existence. And not just obvious talents like singing and dancing or having an extraordinary capacity to understand quantum physics.

But look at energy, right up there at number two in the top ten. Energy is a formidable talent, an unstoppable force for good, available, plugged in and ready to go morning, noon and night. But then again, your eyes might be your talent, shining, engaging, exciting, able to help you to get what you want, make people feel better or safer, or know that you love them. 'He's a natural with kids,' someone may say about someone else. Another talent. Basically, if you can be good at something, it should always be appreciated, or at least acknowledged, as a talent.

Not all talented people are successful, of course. The two don't necessarily go hand in hand. Some talented people have terrible lives and even deaths, sometimes as a direct result of their talent.

The general rule is, however:

Moderate talent + the right attitude = success.

Bags of talent + the wrong attitude = failure.

Making the most of what you have is what really counts when it comes to being successful. It can be as much as 99 per cent knowing what to do and only 1 per cent talent. But that's far more fruitful than having 99 per cent talent and only having 1 per cent of an idea what to do with it.

Look no further than Posh and Becks for the perfect case study. You can say what you like about this pair but the one thing you cannot accuse them of is not making the most of what they have. I am in constant awe of the way they continue to manage their respective careers, marriage and family.

Victoria, the ex-Spice Girl, not the greatest voice ever to attempt to hold a tune, meets and falls in love with David the footballer. A very good footballer, but by no means the best footballer England has ever produced.

They take part in some excruciatingly embarrassing photoshoots to begin with – remember the P. Diddy-style white Rolls-Royce convertible shots that still make anything Katie Price has done look positively tasteful by comparison? And the wedding thrones and Beckingham Palace an' all that other sparkly jazz 'n' nonsense? But they learnt with each mistake and now look at them: they have succeeded in becoming one of the most photographed, enigmatic and LIKED couples of modern times.

They are more famous now than they have ever been, than when Becks was still playing footy and Posh was still miming to backing tracks. It doesn't matter they're not particularly interesting, they hardly say anything and Victoria doesn't even smile any more.

They are officially big news.

So how come?

It's simple, they are a living and breathing work of PR genius.

I remember when Becks held a press conference in Spain, announcing he was leaving Real Madrid to play for LA Galaxy . . .

'The who?' we all gasped.

And for five years.

'Five years???' we all gasped again.

But in the blink of an eye, he'd done his five years, become best mates with Tom Cruise and been hosted at the White House by Mr and Mrs O'President. Becks has since gone on to become one of the world's hottest advertising mules, while Vix has become one of the most successful fashion designers in retail history.

How the hell did they pull all that off?

Becks makes more money now than he ever did kicking a ball around. And Posh has made tens of millions of pounds from first singing and now *haute couture*. Incredible, truly impressive.

Don't get me wrong: I wouldn't want to be either of them for a second, but no one can deny that they have totally rewritten the book of how to milk the holy cow of good fortune.

So, how much luck is involved?

Well, maybe some, but not that much. At least, nowhere near as much as most people think.

Their success is down to meticulous and brilliant planning. In fact, it wouldn't be an overstatement to say they may well be the best-managed double act OF ALL TIME.

Take Angelina and Brad, for example. Here we have the number one megastar couple in the world, but look where they began by comparison. They were both A-list movie stars when they met, both with a history of massively high-profile relationships. So much heat behind them when they hooked up, there was almost a second Big Bang.

Enter the super-brand we have come to know as BrAngelina.

And what a brand.

BrAngelina isn't even a real word, but type B-R-A-N into a Google search and up it pops.

Boom.

Yet here are our very own Posh and Becks, breathing down their necks. That's nothing short of astounding.

Simon Fuller, their manager, is like a wizard with Posh and Becks the perfect apprentices. When Lewis Hamilton joined 19 (Fuller's management company) things didn't work out so well. Hamilton had his own ideas about how he wanted to be perceived and what direction he wanted his life and career to go in. In the end he parted company with Fuller and has since begun to manage himself. With Posh & Becks, however, there has never been any underlying conflict to unsteady the ship.

But there's something else going on here. All the clever PR spin in the world will only bear fruit if everyone involved is prepared to WORK THEIR ARSES OFF.

How about this example of Becks's unfailing commitment to Posh & Becks Inc.

When the Olympic flame arrived at RNLS *Culdrose* back in 2012, I co-hosted *The One Show* live from the event. It was a fantastically exciting moment to be part of. As the gold-painted BA (type) code-named 'Firefly' made its final approach, one could sense the nationwide party that was about to begin.

Chaperoning the flame to Britain were Princess Anne, the Princess Royal; Lord Coe, Chairman of LOCOG; Boris 'Blustering' Johnson, Mayor of London; and Golden Balls himself, Becks – all-round hero and *bona fide* founding member of the UK's original Olympic bid team.

Our Olympic Torch *One Show* Special came and went, the Olympic Flame was lit and the countdown to London 2012 had begun.

But here's the thing:

After we came off air, I had to leave the celebrations straight away to get back home and somehow, someone had wangled me a lift back to London on the golden plane. Not only that, but in the seat where the Olympic flame had been sitting on its inbound flight from Athens. Honestly, it had its own seat next to the Princess Royal. Although when I say *it*, I mean it and five other flames. All flickering away as back-ups should the original flame go out for some reason.

But that's not the story.

The story is, for the duration of the flight as I (seat 1C) was sitting next to the BBC's Sophie Raworth (seat 1D), in front of Boris Johnson (seat 2C) and Lord Coe (seat 2D), Becks was miles back down the aisle in a row on his own.

Why am I telling you this? Because I want you to guess what he was doing while we were all rabbiting over each other and diving into the complimentary champagne. What do you reckon?

Let me tell you.

He was READING A BOOK.

Don't ask me which one, because I can't remember. Actually the truth is, I forgot to look, for which I will always be annoyed with myself. I was so gobsmacked with what I was seeing, it didn't occur to me to check out exactly what book it might be. Purely the fact that it was a book at all threw me right off balance.

Why would Becks be reading a book?

He has never once mentioned books in any of his interviews that I've seen or read. Not once, and yet here he was, nose-deep in print while the rest of us were having a high old time. Or did he simply want a bit of privacy and was pretending to read? Surely not. Had he wanted privacy it would have been much easier for him to close his eyes and pretend to be asleep.

But Becks reading in the middle of a raucous plane full of post-Olympic flame jubilation? I'm just not buying that.

Becks knows that more than anything else, he looks the part. So that's what he was doing. He was looking the part all the way home. Like the members of a boy band whose guitars and microphones aren't plugged in. No one cares as long as we're all playing the right roles.

And WORKING.

Working is actually what Posh & Becks do best. They work really hard, all the time. And that's why they will always have my ultimate respect.

Good luck to them.

Work

Ten Things I Need:

10 To feel relevant.

9 To check my testicles every day.

8 To have a passion outside of work.

7 To have a few good friends.

6 To have a home I want to be in.

5 To be there for my kids.

4 To keep learning.

3 To be able to provide for my family.

2 To be in a loving and stable relationship.

1 To be as healthy as possible.

My All-Time Favourite Restaurant and How I Liked It So Much I (Nearly) Bought It

I do think it's important to underwrite one's future relevance if at all possible. Feeling relevant is a huge factor in how well one ages. Still being part of whichever scene you choose to hang out in has to be a good thing. That's why for years I have hankered after my own proper big-boy restaurant. Having been fortunate enough to eat in many of the very best over the years, I am always amazed, excited and inspired at the tsunami of life that crashes through the door, come lunch or dinner. Players, movers, shakers, chancers, beauties, beasts, the powerful, the peaceful and the downright dreadful. Who doesn't want a bit of that every day?

And the best restaurateurs never want for anything. They get invited everywhere by everyone all the time – hunting, skiing, racing, you name it. They also enjoy the vicarious role of being among life's great connectors, hooking one person up with another for a bit of business here and there or a bit of hanky-panky who knows where. Not that I have any spare time to commit myself to such a venture at the moment, but if it all went tits-up tomorrow, I could think of a lot of worse things I might end up doing.

With this in mind, even though the timing may have been somewhat premature, I decided to investigate an opportunity that came my way, with a view to securing my non-irrelevant future. My favourite restaurant of all time had very quietly been put up for sale. I sensed there might be a deal to be done, and she's a belter, the best of the best, top of the hill, number one.

When I bought Virgin Radio the first thing I did was boldly announce my intentions live on air. It worked then, so I thought I might try a similar tactic this time, only instead of announcing it on the radio I wrote about it in my newspaper column in the *Mail on Sunday*. The world-famous Langan's restaurant, once the shining beacon of the London glitterati, was in need of a new team, a new owner, a new direction and generally being dragged into the twenty-first century.

Now it just so happened that Brian Clivaz, the managing director, and I had exchanged correspondence a week earlier after a chance meeting. Well, I say chance meeting, but ironically it was at the auctioning off of Peter Langan's art collection. The famous collection that had adorned the walls of his eponymous eatery for the last thirty years had become the subject of a much-anticipated sale drummed up to liquidate the beginning of the end. Which it did. And very handsomely, to the tune of almost two million pounds.

Langan was:

A Mad.
B A genius.
C An avid collector of art with an excellent (ish) eye.

Over the years, he had clearly spent every spare penny he had on rare and iconic pieces. Although, having said that, few were as rare and iconic as the prices they realized on the day. Most works went for, get this, five to ten times their estimate. Now either the valuers at Christie's had got their estimates catastrophically wrong, there was something very strange going on, or even more unlikely but increasingly looking like it might be the case, a heady cocktail of the two had taken place.

The legendary Langan's magic had shown itself one final time, his unfathomable alchemy back for a curtain call. The prices went ballistic, proving that some people have more charisma dead than many of those still alive. When Langan set up his restaurant with Michael Caine in 1976, Caine was one of the hottest movie stars in the world; Langan was an outrageous and notorious bon viveur and Richard Shepherd, their chef, was one of only a handful of UK chefs to hold a coveted Michelin star. A triumvirate that turned out to be a lethal combination.

Langan's did lunch and dinner like it had never been done before. Hundreds of covers every day. And the crème de la crème of the world's rich and famous would drop in, to then fall out several hours later – Nicholson, O'Toole, Burton, Taylor, Sinatra, Princess Margaret. Triple AAA* all the way.

Alas, all this was way before my time. But even in the twenty-odd years I've been a regular, the great and good have still been seen there from time to time. It's just that the great and good nowadays are not as the great and good once were. Never mind, we are who we are and we can't be anyone else.

All through *The Big Breakfast*, *Don't Forget Your Toothbrush* and the *TFI* days, I was almost a permanent fixture at Langan's lunchtime.

It was also the place where I made the momentous decision to sell Virgin Radio. My media business was at an impasse at the time, as my backers had just refused me permission to buy the *Daily Star* and *Daily Express* newspaper businesses. Apparently we had done too well, too quickly and no longer needed to 'bet the ranch' – a phrase I'll never forget – on any new ventures. By the way, Richard Desmond went on to buy both and turned them into a hundred -

million-pound-plus business in no time at all – hardly betting the bloomin' ranch!

Anyway, my team were down in the dumps in the full knowledge the controls of the train set had been irredeemably taken from us. Blow them, I said, I know what we'll do, we'll sell up and move on. Six months and a £135 million profit later, that's precisely what we did.

I'm sure I am not the only guy or gal who has benefited from the special blend of 'space and time' that Langan's can lend to an otherwise befuddled and claustrophobic state of mind. It's a big place with high ceilings, a lot of square footage and a huge amount of positive energy, like Grand Central Station without the trains. Sometimes the noise in there at lunchtime is deafening, the backdrop to much scheming and plotting over the years. In fact Langan's might have the most glamorous and starry story to tell of the last four decades, if only she could speak.

Ah, there we are, out of nowhere I seem to have decided her gender. All things great that are not human in my mind are girls: majestic warships, resilient and proud little boats, legendary aircraft and of course beautiful and magnificent old cars.

I think it's the restaurant's magic that drove those prices so high at the Christie's auction. So many people wanted a piece of Langan's, a piece of art that they could hang at home over a table of their own. What then of the ultimate auction lot – the restaurant herself?

'Nostalgia can demand the highest of prices,' whispered a very wise man to me while the sale was taking place. Hmm, words of the magi indeed. Excellent news for the seller but not so great for the buyers if they ever need to sell it on.

There is a similar argument when it comes to Beatles' memorabilia, the most valuable showbiz memorabilia of all. The theory is that its time may peak, like a good wine. Probably somewhere around ten years after the death of whichever Beatle croaks last, as after that the next generation of well-heeled collectors will hold far less affection for the Fab Four than we do now. It's the same with single-seater pre- and post-race cars as opposed to technically much less important Sixties' sports cars. You can pick up an example of the former for a fraction of the far less rare but far more recognizable and usable latter.

How then to go about valuing Langan's? What with all my own emotion tied up in her, I didn't want to become the patsy with so much passion burning in his heart it would lead to a whole load of nonsense burning a hole in his pocket. By the current management's own admission, she needed a complete ground-up and sympathetic restoration, both physically and spiritually. And preferably some time last week or at least as soon as possible. This once-gleaming vessel was halfway to becoming a tatty and lacklustre has-been with wires hanging out of sockets and once-proud staff who looked like they might burst into tears at any moment. The whole thing was in danger of foundering on the rocks. In many ways, damaged goods.

'OK, Brian, I give up. Tell me the price?' I asked.

'The current owner will take £6 million for her.'

Wow. For damaged goods, that's a whole chunk of change.

Yes, £6,000,000 is definitely an awful lot of anyone's money and especially for a restaurant. Even an established one.

But nevertheless my heart immediately pulled out a sledgehammer and started to rain blows down upon my brain. This wasn't just any established restaurant, for heaven's sake. This was the original London grand eatery. The establishment that paved the way for those other Scarlet Pimpernel impersonators that began popping up all over the place in the mid-Eighties and crazy Nineties. Besides, she's my favourite restaurant of all time. Owning and running her wouldn't be the worst default I could choose in order to avoid the showbiz scrapheap. My own lunchtime and dinnertime show, live! Every day.

But hang on, you numpty! You promised yourself not to make any more gleaming errors, no more avoidable mistakes, no more hedonistic passions over what makes sense for the piggy bank. Say it again, and slowly this time.

Six million – that's a lot of broken biscuits.

'We need to look at the numbers,' said my pal, who is also one of my gurus.

I have several father figures whom I go to for advice, my friend Ian being right at the top of the list. He started life as an optician in Hampstead with just one shop. While he was asking his patients, 'Is it better with lens A, or now with lens B?' his more garrulous brother was out cutting his teeth in the London property market. Individually they were all pina but no colada, but when the two of them got together they were unstoppable.

Apply a couple of half-decent minds to a business run in the majority by wide boys and fly-by-nights and watch them clean up. I've seen it so many times. It happens a lot with ex-Formula 1 drivers. They often make five times in the commercial world what they ever made driving a racing car, thanks to their almost autistic ability for analysis, especially when it comes to figures. Suffice to say Ian & Co. now own their own real-life Monopoly board as well as several significant parts of South America. Ian had more advice to quell my trigger-happy enthusiasm:

'Stick to what you know, and even if you can't do that – do anything but invest in a restaurant. Food always tastes better in someone else's.'

He was right on the money again, as wise and as astute as ever. But he could see I was crestfallen.

'What the heck, we'll look at the numbers anyway, if you like.'

I knew he was only humouring me and I should have bowed out, but I so wanted this deal to happen. But then there was the issue of the exit plan.

I learned a few years ago that the thing about going into a business is in fact not the going in at all but the coming out. The exit strategy is King. It's quite bizarre if you think about it. Going in to get out – and the sooner the better – for as much profit as possible.

Transient and short-term, hard-nosed business, dressed up as long-term commitment cut short by an offer 'too good to refuse'. Like always going into a relationship thinking how and when you're going to break up because it's probably just a matter of time, so what's the point in taking the risk to find out otherwise. Perhaps that's why so many businessmen have trouble holding down marriages, because 'long term' per se is simply not in their nature. Just as many of the greatest companies in the world, which have been built up over decades by a single individual with a clear vision and total commitment, are scooped up by a titanic corporate fund the moment that same individual cashes in his chips at life's ultimate cashier's kiosk, and then broken up and sold off.

As I speak, that's where Langan's is, I suppose. I want to commit to twenty years or more of proprietorship, but everyone around me is talking of buy, increase value, sell, which is just not what I'm interested in anyway.

So what's the point?

The truth is, there isn't any.

Me buying Langan's would be yet another square peg in a round hole for the universe to pop out again when I wasn't looking.

For me, nothing's about the dosh alone any more.

It's about having a good time in the process, something the balance sheet has trouble highlighting. It's the happy pounds I'm after.

Pounds are like human years and dog years, as far as I'm concerned. There are different types. There are angry pounds, sad pounds, bad pounds, stressed pounds, shallow pounds, deep pounds but the best of all are the happy pounds.

Never buy somebody else's passion – unless the passion comes with the package. True passion is a whites-of-the-eyes thing, you have to stare deep into someone's soul and hope to see a sign that tells you they mean it.

So many people contacted me with regards to buying Langan's to see if they could get involved. Raising the money would not be an issue. But! I couldn't look them in the eye and tell them I really meant it. Not at the price that was being asked. Whenever other people's money is involved, I think the best policy is to treat it with even more respect than if it was your own. Otherwise you will never care enough to make it work.

Langan's would have to wait: no matter how special and unique it is, it's still just a business and a building and I'm only going to get out of it what I put in. My family needs me much more than any restaurant does and I need my family way more than that.

Life is family. Family is life. That's it. That's the formula. End of story. And anyone who spends a second of their life doing anything else unless they absolutely have to is a fool. Relevance is important but the ultimate relevance is the one we have to our loved ones. Lose that and in the end whatever else you have will be empty and worthless by comparison.

The golfer Sam Torrance was once asked what epitaph he would like his family to inscribe on his headstone. In a heartbeat he replied quietly and succinctly:

He was a great dad.

What could be more relevant than that?

Happiness

The Monk

Matthieu was a young scientist at the start of a promising career when he became disillusioned with life. This drove him to abandon his native Paris and spend the next quarter of a century searching for wisdom and meaning. This he found, like many before him, in the sanctuary of various isolated hermitages situated high up in the Himalayas, famed for their peace and tranquillity. After over two decades of deep contemplation, apprenticeship and meditation, Matthieu was then called back into public life following a challenge for him to take on his own father, as a renowned academic, in a recorded debate. The subject? The meaning of life both here on earth and wherever else it might come into play in the known.

Their exchanges were chronicled and eventually became the subject of a worldwide bestseller: *The Monk and the Philosopher*.

Since then Matthieu has continued to accept his calling to spend the majority of his remaining days – he's now almost seventy – travelling around the world lecturing anyone who cares to listen about the various thoughts and theories he has developed as a result of thousands of hours of meditation. One such talk I was lucky enough to attend earlier this year, as part of my own ongoing research for answers to the midlife questions 'Who am I?', 'What am I?', 'Why are we here?' 'What should I be doing?'

The talk was entitled 'Altruism'.

This was of particular interest at the time because only two hours earlier I had arrived home after attending one of our Children in Need charity events. The event in question was a lavish trip to the Monaco Grand Prix with six couples who had donated almost £1.2 million to the BBC's children's charity for the privilege. I had no doubt that the couples had been sincerely altruistic in their giving. Or was the charity benefiting more from a vicarious side effect than from a genuine selfless act of proactive benevolence? A sentiment that just so happened to be the very crux of what Matthieu had to say.

He claims altruism is a vital quality the human race needs to acquire if it is to stand any chance of survival. By 2030, 300 million of the existing 1.2 billion species currently inhabiting the Earth will have become extinct. The knock-on effect of which will be astounding and irreversible on our planet's diversity. By 2050, Matthieu says, if we continue to carry on consuming the world's resources at the rate we are now, without any increase – which is highly unlikely – we will require two more planet Earths to sustain the supply of everything we need. As that is not an option, Matthieu wonders what the hell we expect is going to happen.

'Of course, it is not in our nature to jump out of the way of a car until it's about to run us over. This is understandable. However, the problem becomes much more issue when the cars eventually keep coming one after the other until there is no longer anything we can do to avoid getting hit.'

He is convinced that's where we're heading, and is confounded by anyone who sees the situation differently. He is in no doubt that they are deluding themselves and anyone else who listens to them. He is on a mission to get us to realize that we have to save ourselves and we need to do it yesterday, not today or tomorrow – by then it will already be too late. He believes if you're not doing something to secure the future within twenty-four hours of reading this, you are accepting the fact that it's OK for our children to witness the beginning of the end of humanity as we know it.

He's also of the opinion there's never been a better world to save.

'Notwithstanding what we are told on the news every day, there has never been less conflict – as long as man and woman have been on the earth. The atrocity of the last two world wars put paid to that. Thanks to radio and television we were shown how horrible, how unheroic, how unwinnable war is, regardless of whichever side claims victory on any given day. There have never been fewer murders, with murder rates globally falling a hundred fold compared to a thousand years ago. The perception is we live in a more violent age, but the truth is that this is not at all the case.'

He is desparate for us to realize we have that ability and means to be happier than ever before. At the heart of this is altruism. So, can we ever become truly altruistic without considering what's in it for us? Even if what we end up doing is for the good of others, will this element of self-interest ultimately negate any positive effects it might have?

Thankfully, yes.

Phew.

Matthieu cites footage of a man caught on CCTV jumping off the platform of an underground station to rescue a man who has fainted and fallen into the path of an oncoming train. The footage shows the man dragging both himself and the unconscious individual to safety with less than a hundredth of a second to spare. Given the time frame, one would assume this has to be an unconscious reflex action and therefore an act of genuinely selfless altrutism.

'Almost but not quite,' says Matthieu. 'It was indeed argued by some that this was an automatic innate reflex action from one human being with regards to saving another. Good news for the individual about to get pulped by the 8.10 from Waterloo, but not good news in that case for altruism. This is because to be truly altruistic, all action must first be considered and then acted upon. Unfortunately, from a purely academic point of view, automatic altruism does not count!

'However, the good news is, I argue that our hero did make a selfless decision, just an unbelievably quick one. Perhaps the quickest decision of his life, almost definitely so. In which case, it was truly altruistic. Otherwise, how come everyone who witnesses such potential tragedies doesn't put themselves in the line of fire to save the life of a relative stranger?'

I can't tell you how life-affirming this was to hear first-hand from such a softly spoken man, respected around the world for his vast insight into caring love and compassion.

Now, the other amazing thing about Matthieu is that he has also been declared 'the happiest man on Earth'. This was the conclusion following a series of neurological tests he underwent over twenty years ago. During which his brain patterns were recorded in various states of conscious meditation for up to twelve hours within the confines of an MRI scanner. The results were literally off the charts, way beyond anything ever witnessed before, proving beyond any doubt that Matthieu had an unprecedented ability to control his brain mind. As opposed to his mind controlling him, which is the case for most of us.

Similar results were recorded when he was asked to meditate on compassion, with the parts of his hippocampus now 'known' to be responsible for the emotion of compassion lighting up like a firework display. In fact, regardless of what emotion he was asked to evoke, Matthieu could deliver jaw-dropping consistency time after time.

With similar calm focus, throughout his talk he continued to guide us through why he was optimistic rather than pessimistic over our future and our potential for collective conscious altruism.

'It's what we humans do. We take or make whaever we need to survive and if altruism is currently the thing, that's what we'll end up turning to. It will become part of our evolution. We move as one because we are one.'

And the evidence for what Matthieu was saying could be seen in the room that night. The venue, Camden Hall – a place I'd visited only once before, to get married to my first wife, bizarrely – was packed to the rafters, a complete and utter sell-out; whereas a couple of years before, the same guy with the exact same message had stood in front of a mere handful of people.

Of course, many people have issues with Buddhism and I can understand why. Retreating to a beautiful mountain for as long as it takes to find yourself is an inherently selfish and self-centred thing to do. While the rest of the world is having to get on with life the best it can, monks are never seen again: what use is that to mankind as a whole? And talking of 'man' kind, women aren't exactly high up in the pecking order in the Buddhist world. A friend of mine's wife and young daughter had to wait outside a Buddhist temple while he and his eldest son were free to enter and see what all the fuss was about.

And as much as I am a huge fan of His Holiness the Dalai Lama, no wonder he's always grinning from ear to ear considering all the gorgeous hotels he gets to stay in free of charge courtesy of all the billionaires and Hollywood superstars who love him so much.

Still, the message that elemental balance is good for each of us and the world as one, is important to get across however that may be achieved. So I'm happy to turn a blind eye to that anomaly if you are. Plus, I did get to meditate with Matthieu, which was wonderful.

'Anyone can meditate, ten seconds a day to start will do,' he purred. 'Think of each session like taking the stopper out of a bottle of perfume, then as the stopper is removed for longer, the more prevalent the smell becomes.'

Our energy during meditation should be directed towards compassion first and foremost, for the world, our fellow humans and ourselves. This is the key to happiness, the kind of happiness that has been proven to be infectious, as opposed to sadness which can affect us all but cannot be taught. This is the defining difference between the two.

Happiness is life's way of letting us know we're getting things right.

PART 2

Marathon Diary

Friday, 2 January 2015

Ow, fuck, I mean – really ow, really fuck. It's 5.15 in the morning and I've just hobbled to and from the toilet for another of my ever weaker, ever more frustrating, ever more worrying pees in the night. The cravings for which seem to keep me awake more than I'm asleep nowadays, feeling like I have a gallon of urine bursting to get out but always culminating in no more than a forced and all too often painful, hot dribble. I need to go and see someone about this. I did a year ago but my doc said it was nothing to worry about, probably a urine infection at worst. 'Certainly nothing to do with the prostate or anything else as potentially sinister.'

I need to go for a big check-up this year anyway. A Mayo-style deal. Mayo, the clinic a good friend told me about. The place in the US that can tell you what nasties are creeping up on you almost before even they know themselves. That's all to come. It's all part of the plan. The plan I'm still working on. The plan that I've been thinking about for the last couple of years.

The reason my knees are hurting like they want to disown me, and the whole of my right leg feels like it has a red-hot poker embedded in it – is because yesterday, 1 January 2015, I ran further than I've ever run in my life before: twice around the lake near to where we live, 9.4 miles to be precise.

Ouch.

Double ouch with bells on.

• • •

It was something I had promised myself I would try to do before the end of 2014. New Year's Eve was my original scheduled date, but as it was my wife's thirty-sixth birthday, we had to go to see my eighty-nine-year-old mum and had agreed to attend a friend's drinks and dinner party, this was not the wisest choice of dates.

Idiot.

One day late was OK though, as long as it didn't spill over into the 2nd. Not that things looked at all promising when I woke up at ten o'clock that morning. My mouth was as dry as the desert, my head was like a cracked bowling ball and my throat felt like someone had poured broken glass down it in the middle of the night. The dinner in question had gone on until 2 a.m. We'd drunk champagne, beer, red wine and brandy. Tash had got up early with our two sons, five-'But nearly six, Dad!'-year-old Noah and two-and-a-half-year-old Eli, whose new game is entering our room just after 6 a.m., as regular as clockwork, declaring his allegiance to Peppa Pig and her family.

By the time I dragged myself out of bed and staggered downstairs, Tash had already been up with the boys for two hours. The three of them were currently mustered at the breakfast table by the bottom of the stairs, midway through porridge, various slivers of fruit and a communal jug of water. Noah was being his usual smiling enthusiastic self, Eli was in the middle of his daily musing on what the heck everything was about, while Tash, quite frankly, looked like the living dead – bless her.

'Babe, back to bed, immediately,' I declared. 'Your turn, it's mine from here.'

She hesitated in that stoic mum way that means, 'Don't worry I'm up now, it's OK.' But for once I surprised myself by saying exactly the right thing: 'Either you go back to bed this instant, or I am. There's no way I'm not taking advantage of this situation if you're going to stay up with the boys.'

'In that case, they're all yours.'

A few seconds later Mummy had gone back to the land of nod, back to the still-warm, gorgeous pit I had left only moments earlier. I felt like shit, but so what? The kids were in sparkling form and ready to eat up whatever this next day of their brief lives had to throw at them. I could have put a movie on, declared a duvet day – both totally acceptable in the handbook of the hungover parent – but neither option would get me the brownie points I needed later on that afternoon to disappear before darkness fell for the two hours required for me to get round my lake twice. This was diabolical planning all round; I'd had a skinful of booze, followed by terrible alcohol-induced sleep, yet here I was contemplating a head-on, serious boys' day out with my sons to give me what remaining chance there might be of retrieving the situation.

The run couldn't wait until tomorrow. In my mind, 1 January is still technically more part of the year before than the dawning of the next. Don't you think? New Year's Eve and New Year's Day are two halves of the same story, the definitive annual two-parter; 1 January simply cannot exist in its own entity, it is the full stop of the preceding twelve months. Therefore 2 January is the true new beginning, like the day after people get married. 'Tis with the dawning of the first complete twenty-four hours after the ceremony that the fairy dust of the big day begins to settle and reality kicks in. So provided I could get my run in on New Year's Day, I would be OK.

But why the time pressure? Well, the truth of the matter is, it was one of many unofficial deals I had made with myself since the idea of this book entered my head.

All my deals with myself are unofficial, in as much as they are never written in stone but hover around me, waiting for the green light. Sometimes weeks, or months, or even years pass by while I let my subconscious mull over what to do. I simply wait until the deliberations are over and the answer pops up, telling me what to do. In this particular instance the answer to the question, or rather questions: Do I think it's important we should all know what it feels like to run, or walk, or crawl a marathon before we die? How would doing so change me as a person? Would doing so enlighten me in any way? And, more pertinently: Do I think I could complete one, even if I wanted to? Both mentally and physically.

With these and other considerations in mind I had taken it upon myself to just make a start. Not running but shuffling.

Every day on my regular commute back home from work I pass Virginia Water on my right-hand side. A beautiful man-made lake commissioned by the Duke of Cumberland as part of his sprawling Surrey/Berkshire game park back in ye olde times of 1753. For a number of months towards the end of last year (2014) it kept catching my eye, each time gradually nagging away at my psyche more than the last. The more I acknowledged the feeling, the stronger it became. Something was telling me I had to stop one day and begin to run. This was the place to do it.

A genuine calling.

And so one day that's exactly what I did. I pulled into the car park, took my parking ticket from the machine and set off anti-clockwise around the perimeter to see how far I could manage before I had to stop for a breather.

Like I say, whether I was actually running or not wasn't the issue. All I had to do was effect any movement other than walking for as long as I could, hopefully getting a little sweaty and out of breath in the process.

I didn't care what it looked like, as long as there was an outside chance it may become sustainable. I mean, we are talking way below even the level of jogging here. In fact, during one of my first 'shuffles' round the lake, two power walkers overtook me. I didn't mind, and they were far too polite to giggle, although they did go respectfully quiet as they carried out their manoeuvre, like a stream of traffic passing a hearse.

They had their agenda and I had mine.

All I was concerned with in those early outings was to make it around the lake, any way, anyhow.

The first time I shuffled for perhaps a few hundred yards short of a mile before taking a break, and then perhaps four or five times after that. But the feeling of satisfaction I felt for the rest of the day, right up until I was in bed and dropping off to sleep, was immense. I couldn't wait to do it again the next day and then the next and the day after that.

The first few days of shuffling saw an exponential increase in stamina.

On only day two I could make it round having just paused three times.

Day three twice.

And then on day four I made it round all the way without stopping once.

Even though I was moving painfully slowly, glacially almost, I convinced myself I was now a runner.

Every day I felt secretly great. A similar feeling to when as a teenager you finally bag a girlfriend, but only you and she knows, that feeling when the world seems so much more exciting and shiny and bright than it did the day before.

If this was how running/shuffling was going to continue to make me feel, I simply had to carry on.

As my confidence grew and the car park tickets began to stack up, my shuffling pace increased until I could complete my beloved circuit in under an hour, then fifty minutes. On Christmas Eve I even managed to record a personal best of forty-three minutes – though admittedly it nearly killed me.

'I won't be doing that again anytime soon,' I said to myself, still feeling faint fifteen minutes later. By this time I had already started to flirt with thoughts about the 'M' word. I figured with the right amount of preparation I could probably shuffle a marathon, but not if I messed my joints up needlessly 'running' as fast as I could.

I don't take many things in life seriously but when I do, I go to a different place. I wish I went there more often as it seems so much more peaceful than where I normally exist, but I suppose that's the deal. We have to really want something to stand any chance of experiencing it. And my main focus here was endurance. So, why go quickly? Why punish my 48-year-old joints and lungs more than I had to, especially if in doing so I risked jeopardizing my chances of ever making it around 26.2 miles.

Sure, it was good for my ego to know that I could probably bust the forty-minute mark, but that's not what this was about. For this to work it would have to be an anti-ego process. I wanted to figure out my realistic chances of running/shuffling a marathon without stopping, so excessive speed (i.e. in my terms – or perhaps that of a sloth) was of no consequence. I promised myself I would never let such vanity enter my 'training' again.

Wow, now there's a word: 'training', which I suppose was valid. After all, that's what I was doing. Training . . . perhaps . . . for . . . a marathon.

As the shuffling continued, the quietness began to creep in. Quietness, I have found, is a usually very welcome ingredient to most recipes to do with creativity or positivity. In fact I can't think of a single instance where the opposite has been true.

I was further buoyed when my running became ever quieter, lighter, as did my breathing, my thinking, what I was doing had quickly transformed from an uphill struggle into a daily release and endorphin high. Ergo, I continued to look forward more and more to my shuffles around the lake with each new outing.

The moment I jumped in the car I started smiling from the inside out. The plain fact is that by the time I returned home again, I would have experienced another hour, minimum, of something that was unquestionably doing me, as well as those around me, a whole heap of good.

I had also, almost immediately, begun to lose weight. Not a lot, but a few pounds. My skin felt tighter under my arms, my middle-age podgy back-fat seemed to be showing signs of disappearing – all because of doing something bit by bit, day by day, quietly, calmly and thoughtfully. Even making sure I had the right change for the meter in the car park gave me a sense of self, bringing back memories of asking Mum for the 20p subs for scouts of a Monday when I was eleven years old.

Shit. Life really is so simple. How come we let it get away from us?

And so it was all going swimmingly, with the question 'when and how will I know whether or not I think I should attempt a marathon?' happily simmering away on the back burner.

But why, other than the reasons I have already specified, had this idea entered my thoughts in the first place? Well now, that's where *Call the Midlife* comes in.

As I witnessed the beginning of my fiftieth year on the planet, a milestone in anyone's life and an experience I wanted to write about, hopefully slaying the Midlife Crisis dragon in the process.

In order to make sense of all the ranting and raving, and to tie up any loose ends, I needed an ultimate destination at which to end my journey. The marathon, I decided, would give that journey purpose. But if I was going to succeed it would need to be the most doable, achievable, non-midlife-crisis, non-painful marathon of all time.

So now you see why, before embarking on this journey, it was vital to carry out a preliminary assessment to establish whether I stood the ghost of a chance of pulling it off – and emerge still standing at the end.

Once around the lake without stopping became twice around the lake without stopping.

The first time I attempted this, it brought all the memories of my first shuffling day flooding back.

The same trepidation, the same nervousness, the same intrigue. And in many ways a similar outcome. I didn't make it all the way round the second circuit without a break. In fact I stopped twice but that was OK. There was no rush. Two laps was now the norm. Continuity would come soon enough. All I had to do was stick at it.

Hence that New Year's Day run.

'Dad, what shall we do?' asked Noah.

'Come on, boys, we're going out.'

EXTERIOR: Guildford Town Centre

New Year's Day, 10 a.m.

It's dead, and I mean really dead, but all the shops are open. What happened to the January sales? I know the answer. The same as pub opening hours. They got too loose for their own good. Too many pre-January sales. Another example of a short-term high, long-term low marketing ploy. But with zero strategy. I see it all the time nowadays. Note to self: Don't get me started. (I'm becoming more grumpy, not necessarily a bad thing – we'll get on to that later. How we become the old curmudgeon kids can never understand.) Anyway, the huge positive of the fucked-up high streets of Great Britain's strategy is that Noah, Eli and I basically have the whole of Guildford to ourselves.

We select parking for two hours, which should be plenty of time. We only intend visiting four outlets: one toy shop, Argos, a coffee shop and the Cornish Pasty Company. We spend half an hour in the aisles of the toy shop and approximately the same flicking through the myriad pages of the toy and games pages of the Argos catalogue. We then take fifteen minutes' thinking time to consider what to purchase over hot chocolates and croissants in Caffè Nero, two minutes picking up a 'traditional Cornish', and then back to the toy shop, which wins.

It's Lego again. The world's No.1-selling toy. Back from the dead. No fucked-up strategy for the Danes. Get those guys to run our high streets.

The boys cannot believe they have a bonus present after Christmas. They are beyond happy in the back of the car, beaming. As is Mummy when they arrive home. Tash couldn't be more grateful for her extra hours in bed. Straightaway I wade in. It's the only way, when it comes to brownie points – spend them quickly before they expire.

'OK if I go for a run?'

'Sure, baby.' Behind her the kids are already ripping open their boxes, the fire in the living room flickering away. 'We'll build, you shuffle.'

Perfect.

• • •

It was 2.31 when I left the house and by the time I returned I would have orbited my lake non-stop twice. It was as simple as that, like waiting to see the headmaster at school: regardless how it ended, this was definitely going to happen one way or another. A fail-safe thought process that I employ on a regular basis, usually in situations where I would otherwise get sick with nerves or my brain would go into meltdown over what I might be about to get spectacularly wrong.

The 4.7-mile loop around Virginia Water is glorious indeed. The gloriousness helps; it's absolutely beautiful out there. From that first ever shuffle I always set off anti-clockwise, turning right from the café at the gates towards the totem pole and Guards Polo Club, up to the top, over the bridge and then back down the other side parallel with London Road, the link between Wentworth Golf Club on the A30 and Ascot village. This way round, it's the rough before the smooth, the first half gently undulating and winding, and over twice as long as the flatter, straighter home leg.

My legs felt good, much better than I expected them to. My breathing was steady and my focus/concentration, which was my biggest concern, was OK too. This was what had bothered me most about the prospect of doing a marathon: could I just keep going mentally? How does one cope with the fact that after running 6 miles, there's still 20 miles and 385 yards to go? But 'No problem,' I thought, halfway round the first loop. As usual, it was about breaking it down. Like a big fat juicy steak. Slice by slice, bite by bite.

I approached the end of the first circuit, the last corner by the waterfall where there are always smiling couples and giddy families posing for photos. A few seconds later, I reached the point where I used to pull up in my one-lap days and treat myself to walking the last hundred yards while looking back at the vast body of water I'd just stretched out like a huge mirror disappearing into the trees on the horizon. But there would be no pulling up today, or at least that was the plan.

Gently I shuffled on past where the main path breaks into two, the outer loop and the inner loop, my loop, and off I went again. Just that moment alone was worth the journey.

Again, quietly and calmly, another running first.

Real joy.

This was something I had been thinking about for weeks, months even. Like I used to when I was a kid. When we had time to con-template and really think about the things we wanted to do. By hook or by crook, by the time I finished, in the dark, I was deter-mined this would be the longest run of my life thus far.

And I did it.

I bloody did it.

I creaked out of the park gates after affording myself a walk for the last couple of hundred yards.

I could barely lower myself into the car but I didn't care.

I arrived home still creaking, and by then also simultaneously seizing up, but I was delirious.

'So far, so good,' I said to Tash, before explaining what I'd done.

'You did what? Wow! How?'

I felt amazing. But how else did I feel? How was it supposed to feel? I purposefully hadn't read up on anything to do with long-distance running. Prep, execution, aftermath – nothing. I didn't want to be Textbook Johnny. Never have done.

I have a friend who insists on forever telling me a quicker route whenever we're going anywhere in the car, even when we're not late, going somewhere nice and it's a beautiful day. Why? What's the point? Who cares? What are we going to do with the extra five minutes we save when we do finally arrive anyway? He'll probably spend it checking emails that don't matter. I've never asked him but I bet he's Textbook Johnny.

It may on the other hand be because I don't like being told what to do.

'But surely,' I thought to myself, 'of all things, when it comes to something as basic as running, we should just run, like we just read, to ourselves and for ourselves. Figuring out how it works for us as we go.'

There are countless books on running, thousands no doubt – not that I've checked, but there must be, just as there are now special-ized running shops. Yet surely 99.9 per cent of what we need to run we already have.

Body? Check.

Two legs, two arms? Check.

Eyes, ears, mouth? Check.

Lungs and all other major internal organs? Check.

Of course, I was entirely wrong. If I'd read about how to cool down, for example, I'd know that what I was about to do next was the opposite of what was good for me.

'OK if I nip up for a bath?'

'I think you deserve one,' replied Tash.

● ● ●

Morning after my heroic two laps of the lake the day before.

I wake up, peaceful, rested. Mmm but there's something else. My whole right side below the waist has acquired a pulse all of its own. A dull ache from my hip down to my ankle. But no matter, something has to give; I am forty-eight years old and have never done anything close to this before. If this is as bad as it is going to get, I can cope – as long as I take things steady from here on in.

Then I climb out of bed.

My knees have never felt like this before – I don't even know what this feeling is. The closest I can think of is a combination of brain freeze after too much ice-cream and when the school bully bent your fingers back in the playground at break time.

There will be no running today. Not even a three-mile recovery run. (I later discovered there is no such thing as a recovery run, it's a huge myth.) It's now that I start to wonder about those dreaded textbooks. 'They're bound to be crammed with dilemmas and experiences of this nature,' I think out loud.

Even closer to hand, of course, the ever-present YouTube with its millions of 'how to?' posts. I have to admit to a hefty slice of hypocrisy where these are concerned. There's nothing like a YouTube 'how to . . . ?' session. Although I must confess to often confusing merely watching how to do something with then convincing myself this almost means I've actually done it.

'Still, I must resist,' I tell myself. 'It's my way or the highway.'

Double idiot.

It was at this precise moment I first began to feel ever so slightly like an ass in running denial.

_____

Saturday, 3 January 2015

Twenty-four hours later, I wake up and my right hip feels like it's on fire. Even worse than last time, my red-hot poker moment.

Oh dear.

Doctor!

• • •

All right, I capitulated, or panicked, or both – more likely both. I confess I turned to Google. I decided to allow myself just one search to start with. I figured this would make me focus on what I really wanted to know, as opposed to scatter-gunning for anything and everything.

After thinking long and hard, this is what I typed:

What does Paula Radcliffe eat?

It turns out that Paula likes breakfast cereal and snacking on bananas and dark chocolate.

Oh joy!

I love bananas and dark chocolate!

I want some now.

I wonder if melting the chocolate over the banana makes any difference to its health benefits.

Quickly, I checked.

Answer: absolutely none.

Brilliant.

Chocolate with a minimum content that is 70 percent dark can protect against heart disease, high bloodpressure and many other well-known and feared health hazards. Plus it has essential trace elements such as iron, calcium and potassium, is full of lots of friendly vitamins and tastes gorgeous. This was all almost too good to be true. But it is true.

Back to Paula briefly. Firstly another 'Oh joy' moment – she and her husband Gary REGULARLY LIKE TO EAT STIR FRIES.

Hallelujah. She also loves a post-race bowl of chips or cheese sandwich swilled down with a glass of wine. I'm actually hearing angels now.

I read on. The woman is amazing. My new immediate hero. Do you know that she continued training right up until the DAY BEFORE she gave birth to her daughter Isla?

OK, calling all fatties, that's the end of all your lardy excuses to stay on the sofa, right there.

And that was it. From that moment on I read anything and everything I could get my hands on about the running greats and their individual regimes and idiosyncrasies.

All the reading in the world, however, was not going to stop me from falling apart, which was looking increasingly more likely with every fresh shuffle. It was time to seek the help of yet more professionals – first stop, the local chiropractor.

'Yes, someone can see you,' said the nice lady on the other end of the telephone. 'But not until Monday, 11 a.m.'

Monday, 11 a.m. it was then.

• • •

After being examined and then cracked and twisted for a good quarter of an hour or so, I asked Phil the chiro what he thought my realistic chances of getting through a marathon at the end of April might be.

'Physically you could probably manage with regular sessions here, but how long have you been running?'

'Four weeks,' I answered.

'Oh, really,' he squeaked in that high-pitched tone of someone trying to suppress their surprise. It was obvious he thought I was pushing it a bit – but kindly agreed to help me the best he could if I wanted to try to go for it.

Done.

Phil was officially the first member of my secret back-up team.

• • •

Crunchtime:

'If I can make it around the lake THREE times without stopping, as long as it's before a hundred days to go, anyway, anyhow, I will investigate the possibility of gaining a late entry into the Virgin Money London Marathon.'

But until then I was not allowed to even look on the website. Again, when it finally came to it, I was a day late, not actually taking up my challenge until January. On this occasion I didn't run all the way but nor did I actually stop. I shuffled two and a half laps and then had to walk twice before just about making it round. It was by no means pretty but I'd one what I set out to do.

Bingo! I was clear to proceed.

That evening there were two things I specifically didn't do.

1. I didn't have a hot bath, having now read up on the fact that hot baths are no good for your muscles whatsoever after a long run, even if they feel like heaven at the time.
2. I decided not to tell anyone I didn't have to about my marathon ambition. I didn't want it to become the calling card of all my conversations between now and when/if it happened. I also wondered whether or not it would be possible to train for a marathon in secret.

The next day I contacted the organizers, requesting a secret place. The usual deal being that they are happy to give well-known faces late entry in return for the odd promotional photo or a magazine piece article. I was asking for the opposite.

'But think of it as a twist,' I enthused. 'You've got loads of celebs talking about their training and preparation beforehand, but you've never had someone pop up from nowhere on the start line on the day. Least of all someone like me, not exactly renowned for running or fitness of any kind.'

I'm not quite sure where, but somewhere during the conversation I must have said something right, as a couple of days later they agreed to facilitate my ruse. In fact, once they had signed up to the idea they very quickly became as excited about the subterfuge as I was.

The plan was as agreed.

As few people as absolutely necessary would know about my involvement until the morning of the race. After that, both at the start and finish line, I would have as many photos taken as they wanted and talk to every news crew in town. It would be the least I could do.

This was really it. I was in. I had to do it now. There was no way I could let these nice people down after they'd gone out on a limb to help me.

Responsibility, an excellent incentive.

• • •

The next day my thus far ad hoc shuffling could be officially upgraded to an actual marathon training programme.

I cannot tell you how excited this made me feel. Like I hadn't been for years.

The internet is perfect for things like marathon training plans.

There are dozens of them: the BUPA Marathon Training Plan, the Lucozade Sport Marathon Training Plan, all with various time frames and beginners, intermediate and advanced options. In the end, perhaps due to a warm glow of loyalty, I opted for Virgin Money's own official training plan.

Not that there's much to separate any of them.

Boom, I was in.

Double boom.

Technically I was ahead of the mileage.

But, according to what I was looking at, my 'training' thus far was all over the place and would be no use whatsoever come 26 April. Unless I began to adhere immediately to 'The Way'.

What was also a concern was that my whole body, especially my legs, was beginning to feel like it were made more of glass rather than stretchy skin, muscles, tendons and bones.

There was no longer any doubt, what I had suspected for years was true – when it comes to physicality, I am indeed one of nature's more fragile beings. But fragile or not, I was going to do my utmost to get through this marathon, even if it meant crossing the line in several different pieces.

Training for a marathon is unlike any other regime I've experienced. If you miss a day while writing a book, for example, you can write for twice as long the next day. If you miss a day while training for a marathon, that day's lost for ever. You can play catch-up but it throws everything else off. Getting the running days in at the right time is important, but just as important is getting the recovery and rest days right as well. One of the things I'd been warned about was people not adhering to their training programmes early on and then ending up having to overtrain the closer they got to race day.

Saturday, 17 January

100 DAYS TO GO

First official training run. Back to a heavenly just once around the lake but at a new, quicker pace. The pace I'll need to maintain for six times that distance if I'm to stand any chance of breaking five hours.

MARATHON LORE:

UNDER FIVE HOURS IS WHAT'S REFERRED TO AS A
'REAL MARATHON' – ANYTHING OVER FIVE HOURS
COULD BE DEEMED A QUICK WALK.

Out of breath virtually from start to finish. Recovery quicker than expected. Worry level, high.

Duration: 45 minutes with new 10-minute walk cool down.
Distance: 4.7 miles.

Sunday, 18 January

99 DAYS TO GO

Family day: once round lake, fits and starts of running while taking turns chasing kids with Tash.

Duration: irrelevant. Fun and fresh air had by all.

Distance: 4.5 miles.

Monday, 19 January

98 DAYS TO GO

The most beautiful day. A dazzling low winter sun, clear blue sky, 3 degrees. Days don't get more beautiful. Once round the lake, new pace. Legs tired but relatively comfortable. Quick recovery.

Distance: 4.5 miles.

Tuesday, 20 January

97 DAYS TO GO

Have to stay in town as going to meet the Duchess of Cornwall in connection with my '500 Words' – an annual writing competition for children of thirteen and under. Ended up going to Clarence House in my camper van. 'Are you intending on staying the night?' she asked as I pulled into her garden. 'You're more than welcome.'

Lovely lady.

We had several cups of tea and a plate of biscuits, during which she agreed to host this year's final over the road in St James's Palace. Wow, the kids will be thrilled, as will the BBC.

Anyway, back to the training the day before: Radio 2 to Hampstead Heath running and walk back. Wholly enjoyable even though Central London to Hampstead is basically uphill all the way.

Distance: 8 miles.

Wednesday, 21 January

96 DAYS TO GO

Excited for three reasons. Going to be working with the Duchess of Cornwall again, this time spending two hours at a primary school in Haringey, where she'll watch while this year's judges and I workshop some of the children on various methods of storytelling; then going home to see my new grandson, Teddy Rupert. He's come down 200 miles from up north with his mum and dad to see us. He's only twelve days old! Ahh bless!

And my midlife new motorbike is being delivered. A BMW 800.

Running: once round the lake, very relaxed. Super-relaxed.

Distance: 4.5 miles.

The Midlife Motorbike

The longer one experiences life, the more one comes to the conclusion that, barring war and famine and other reasons why one might end up destitute, helpless and hopeless, life is about coming up with reasons, tenuous or otherwise, to justify doing the things we want to do.

So here I am contemplating my fiftieth year, which already consists of signing a contract to bring back *TFI Friday* and committing to run the London Marathon, while figuring out my commitments in the summer: two four-day CarFests, one Dine & Disco weekend, the Monaco Grand Prix week and the London to Brighton Car Run (driving a vintage bus) all for Children in Need. How the heck am I going to squeeze all this in with a daily radio show, the weekly Friday edition of *The One Show*, an 89-year-old mum, energetic wife, three kids and now a grandson?

'Well, one thing's for sure,' I told myself. 'It doesn't help that I get stuck in traffic most mornings on the journey back and forth to Ascot.'

And then I think, 'Motorbike!' It's the obvious answer, isn't it?

I've owned several motorbikes in the past: low-powered machines as a teenager and then a Triumph Thruxton when I first met Tash. She had a full licence and a Triumph Bonneville to go with it. The fact that I ended up returning my Thruxton to the shop, unable to rev myself up enough to take the test is another matter.

Ever since then I'd been trying to convince myself I was anti-bike, more out of bitterness than sincerity. However, the fact remained: I'm a wannabe biker trapped inside a lily-livered non-biker's body.

But where to go and what to do?

I thought I'd buy the machine first, stare at it for a few weeks and then muster up the necessary to do whatever it took to gain my licence. Fully aware this exact method had failed before, I pressed on regardless. It was time for a boys' trip, but not before some in-depth online research. The Internet comes good again.

I have always had a soft spot for the Kawasaki Ninja, the dream machine Tom Cruise whisks Kelly McGillis off on in *Top Gun*. A nice bit of Eighties kit, rideable, more reliable than something really old and a very cool-looking thing all round.

Google Images: Mmm, yes please.

I've only ever dealt with two motorcycle shops in my life and even though almost ten years had passed, I remembered how well they both treated me. I think most bike shops are generally this way. I would be doing business with one of them again this time, that much I'd already decided.

'Hey, Chris, great to see you again,' said Mark from Haslemere Motorcycles, with the same irrepressible enthusiasm as when we last met a decade ago. 'Tempted to have another go, are we?'

'Yes, actually. I was thinking about a *Top Gun* Ninja.'

'Interesting!' he replied in the same high-pitch tone Phil the chiropractor had employed when I informed him of my secret plans to take on a marathon.

'They're good and exciting and iconic and all that, but they are more hobby bikes than daily commuters.' Which is garage speak for, 'You'll probably spend more time wondering why it won't start than wondering where to go once it has.' Of course, I should have known, it's exactly the same with old cars. Mine all work – just never all at once.

The upshot of my visit to Mark was the purchase of a glorious 1999, one owner (ex-Lightning pilot), 32,000 miles, Honda VFR800 touring sports bike. More born to be mild than born to be wild, as I later found out. But the point was she looked the part, which is often mostly what it's about for me. When it comes to anything with wheels, I'm much more an aesthetics man than a power-hungry speed freak.

'Don't get me wrong, she has some decent poke,' said Mark, 'but she's not the kind of bike that's going to throw up any surprises without warning. As always, it's still about the nut behind the handlebars. She's as friendly, obedient and reliable as these type of bikes come.'

The next day, Richard Hammond was due on the show to help us launch 500, having very kindly agreed to be our head judge again this year. His third year in a row. A big (little) biker himself, I whispered to him for his opinion.

'What do you think of a Nineties VFR800?'

'Ooh,' he cringed. Then he yawned.

Hang on a minute, here was Richard now doing the same face about the bike I had bought as Mark had done about the Kawasaki Ninja that he'd told me not to buy.

'Well how about an Eighties Kawasaki Ninja then?'

'Ah, now that's a bike.'

D'oh!

I chose not to take the conversation any further. I'd paid for the VFR anyway.

'What you might want to consider for everyday use, though, is a brand-new BMW F800. They're the nuts. A real mile muncher. I've got the 1200 version, state of the art, telephone, sat-nav – the lot.'

Mmm, so what I really needed then was the Honda for weekends, the BMW for schlepping back and forth to London and the Kawasaki Ninja to drool over through the kitchen window, which looks straight into my garage. Perfect – three reasons to buy three bikes.

I really needed to sort out that licence.

But then, no, surely this couldn't be true.

'Hi, it's me.' It was The Hitman, His real name Hiten. He's Indian and has been my assistant forever. 'Er, why do you keep saying you don't have a motorcycle licence on the radio?'

'Well, because I don't.'

'But you do, you've had one for years: Category A – which means you are qualified to ride any motorbike without restriction, any motorcycle on the planet. You are Mr Super Bike if you want to be. It's a test you must have taken years ago. Anyway I've checked with the DVLC and they've confirmed that is one hundred per cent definitely the case.'

Was that those angels I could hear again in my head?

I have forgotten many things in my life, like going to Japan to make a TV show, for example, but taking and passing my motor-cycle test? Surely even I would be able to remember that.

But Hitman was insistent.

'You're also qualified to tow a trailer, drive a bus with not more than a certain number of non-paying passengers, and loads of other things. Apparently, Hits said, it was all to do with when I passed my test. Back in the good old days, passing the one basic driving test meant you could drive most vehicles ever invented.

After this hugely welcome news, it quickly began to sink in that all I had to do was get a bike delivered, get it insured and, after a few sessions around the local roads, I could be on the way to London five minutes later.

Hence Hammond's recommendation of a (nearly new – 4,000 miles) BMW F800 GT rolling off the back of the local franchise dealer's truck forty-eight hours later.

A nice man by the name of Paul had sorted me out and I was good to go. Not that I went anywhere for a few days: it had been below zero for over a week. The heart was willing but my nuts were not. Me, two wheels and the M25 would have to wait. For now.

As news of my new two-wheeled purchase leaked out, the general response was, 'Please sell it immediately, you're going to kill yourself.'

Except for Tash, who said, 'I think it's a great idea.'

Hopefully for the right reasons.

Thursday, 22 January

95 DAYS TO GO

Started my run from home wearing my running watch for the first time. A game changer.

Distance, time and pace. It enabled me to make up runs, turning left or right, knowing how far I've gone and when to turn back for home. A revelation.

Duration: 2.5 hours.

Distance: 12.6 miles.

Friday, 23 January

94 DAYS TO GO

No run. Went for a walk instead. Followed by an hour of sauna sessions in between radio show and *One Show*. Legs felt great.

Distance: 5 miles.

Tuesday, 27 January

10-DAY DEBRIEF

Amazing what you can do with a wee bit of discipline. Really never thought I would be here in life. Regardless of what might happen come race day, I'm thoroughly enjoying the regimen of training for a marathon.

I've taken to using a mid-run checklist based on what I was taught learning to fly. It's called the FREDAT check and involves scans of the instruments to ensure nothing is obviously about to go wrong. Here's how I adapted it:

Flying:	*Running:*
F = Fuel	Legs
R = Radio	Breathing
E = Engine	Lungs
D = Direction	Direction
A = Altitude	Mental state
T = Transponder	Arms/upper body

These 'onboard' checks help me to assess what part of me needs a rest and when. Legs tired – give it more arms. Breathing too heavy – ease off. Mind wandering –relax, try to come back to the moment. No use my body being in the park if my head's still at work.

Also for the second time in my life after my encounter with Guy, the sleep Doctor, food has become an important commodity as opposed to an indulgence or treat. For the most part I'm now only eating what I know is good for me and what's going to help me on my next run. Lots of porridge in the mornings. No bread, no crisps, lots of chicken and tuna. Have also fallen back in love with milk. An ice-cold pint from a glass is the first thing I have when I get back in from a run.

I'm sleeping better, with hardly any nightmares recently. Sharper at work. All good. Very little bad. Body's still in bits, but you can't have everything.

Saturday, 7 February

79 DAYS TO GO

Noah's birthday weekend, even though it's not actually his birthday for another three days. He's asked to go to a soft play area with some of his mates. It's a mums thing. I've agreed to take them all for pizza later. I run down to the lake where I do 5 miles of gentle jogging interspersed with half-sprints every 500 yards or so. It's almost fun, but not quite. Then again, if anyone had told me two months ago that it would even come close to fun, I wouldn't have believed them.

Walk home from the lake.

Distance: 7 miles.

Sunday, 8 February

78 DAYS TO GO

Another rest day from running but I throw in my first gym day. Cross-training highly recommended. Twenty minutes of gentle bike, light weights – upper body, sit-ups. Important not to let the rest of your muscles get left behind. Hugely important to keep body shape in proportion.

Monday, 9 February

77 DAYS TO GO

First three-stage run. Lots of firsts, keeping it interesting. Jog down to lake, step up pace for a bit, and again a bit more. Walk back home.
   Duration: 90 minutes.
   Distance: 6 miles.

Tuesday, 10 February (Noah's sixth birthday)

76 DAYS TO GO

Read Mo Farah's training schedule. Do you know he does a marathon every Sunday come rain or shine, no matter where he is in the world, fifty-two weeks of the year? But that's not the big thing. Each week's marathon is part of a 135-mile-a-week regime and is followed every Monday by a recovery run of 10 miles in the morning and a *further* 6 miles in the afternoon.
   Inspired by this . . .

Wednesday, 11 February

75 DAYS TO GO

Tempo run (I've started using the fancy terms now, not that I am completely sure exactly what they mean) in the morning. Distance: 6.5 miles, which includes (via my fancy watch) not one, not two, but *three* new records (it does all this for you even if you don't ask).

Easy run.

Afternoon: another 3 miles.

Weird but hilarious. My legs are aching so much from the morning I find it really difficult to run for the first mile in the afternoon, but then everything starts to click back into place and come on song.

Are the constant miles paying off? Careful, Evans, you know what they say: 'Pride comes before a fall.' You of all people should know that.

Friday, 13 February

73 DAYS TO GO

Run to Primrose Hill in London from Radio 2 to look at a house. Always fantasized about becoming a Primrose Hill Billy. Lived everywhere around there but Primrose Hill itself. Camden, Belsize Park, Hampstead.

The house is gorgeous, way out of my price range, but I put in an offer regardless. As a very wise mate of mine always says, 'Just get in the deal'. The finer details (i.e. money) can be ironed out later.

During the run back through Regent's Park, very light jog, saw a woman with an absolutely beautiful action. Mid to late thirties, so graceful, balanced, symmetrical. Stunning. Can't stop looking at the way people run, all shapes and sizes, each with their own unique style.

Distance: 5 miles.

Saturday, 14 February

72 DAYS TO GO

Tash and I don't do Valentine's. Although we have booked a table for dinner at Tom Kerridge's pub, the Hand & Flowers in Marlow; it sports two Michelin stars and is one of the greatest food experiences on the planet. We are not, however, going to be one of the millions of Valentine's Day tables for two, we've booked to go with

Ben and Charlie, a couple we met via Noah's school, plus a guest star last-minute addition to our party, the weather lady Carol Kirkwood. Random, but hey, I work with her every day, she's such a positive force and no one who doesn't want to should be on their own on Valentine's. Those are the rules.

Also woke up this a.m. to the stark reality that tomorrow is ten weeks to go to the London Marathon. This has always been the most significant milestone for me. This is where the serious countdown begins. Everything I've done before has been trial and error and extemporization. From now on, everything will have to be super-structured and set in stone, or at least as much as it can be. I'll have a mini blow-out tonight and then I'll knock the booze on the head completely, except for a couple of birthday lunches I've committed to between now and race day.

Having said that, we're also booked to go to the South of France for two weeks at Easter. Mmm, not ideal. I suppose this means I will need to try to complete my big pre-race run of 22 miles at marathon pace before we embark. Oh dear, looking at the calendar, that's in just five weeks and six days from now. Gulp.

Chiropractor's first this morning and then a run from there, central Ascot to Noah's school to pick him up from Saturday-morning football.

Duration: 75 minutes.

Distance: 6 miles.

Monday, 16 February

70 DAYS TO GO

When I first attempted to run round the lake I made a deal with myself that I had to do the full distance before I allowed myself to get back in the car and drive home.

Today I've made a similar deal with myself, except instead of just over four miles, this time my target is 15 miles. Whatever happens I will not return home until I've completed 15 miles some way, somehow. Crawling is always an option.

And so off I shuffle, turning right out of my house, no phone, no nothing except the clothes I'm wearing and my running shoes.

My running watch is fantastic, the most important thing currently in my life after the roof over my family's heads. I love the fact it allows me to go out and make up a fifteen-mile spontaneous run.

After an hour on the road I've covered my standard 5 miles but can't even think about turning for home yet, as that would leave me 5 miles short. So I start throwing in extra loops or back doubles, a mile here, a mile there. My watch will sort it all out.

Just over 10 miles and I begin to struggle. My lungs are completely fine, I could stop and not even be out of breath, it's amazing how they adapt to a different frequency of breathing. Worth taking up running just to know what that feels like. But my legs are really not happy; once the mileage reaches double digits they begin to feel heavy.

To make it home, the last 3 miles include three or four walking breaks for a good minute or so. Still, not bad for a beginner. I've completed 15 miles plus an extra mile for the cool-down walk home afterwards. My watch flashed up two new records:

One: new quickest 10k.

Two: longest run yet.

Duration: 3 hours 1 minute 37 seconds.

Not quite sure of what any of that means right now.

Just glad it's over.

Tuesday, 17 February

69 DAYS TO GO

From what I learnt yesterday and with now less than ten weeks to go to the marathon, I begin to accept that a sub-five-hour time is probably not realistic. I decide that perhaps a more achievable but equally fulfilling goal might be to attempt to complete the marathon without stopping regardless of what time it is. I really was quite broken during the last 3 miles of yesterday's run, yet in the marathon I would still have another 11 miles to go.

Recovery run: 45 minutes.

Distance: 3.5 miles.

Wednesday, 18 February

68 DAYS TO GO

Big day. I have decided to buy some proper running gear. It's time to get used to what I'm going to be wearing on race day. I run from Radio 2 to Kensington High Street, which I thought was about 5 miles away. It's not, it's less than 3. NOWHERE IS AS FAR AWAY AS YOU THINK IT IS! There's a running shop there – in fact, there are more sports shops on Kensington High Street than any other high street in Britain. I haven't checked, I'm just guessing, as there are no fewer than six within two hundred yards of each other. There's also an inordinate number of banks and travel agents, for some reason.

I purchase some running leggings, some shorts, a top and a jacket. That's it, I have now voluntarily joined the MAMIL crowd. My name is Chris, I am a Middle Aged Man In Lycra. I promised myself this would never happen. D'oh!

But what a difference my new super-light outfit makes. Especially the leggings, they immediately lend more support to my legs and my knees are fairly singing with joy! I now also look (a bit) like a 'proper' runner. I bounce back to Radio 2 through Hyde Park and down Oxford Street. I am Tigger.

Duration: 1 hour 20 minutes.

Distance: 6 miles.

Thursday, 19 February

67 DAYS TO GO

Tash and the kids have come to see me in London. We hang out together all day and end up in a brilliant Chinese restaurant. It's called Feng Shang Princess and is an actual floating Chinese barge on the Regent's Park Canal just by the entrance to London Zoo. I highly recommend it.

It's also one of the first places I was taken by record companies when I was a young producer, during the days when they still had budgets for boozy lunches to schmooze young innocents into playing their artists' products on the radio. In fact it was this very restaurant where Kenny Everett found himself on the receiving end of one of the most original and memorable plugs of all time.

He was taken there by a couple of record company guys, one of whom excused himself to go to the toilet halfway through lunch when in fact what he was actually going to do was jump in the canal, swim up to the porthole by the table Kenny was sitting at and tap on the glass, brandishing the seven-inch single he wanted Kenny to play.

The next day Kenny went on the air, told the story and played the song.

Job done.

Today was special for us because it's the first time we'll have ever been out for dinner as a family. Sure, we've eaten out together before, hundreds of times – pizza, fish and chips, or a pub lunch – but this was our first time, just the four of us of going out purely for dinner.

The greatest meal of my life to date.

Distance: 0 miles. Who cares?

Friday, 20 February

66 DAYS TO GO

A friend has taken over the Kensington Crêperie. We decide we have to go and make it the bookend family lunch to the family first the night before. The thing is, I don't even like crêpes, or at least I thought I didn't. Turns out I not only like them, I love them.

This place is so busy, they are turning tables every five minutes. Even though it's freezing cold outside, there is an ever-present and enthusiastic queue. Jeez, why aren't crêperies as big as Domino's?

The menu is amazing, sweet and savoury, simple, tasty and of the highest quality. And the sheer energy in the room is electric: kids, parents, grandparents, young couples, people on their own grabbing a quick bite, everyone smiling, laughing, chatting away furiously. Magnificent.

I have a little bit of everyone else's savoury main as well as my own, plus a rum and raisin (with real rum – woohoo) and homemade ice cream as a dessert. Why? Because I can. Because I am going to run back to work, by which time whatever calories I have taken in will have been burnt up in the fuel tank again.

I LOVE RUNNING.

Duration: 1 hour 10 minutes.

Distance: 6 miles.

New record: fastest mile – 8 minutes 46 seconds. The crêpe diet may well be the way forward.

Saturday, 21 February

65 DAYS TO GO

Another muscle and joint-saving mercy mission to St Phil the chiropractor at 8.15. Phil is working wonders. Without him, there's no way I could be putting my forty-nine year-old bag o' bones through anything close to what I'm getting away with. Every weekend he straightens me out to fight another day.

Today, as well as the usual glorious neck, back and hip adjustments, he's working on my leg length and the arches of my feet. 'We all have confused feet as nature gave us arches to cope with rough terrain but then we all started wearing shoes instead and messed up her design. Now when we do walk barefoot, most of the floor our feet come into contact with is flat, which causes our arches to move the keystone of the bridge of each foot so it's out of line from where it was when we were born. This in turn can throw our ankles, knees and hips out of kilter and ultimately the whole of our skeleton. Another case of us being our own worst enemy. Shoes are like porn: good up to a point but detrimental thereafter.'

• • •

The thing about running is how little gear one needs to do it. That's what I love about it, as well as the honesty. Which I suppose is part of the same thing. You can run almost anywhere, anytime, it's a fantastic way of seeing and appreciating wherever you are. And the most important thing for me is running comes from within, a direct reflection of who we are. It brings out our natural rhythm, what's on our mind, how much fuel we've got in our tank, how tense or relaxed we are, the you of you.

I've noticed more and more, when I get home from a decent run, say an hour or more, all I want is a glass of water or a glass of milk, which tastes better than any glass of champagne or wine I've ever had.

The only feeling I can compare it to is when I'm with my children, watching them laugh uncontrollably or seeing their furrowed brows when they are giving something 110 per cent of their concentration. It's that golden moment when nothing else matters, when for a fleeting few seconds life feels the absolute best it possibly can. When we come closest to realizing why it is we're here.

I am almost certain that from now on, for as long as I can, I will run. I love it. Oh absolutely bloody love it. God knows why I started running that December afternoon back in 2014, but rest assured I will be running most December afternoons from now until my legs and the rest of my body have had enough of me.

Monday, 23 February

63 DAYS TO GO

The target is 18 miles. And it has to be running all the way with any cool-down taking place afterwards. Taking my GPS watch and making the route up as I go along. After setting off at the lake – good karma: where it all began – I follow my nose cross-country towards Windsor. I have a vague idea of the general direction I need to be going, buoyed by the fact that after four and a bit miles I come to the giant statue of a horse at one end of the Long Walk.

Stretched out in front of me, there it is, leading all the way downhill before it levels out and leads right up to the gates of Windsor Castle: a truly beautiful sight, a wonder to behold.

I run all the way up to the gates, touch the wall, turn around and come back again. It soon becomes obvious why it's called the Long Walk – it's 1.7 miles from castle to statue. I begin to calculate how far I will still have left to run once I've doubled back to the copper horse. The answer is 9 miles. Half of my required mileage.

As I run, I'm constantly checking the legs versus the lungs, versus the head, versus the arms. I make it to the half-marathon point of 13.1 miles for the first time ever without stopping. As my watch buzzes the news of my fifteenth completed mile, I'm still going. This is also now the longest run of my life. Suddenly the prospect of only 3 miles left feels like a walk in the park compared to what I've already achieved. Two months ago, anything over 3 miles would have had to include a walk in the park.

But not so fast, sonny. Here we go again: things begin to seize up. All the trouble is below the waist, as usual, with my breathing still as calm as if I were inback home watching *Chariots of Fire* with a cup of hot chocolate on the go. I head back towards where my car is parked, just in case. No point in overdoing it. Never any point in overdoing it.

Seeing the car relaxes me. I'm a mile short of my target so I run round the car park praying for my eighteenth mile to buzz up on my wrist.

Eventually it does.

I grind to a halt.

I fall into the car.

It's all I can do to lean out of the window and put my ticket in the slot. I'm home within three minutes, but Jesus Christ, my legs. It's like someone has swapped them for lead. I have to keep them moving: ten minutes of a good session of post-run stretching can offset days of needless aching.

I decide to jog back out of our gate to the local shop. By the time I get there, it feels as though my legs might actually have taken root.

I buy four bottles of Lucozade Sport – the ads claim the electrolyte aids recovery. That'll do for me, I can always sue later.

Duration: 3 hours 30 minutes.

Distance: 18 miles.

YES!

Tuesday, 24 February

62 DAYS TO GO

Not running ever again! Joking. Actually feel quite OK. I mean, everything's a little tender, and there's evidence of virginal nipple rub and two quite serious blood blisters on my toes, but I thought I'd feel a lot more broken than I do.

Rest.

Yes please.

Wednesday, 25 February

61 DAYS TO GO

Was going to run today, just a short recovery run – helps flush the system, or so I've been reading. Actually went out but stopped after a few yards. Legs are much more tired than I realized. I am much more tired than I realized. I'm not hurting but I'm empty.

Thursday, 26 February

60 DAYS TO GO

Feel similar to yesterday. Lots of articles advise against pushing after a big run but I'm going to see how it feels.

I stay out for almost exactly an hour. Not great but not terrible either. I'm very careful to listen to my body the whole time just in case.

Duration: 5 miles.

Friday, 27 February

59 DAYS TO GO

First run between the production meeting for *The One Show* and the show itself. How times have changed! When I did *TFI Friday* we'd be in the pub all day, kicking our heels over six or seven pints of Guinness with a whisky chaser after every one. Now here I am, throwing in a quick hill-run to North London before the dress rehearsal.

Duration: 1 hour.

Distance: 4.5 miles.

Saturday, 28 February

58 DAYS TO GO

As I run to the curry house where we left the car last night, I reach the conclusion that curry is not a meal I'll be having the night before the marathon. When curry wants out of your colon, it doesn't mess around, nor does it give you much warning. I get caught properly short.

But it's 9 a.m. I'm in well-to-do Sunningdale for crying out loud. I look for a bush or a back alley, an involuntary exodus is only seconds away and I'm definitely going to shit my pants. I can see our car in the lay-by on the other side of the level crossing opposite Waitrose, but there is zero chance I'm going to make it.

I am walking extremely uncomfortably and awkwardly in an attempt to assuage my quickening contractions and deny gravity, but it's too late; exponentially the situation has intensified from a code red to a full-on code brown. Movement is taking place, I am my three-year-old, late for the potty. Thank Christ I'm wearing my running leggings, otherwise this would be even more of a disaster. I was about to find out their threshold with regards to containing human excrement.

I gingerly squelch into my car seat. The stench is overwhelming, I feel like I might pass out. What else can I do, though? I just pray

178

when I arrive home my wife and kids will have already left for Saturday-morning football club.

They have, thank God. I begin the clean-up operation: it's horrendous and gets a lot worse before it gets better. No more running after a curry. In fact no more curries at all until after 26 April.

Duration: what seemed like forever.

Distance: 3 miles running, including the last 200 yards of strained grimacing, 3 miles back home trying not to pass out at the wheel.

Sunday, 1 March

57 DAYS TO GO

No run.

Monday, 2 March

56 DAYS TO GO

I've been contemplating how far to run today. I know I can do 18 miles without stopping and technically I'm a week or two ahead of that distance. Seriously considering giving myself an easier week all round. Lots of experts recommend this. It seems to make sense, so I decide to run 10 miles as quickly as I can.

Except then I remember reading a few articles that point out a shorter, quicker run can be harder to recover from than a much longer, slower one. I check myself with this fact and decide instead to run a fast-tempo 10 miles but quite a way off my limit. Suddenly, I'm looking forward to it much more. The decision feels right . . .

• • •

TWENTY (!) MILES LATER

. . . Hang on, that didn't pan out as I intended. After a couple of miles I found myself running past the house in Camden where Amy Winehouse died. It's in the same square where my wonder-

179

ful ex-wife Billie Piper now lives, which in turn is only a few hundred yards away from the flat where I first lived in London after I hopped off the train at Euston way back in 1989. A day I'll never forget, armed with little more than an old army bag stuffed with several pairs of jeans, a few T-shirts and a heart full of hope.

Invigorated by thoughts of the past, I looked up: the sun was shining, I had the rest of the day untouched and suddenly I changed my mind. Fuck it, I thought, let's go for the 20-miler, taking in the houses I've lived in since arriving in London.

I've always been a North Londoner. You either are or you're not. I've lived in North London longer than anywhere else since I was born, something else I only realized during this run. Now I had committed to 20 miles, I would be out for at least four hours so I would need all the thought material I could muster. That's one of the challenges of a long run: what do you do with the head time available? I would run a sightseeing tour of my own past. After Camden I would need to turn left and head down into Kentish Town, before veering right and directly north again to Parliament Hill and Highgate.

One mile for every year I'd been down here. That worked.

Within ten minutes I was coming up to The Forum, formerly the Town & Country Club, the first place I ever saw Texas, David Bowie and a shedload of other solid-gold performers. Then I glimpsed the car park round the back and was reminded of the time a confused but enthusiastic Robbie Williams beckoned me into his Range Rover to play me a CASSETTE of a new song he'd just finished, one he was sincerely hoping would consolidate his post-Take That solo career. The tune was dominated by a sample of the haunting strings loop from *You Only Live Twice* and went on to be a worldwide smash ('Millennium' – you may be aware of it).

Next on my tour: five minutes up the road, a gorgeous old terraced house I rented for a while shortly after landing my life-changing job on *The Big Breakfast*. This was most memorable as the house in which I was 'hit' by Noel Edmonds live in front of fifteen million viewers on BBC1 back in 1993. I was sitting picking my nose on the sofa, watching my favourite show when Noel clicked his fingers and boom, there I was, live in my own living room after his technicians had spent the whole day wiring up secret cameras all over the place.

After passing there I filtered left into Hampstead Heath, following a route that would take me all around the perimeter of its vast expanse. I love Hampstead Heath, and I've made many big decisions in my life while ambling along its paths. There was a period when I walked there every day without fail to sit atop its highest point on a bench from which you can not only see the whole of London's dramatic skyline but right across into Kent, the Surrey Hills, Berkshire and Buckinghamshire.

That said, I'd never taken in the extent of it before. My goodness it's huge, and much hillier than I realized. Half an hour later I was breathless running up a steep incline past Kenwood House, a former stately home that sits on the northern edge of the Heath. I needed a break soon and I got one: the next mile, heading south, was downhill all the way. It took me past the studio flat which was the first London property I bought. It cost £105,000 back in the early Nineties and was no more than a large room with a galley kitchen, a bath in the corner and a ladder up to a galleried bedroom. Crazy times, crazy prices. Nothing has changed. When I put it on the market, Tori Amos, the Cornflake Girl, came round to have a look. Like me she fell in love at first sight, but in the end had to pass as she couldn't figure out how to get her grand piano up over the roof and in through the French windows.

A few hundred yards on, a right and a left and I was outside what's now a trendy bar but was once the Haverstock Arms, the pub I used to go to every single day for ten years. The pub where I met hundreds of 'friends' – and probably spent close to a million pounds. With friends like that . . .

One of the old signed *TFI Friday* desks (there were three!) was hung there on the wall. It was also the place where I first hatched the idea of *Don't Forget Your Toothbrush*, my hit game-show for Channel 4 and the venue for the wake of my old friend, the actor

Ronnie Fraser. The man who taught me to drink, laugh and not take showbusiness at all seriously. He should have known, he was first in his class at RADA in the fifties and was best friends with Peter O'Toole and Sean Connery, both of whom were pallbearers at his funeral. I can vouch for this, as I was the one in the middle with James Bond behind and Lawrence of Arabia in front.

Stellar times.

Up Haverstock Hill next and past several more flats I'd lived in at one time or another. It was beginning to sink in just how peripatetic my twenties and thirties had been. The first mews house I rented was next, a tiny place but with a huge sliding window on the first floor that opened up the bijou living room to the whole world. A few hundred yards on and the mighty Steele's Road, named after Sir Richard Steele, the eighteenth-century writer-politician who co-founded the *Spectator* magazine.

This is the road famed throughout the Nineties and early noughties as the real Stella Street, home to Bob Hoskins, Jude Law and Sadie Frost, Noel Gallagher, David Walliams – and lots of other household names who still live there. My house was the one closest to the pub at the end of the street on the left and most memorable to me as the first house I sold, thinking I'd done really well by making a ten per cent profit.

Not bad short term but a disaster long term as three years later its value had doubled. You know that phrase: 'first profit; best profit – first loss; best loss'? Well I think that's for the most part, absolute rot.

After yet more reminiscing and memories, all of them fond – what's the point in remembering the not-so-good times? – I found myself jogging through Primrose Hill, which has to be the prettiest village in North London, somewhere I've always hung out in but never actually lived.

'God I love it here,' I said to myself. There's the hill itself, the first-ever UK park gifted to the public, the church, the canal, the curved parade of rainbow-coloured shop fronts, cafés, restaurants and a cast of locals all playing their own bespoke role in The Primrose

Hill Show. And then there's the paparazzi trolling up and down in their various mini-vans with blacked-out windows, hoping for a fifty-quid snap of Robert Plant nipping out for a loaf, Liam embarking on an afternoon drinking session, or Andrew Marr having an impromptu get-together with apparatchiks in the local French bistro. But it's the houses with their infinite views across the city that are the real stars of the show. All of them, without exception.

'Why did I never buy a place here when I had the chance?' I mused. 'Mmm,' I thought, 'I wonder if my offer's been accepted yet?'

Ten minutes later and I was idiotically trying to weave in and out of the pavement traffic of rush hour on Baker Street.

There I was, moving twice as fast as everyone else amongst a human throng that was ten times more stressed than me, too busy looking down at their smartphones to watch where they're going or see what might be about to run them over. I hit my first pedestrian-crossing red light – which gave me time to check my GPS watch to see how far I'd run and how long I'd been out.

'Shit, fuck, no! You cannot be serious. There's no way I've only done ten miles!' But it was true. I'd taken in a massive loop of Camden, Kentish Town, Belsize Park, St John's Wood and THE WHOLE OF HAMPSTEAD BLOODY HEATH and still I'd only covered 10 miles and been out for just under two hours. 'Now, how the heck, where the heck, am I going to get my other 10 miles from?' I was running out of London.

Immediately I headed to Hyde Park. Thank goodness for the Royals. I would run the outer boundary and then past another house I used to own in Belgravia, which made my Steele's Road property wheeling and dealing look like financial genius. I bought this one for £1.5 million, thought I'd rung the bell when I sold for £1.6 million five years later. Last year the same house sold for £32 MILLION! That which does not destroy you only makes you stronger.

Deep breath and move on, literally, down into St James's Park, Green Park. 'That should do it,' I told myself.

Wrong!

As I approached Big Ben with the band of the Household Cavalry going through marching drills in the courtyard on the right-hand side, I was still 4 miles short of my 20-mile target. I couldn't believe it. I thought back to my first ever shuffle/run in December 2014 when I couldn't make it around the lake at Virginia Water. Now here I was, getting frustrated that I still had that much left to go, not because I didn't think I could keep going but because I couldn't work out which route to take.

Almost without realizing it, I made my way across Westminster Bridge and a few minutes later I was heaving myself past County Hall to join the Jubilee Walk. Here on the South Bank there were tens of thousands of people to negotiate. Not to mention hundreds of lunchtime runners, every single one of whom, regardless of size, build, age, shape or ability was overtaking me as my legs began to grind to a halt. Shit, they were hurting. I only had two miles to go exponentially but I could barely move another two steps. These were the most extreme physical sensations I had ever experienced.

In the end I just about made it back to Broadcasting House, whereupon I asked myself:

'If I absolutely had to, if my life depended on it, could I have somehow run another 6.2 miles, making up the full marathon distance?'

To which the answer was an emphatic no.

Friday, 6 March

52 DAYS TO GO

First group run with the radio team – somehow we'd all signed up to do the Windsor Half-marathon on 27 September. Plenty of time to prep and the perfect smokescreen for more secret training. Turnout: 3 people.

Distance: 5 miles, with a coffee and croissant stop half way. Very civilized.

The offer on the house I can't afford has been accepted. Even more civilized.

Sunday, 8 March

50 DAYS TO GO

STILL HAVEN'T TOLD TASH.

Now more like a lie than a secret. Because of my chaotic work life she is used to me being in and out of the house sporadically. She's aware I'm still running and very pleased that I'm getting fit and finally looking after myself. But she has absolutely no idea a marathon is in the offing. She's the athlete in the family, not me. In fact Tash would more likely expect my mum to run a marathon than she would me.

The longer my secret goes on, the more frightened I am of eventually telling her. Like taking too long to say you're sorry for something.

Tuesday, 10 March

48 DAYS TO GO

My right foot has been hurting like I don't know what. My chiropractor says it may be *plantar fasciitis*, but should be OK to run on as not too bad. I'm massaging it by rolling it on a golf ball whenever I get the chance. Sounds mad but it works.

I try a gentle few miles; foot feels OK, so I decide to make this a long run of exact half-marathon distance. I also practise nutrition and hydration for the first time at 7 miles. Seems to help more than I realized it would.

Duration: 2 hours 10 minutes.

Distance: 13.1 miles.

Thursday, 12 March

46 DAYS TO GO

Tuesday's run nearly killed me. Could not have run another yard. So, a nice time but I need to know I can run 26.2 miles and not 13.1. That's the goal, that's the aim. It's so easy to get distracted when you've been doing this for a while. As shorter distances get easier, the temptation to become full of oneself is ever present. Must remain humble. Must presume the worst. What is it the SAS say: Train hard, fight easy? Yes. And keep it to yourself while you're at it.

Today it's a lovely day and I just want to amble in the sunshine and figure out the rest of my life. So I opt for a quite useless pootle around the lake where it all began, with a few half-hearted interval sprints. Soon my right foot is playing up again. One way or another I get around the 4.5 miles in about fifty minutes, which would have been a dream when I first started a couple of months ago. Such thoughts, however, are counter-productive at this stage.

The highlight of my circuit was seeing the England rugby coach, Stuart Lancaster, deep in thought doing his own walking lap. I've seen him here a few times now. England's RU training camp is down the road. Always looking straight ahead, always focused but always wearing a bright white England rugby jersey.

Duration: 50 minutes.

Distance: 4.5 miles.

Friday, 13 March

45 DAYS TO GO

Comic Relief Day. Red Nose Day for most, another red-face day for me. Our second Windsor Half team training run. A much better turn-out this week: double from last week, six of us show up.

We run to Primrose Hill and around Regent's Park. Coffee stop in the village, jog back: 5 miles, lovely job. Everyone did really well, considering. I sneak out for another 3 miles to try out my new target marathon time of 11-minute mile pace. It's OK but my legs begin to hurt. If you have the luxury, listen to your body. With six weeks to go, I do – just about. I turn for home. Night off *The One Show* so it's back to Ascot early for what is effectively a long weekend. I arrive home at 2 p.m., have a bath. Lie on my bed and check out all the best training plans. How are they looking with six weeks to go?

More to the point, how is what I'm doing looking with six weeks to go?

It's looking OK but I sense more and more my training is becoming a balancing act of what my mind wants to do, conflicted with what my body is able to do.

Sunday, 29 March

28 DAYS TO GO

We're in France on a two-week family Easter break. The vacation party consists of all three of my kids, Noah, Eli and Jade, my grandson Teddy, Jade's husband Callum, Jade's mum Alison, her husband Anthony and my wife Natasha. Of course, this is not ideal from a preparation point of view, but I'm only trying to run the London Marathon, not scale the Empire State Building in my bare feet. On the plus side, there's going to be plenty of time to nip out for short runs and for the three long runs I need to tick off – a 10-miler, a 15-miler and a 20; the various coast roads available will be nice and friendly and flat, as well as interesting and new. I'm both nervous and excited, the perfect combination.

Our first overnight is in St Tropez. I decide to get up early on the Sunday morning and get my 10 miles in the bag straight away. I run to the next village. It's 9 miles there and back, so I run once around St Tropez on my return which just about gets me to my target. Good. Excellent, in fact. Hardly any discomfort apart from the now usual twinge of fragility in my left knee.

Tuesday, 31 March

26 DAYS TO GO

'Are you excited that it's your birthday tomorrow, Dad?' asks Noah.

We're having one of our pile-on-cuddle chats. I'm lying down and he jumps on top of me – actually, dives on top of me and stays there, stuck like a limpet, usually with his cheek somewhere around my ear so he can whisper confidential father–son messages in my shell-like. He would happily stay there all day carrying out covert negotiations. I would happily let him. Moments of gold. Heaven on Earth.

'Of course I'm excited, it's my birthday,' I reply.

And it's true. How could I not be? I'll be spending the day surrounded by my three children, my grandson, my daughter's mum and her husband and my own wonderwoman, my wife Natasha.

Later, over dinner, I go into a quiet paranoid cold sweat as the thought hits me: 'Oh my goodness, what if everyone around the table thinks this was planned as a "Happy birthday – how great am I! Come stay on my big boat in France so I can show you!" week? Aaaarrrrggghhh.'

We only booked this week 'cos it's the first week of the kids' Easter holidays. The fact that my birthday falls on the fifth day of our vacation is pure coincidence. Due to Easter being its usual movable feast from one year to the next.

Healthy paranoia? No such thing.

It turns out to be quite a weird night. After we watch *The Game*, starring Michael Douglas – somewhat far-fetched, but entertaining nevertheless.

As a child, Douglas's character witnessed his father commit suicide on his forty-eighth birthday. To help him come to terms with this as he celebrates his own forty-eighth birthday, his younger brother, played by Sean Penn, commissions a special event company to stage a bizarre game which ends with Douglas – SPOILER ALERT – unknowingly replicating his late dad's death plunge. This involves him jumping off a building and crashing through the glass roof of a banqueting hall into his own party.

Incredulous and still alive, it ends with him chinking glasses with his little bro at the bar as Sean picks up the tab for the whole shenanigans.

Told you it was a little far-fetched.

But Michael Douglas playing a forty-eight-year-old? You know how you first start to realize you are getting on when policemen look like teenagers in fancy dress and the Prime Minister is younger than you? Well, watching Michael Douglas celebrate his forty-eighth birthday on the eve of my forty-ninth took that feeling to a whole new dimension.

After Tash and I turn in, I lie in bed in our cabin having a quiet moment wondering what I think now there's under half an hour to go before the onset of my fiftieth year on the planet.

Age doesn't matter, it really doesn't. I truly believe we are as old, or hopefully as young, as we feel, but it is a fantastic yardstick to help us judge how we're doing. That's its most useful purpose. I suppose that's why I have become obsessed with countdowns, simply because they are a way of compartmentalizing our minutes, hours and days into units of gold that need to be spent wisely.

This holiday has been part of a huge countdown. From the first day I started back at work this year, I made a mental note: 'Sixty radio shows to go till our family holiday on the boat.' Sixty shows back to back is by far the longest run I've ever done. And even though I love my job, the first thought every morning as I stumbled into the shower was, 'Another day to cross off on the countdown to France.'

Wednesday, 1 April – 49th birthday

25 DAYS TO GO

'The night is darkest before the dawn,' declared Christian Bale's Batman, by far the best Batman of all time. And so came April the first, the date this demi-centenarian began his march into the second half of the only century he was ever going to get to play at being a human being.

I'm about to get up to dutifully record my thoughts on this very subject when I'm grabbed by the wrist. My wife is extraordinarily strong for her size, with a vice-like grip which can be both reassuring and menacing in equal measure.

'You can't get up, the kids are doing something special for you,' she whispers through threatening gritted teeth. I get the point immediately. Moments later, as if on cue, in come the boys wearing matching striped pyjamas and brandishing four presents, a card and a balloon.

More gold.

More 'I love my life.'

The four presents include a new edition of Plato's *Symposium*, to replace the one I lost last year, and a first edition of *The Complete Book of Running* by James F. Fixx. This is a legendary book about running written way before the culture of weekend supplement fads. Jim Fixx, although he unfortunately met his demise while out running one day, is renowned and credited with observing and then stating many things about running that had never been put into words before. I couldn't wait to read it – the perfect holiday read with less than a month to go to my secret marathon. It's almost as if my wife knows what I'm up to.

Mmm.

'Perhaps all wives do, all the time, whether they choose to admit it or not,' I wonder.

All day I receive a steady stream of best wishes and many happy returns via, text, email and Twitter, but something else that has been catching my eye lately are the tweets suggesting I try the pose method of running to help avoid the various aches and pains I've been bleating on about.

After lunchtime I find myself with a quiet hour or two of unexpected me-time while the rest of the gang wander off into town on various missions involving papers, ice cream and sun-block. Contemplating how to spend this priceless window of opportunity, I plump for researching the pose running method and decide to save my Fixx book for my second week away – a decision that will turn out to be a huge mistake as I will not read this excerpt until it's too late: 'Never change your routine at the last minute before embarking upon something you know for sure your old routine will get you through.'

The Pose Method

Within seconds of opening my Internet browser I was presented with countless articles and videos on pose running. There I was gripped by what I was seeing on the screen of my Samsung tablet. If these testimonies were true, this could revolutionize my marathon experience.

Basically the pose method makes use of gravity to aid the muscles when running. It's described as a controlled falling, based on picking up your feet underneath you as opposed to stretching out your legs in front of you. Effectively this means that your body leads while your stride takes place behind, merely to stop you hitting the ground. It claims minimum effort, stress and strain on all the joints and muscles that normally come under fire when subjected to excessive mile-munching.

I couldn't wait to try it out to see if it lived up to the hype, which also included a significant increase in speed, even for a beginner.

Having only used approximately half of my designated me-time, I figured I could sneak in a quick 5 miles playing with my new wonder method. Within minutes I had got the gist and was experiencing the sensation of some invisible force pushing me along with their palm gently resting in the small of my back. Hinging at the knee, drawing my foot up underneath via my hamstring really did feel a lot easier than reaching out one foot in front of the other.

Another key to successful pose running is to have a strong back, with a very slight forward incline, looking straight ahead all the time. It feels weird at first but quickly becomes comfortable, at which point one really does start to experience this mystical sensation of grace and lightness its exponents talk about.

I let myself settle for a while before having a look at my watch to see what pace I was at. Bearing in mind my usual target pace for a mile is 11:00, can you imagine my surprise when I looked down to see the figures – 9:40!!! What? I couldn't believe it. Now and again these satellite running watches do experience the odd malfunction, so I left it for half a mile before checking the display again. This time my pace had dropped to 9:30. OH – MY – GOD, this was incredible!

And the sudden increase in pace wasn't the only benefit. When I arrived back at the boat 4.7 miles later, I had barely broken sweat. For the rest of the day I felt like I'd won the lottery but wasn't allowed to tell anyone until my ticket had been officially checked.

I couldn't wait to run again the next day.

Meanwhile Jim's legendary book remained on my bedside table untouched. Oh, how I wish I'd opted to read his received wisdom instead of clamouring for some 21st-century woo-woo wonder method.

Thursday, 2 April

24 DAYS TO GO

Tash comes running with me, same route as yesterday: turn right off the back of the boat down to the sea wall back through the famous tunnel – the opposite way to that which the cars go in the Grand Prix. Then up past Jimmy's Bar, heading towards Italy, before turning left at Monte Carlo beach to run back towards Casino Square, down with the port on our left-hand side, and back to the boat.

Again, 4.7 miles, again, super-quick (for me, that is) and again, almost completely effortless. And we'd even stuck a sprint finish in along the swimming pool section!

But oh dear. The morning after the two pose runs the couple of days before, my right Achilles feels like it has a dagger sticking out of it. Whatever the pose method is good for, I must have been doing something wrong and this is the result. I struggle to make it up the four stairs to breakfast and don't go anywhere near my running shoes for the rest of the day.

Friday, 3 April

22 DAYS TO GO

Everything I have been told about the marathon is coming true. Especially the injury bit. The razor-like right Achilles issue is just the latest in my continuing journey on the discovery of running pain. But a very wise lady I once met told me, 'We humans have an uncanny knack of finding exactly what we need, exactly when we most need it, if we have our eyes and ears open to see it and hear it, that is.'

These are words I often think about when I'm stuck in a corner from which I can't see any obvious or immediate way out. And with her wise counsel still resonating in my ears, sure enough help appears on the horizon in the form of one of my few true and trusted friends in the world: Jen.

She and her husband, Big Kev, have arrived to join us for a few days of our holiday, swapping with my daughter and her gang, who flew back to the UK on Good Friday.

Now, the rather fortuitous thing about Jen is that not only is she a qualified personal instructor but also a veteran of several marathons and half-marathons. After a brief doctor/patient consultation Jen sets to work, going crazy with her thumbs up and down my shin bones for about ten minutes. It's uncomfortable, to say the least, but nothing compared to the second session she was about to dish out.

'Your calves are like rocks even when you're just standing up – that's not normal,' she announces. 'I'm going to have to resort to the ice-cold Coke-can makeshift roller method. Please resist the urge to punch me, regardless of how much you might want to in the next fifteen minutes.'

There follows an intense period of deep-tissue massage the likes of which I had no idea existed, during which I scream like a banshee from beginning to end. It's a strange pain, the strangest I've ever experienced. Even though I find it generally unbearable, I don't want her to stop because I know it's doing me good.

Saturday, 4 April

22 DAYS TO GO

Whatever Jen did, it's enough for me to at least attempt my 15-mile penultimate pre-marathon long run on schedule. With three weeks to go, I should be doing 18 miles this weekend and 20 next, but that's just not going to happen. So I'm going for 15 today and then a final 20 in seven days' time. And then nothing whatsoever until race day itself. It's a high-risk strategy, and one you won't find in any marathon training plan anywhere in the world, but I just don't think my body can cope any other way.

My alarm wakes me at 6.30 a.m. French time. I rub Votarol cream into any parts of my legs that are prone to pain (basically all of them). I then take two Ibuprofen. I make a double espresso, down half a litre of water and go for an insurance comfort break just in case. I check my socks and shoes for sand, stones and grit, and I'm on the road at almost exactly 7 a.m.

There are twinges of potential muscle and joint breakdown in several places below my waist. Real or imaginary, I simply don't know any more. After 2 or 3 miles my suspect right Achilles starts to tighten so I begin to roll it out while I'm running. This feels as though it will get me through what I need to do. My pace is the slowest it's ever been, hovering around the twelve-minute mile mark. I could probably walk faster but I don't care as long as I can bank the 15 miles one way or another.

My Achilles remains on the edge the whole time, my left leg the hero of the piece doing everything within its power to drag the right leg through. After 9 miles this over-compensation begins to take its toll and my left knee collapses in a howl of protest. I have to pull up immediately. I get my elbow in there straight away, the Paula Radcliffe method. It's a useful little slice of masochistic emergency therapy she shared with me when we met at the radio show a few weeks ago.

It's 8.55 a.m. and I'm leaning against the sea wall somewhere between Cannes and Antibes, digging my own elbow as hard as I can into the skin directly above my left kneecap as far as it will go and as much as I can bear. Twenty seconds later and I'm back pacing, placing one foot in front of the other as gingerly as I possibly can. Still rolling my right foot from in to out with every ground strike while simultaneously running with my left knee pointing outwards and my left foot side striking the tarmac. I am a running mess. I believe this is referred to as crisis running. I have to get to 15 miles this weekend otherwise what is already becoming an ever slimmer chance of completing the marathon will begin to vanish irretrievably.

I return to the port, where I stowed a bottle of water and Ibuprofen on the way out. After 11 miles, I stop and down the water plus two pills. But the moment I come to a halt, anything that's vulnerable begins to either seize up or sear with pain – in some cases both. Sharp pain, dull pain – you name it, my legs have become survival specialists. A month ago, had I felt even close to this I would have stopped and hobbled for home, but this is a must-finish situation. I have to get going again as quickly as possible. The only risk now would be not to take the risk. The calendar is against me.

By this time the rest of Cannes is awake, the bright young things of the new generation out jogging, interval training and stretching on the beach. They look like works of art peeled from the glossy pages of *Vogue, Cosmo* or *Men's Health*. I know I look pitiful by comparison but I have just run a very quiet, very private, very painful, very slow half-marathon and I still have 2 miles to go to reach my 15-mile target. So, with the greatest of respect, fuck them. I need to get this done.

I make it back to the boat with 0.2 of a mile still to go. I run past our berth on down the pontoon until my watch buzzes fifteen zero zero. Finally.

Again, I contemplate what I always do after a long run: whether if I absolutely had to, could I carry on and somehow and run an additional 10 miles. The answer is an emphatic no. Besides, it would have to be 11 additional miles. That's how tired I am: I can't even subtract 15 from 26. I know that millions of people run marathons all over the world, all of the time, but I'm trying to run mine and frankly it's proving a lot more difficult than I ever thought it would be.

Duration: 2 hours 58 minutes.

Distance: 15 miles.

Saturday, 18 April

8 DAYS TO GO

Many Clouds won Saturday's Grand National back in England but looked as though he might keel over at any moment after he crossed the finishing line.

'He's OK, he's OK,' murmured a stable of obviously nervy television commentators, somewhat unconvincingly.

'Er, no he's not,' shouted back millions of us watching the poor beast live on telly all over the world. He looked dead on his feet, poor thing. Talk about wobbly, this poor chap looked like his muscles had been replaced by whatever that stuff is they put in a lava lamp.

But that's not the bit of the post-race drama that most piqued my interest. I was most focused on what Oliver Sherwood, the trainer of Many Clouds, said in his post-win interview: 'The horse didn't do anything after the Gold Cup, barely anything.'

Well, eureka, that was it. There was the answer to my marathon dilemma right there.

That's what I would do. I would become the human equivalent of Many Clouds. For the next fourteen days and nights I would do hardly any exercise whatsoever, other than to keep myself flexible and 'tickle' my muscles awake every now and again, something else Paula advised me to do a couple of weeks back. Weight gain might be an issue, especially without the incentive of having to run the next day, but that's a bridge I will cross when the bathroom scales call for it.

Sunday, 19 April

1 WEEK TO GO

Haven't been this nervous about anything since I was a kid. Here I am, still with seven days to go, it's 6 a.m. and I am downstairs on my own, like a child on Christmas Day wondering whether or not he should open his presents before the rest of the family awake from their slumber. I am just so out of my comfort zone.

A week of total rest, the first since I began my shuffling/running adventure at the end of last year. Not one hour has passed by in the last one hundred and sixty-eight that I haven't thought about my knee or my Achilles or my ever-troublesome hamstrings. And there's no doubt I felt fitter a few weeks ago than I do now. And lighter. My belly's back, my diet's not what it has been and my sleep patterns are all over the place.

I'm up early today in the hope that I can knock off a few miles to get things going again. It's not what I said I was going to do: rest completely until the marathon, but I just don't feel that's the right thing to do anymore. I know every pound I put on will have some sort of effect on my ability to get round as efficiently as possible, plus I need to give the muscles that are working at least some chance of retaining their momentum. And then there's the wind issue. When I run, I am far less bloated; at times this week I've felt like an over-inflated party balloon. I really need to fart, a lot.

I had a quick look at a few training plans last night to remind myself of where I should be with a week to go. Most of them advise something along the lines of an 8–10-mile run this weekend, followed by two or three easy runs ahead of next Sunday. There's no doubt about it, my regime has gone way off-piste over the last three weeks. Those two days of supposed miraculous pose running while I was in France really messed me up.

Nothing wrong with the pose technique per se, just stupid of me to try it out with so little time to go and messing my knees and calves up. Still, I am where I am, so it's no use wondering where I would be if I'd got on another train.

Over my self-imposed last week of non-activity, I have more than tried to compensate by reading a few more books about running. *Born to Run* by Christopher McDougall, *What I Talk About When I Talk About Running* by Haruki Murakami and my favourite, *Run or Die* by Kilian Jornet, one of the most committed and successful extreme runners the world has ever seen.

He even talks about when he was so tired attempting to break one of his own many records, he actually fell asleep while running, like an exhausted driver might at the wheel of a car. When he came to, he was still running but a hundred yards to the left of where he needed to be. Incredible. He also talks of days when he has been so stiff in bed that he can barely move one locked leg in front of the other to get to the toilet, even though he's due to run 50 miles half an hour later. Then there was the time he took the wrong turn after running all day when it was already dark, and he didn't know whether to stop and ask for shelter or carry on as he still had 30 miles go before he reached the camp where his team was waiting for him. Go online to see footage of him flying down snowy mountain ranges and skipping along deathly ridges thousands of feet above sea level like a kid playing hopscotch in a playground. Incredible stuff, incredible guy.

On the other hand, and I know this is going to sound pathetic, at no point does he talk about a pulled muscle or feeling a bit of extra timber around the old waistline. One man's exploding heart and blood curdling at the back of his throat (something he references on more than one occasion) is another man's fifty-year-old frame trying to hold up for dear life.

Anyway, whatever, I can't put this off any longer. My lake is waiting for me and if I don't get out there soon, Tash and the kids will be up wanting Dad for general Sunday-morning fun and mayhem and that will be that.

Now, talking of Tash, with only a week to go and my marathon-eve hotel room booked, I think I'd better tell her what I'm up to.

Gulp.

Monday, 20 April

6 DAYS TO GO

A good night's sleep makes the world seem a whole lot more reasonable place to be, don't you think?

My 67-year-old Indian accountant, Kirit, who's been with me through thick and thin, both good times and bad, when I've been wedged up in the black or teetering on falling into the abyss on the wrong side of the red, loves sleep. What is more he's really, really good at it. If he finds himself with a spare half-hour with nothing to do, regardless of whether he's particularly tired or not, he will just fall unconscious.

'I adore sleeping, I do it whenever I can.'

Not that he's lazy, or apathetic, or obese; he's as skinny as a rake, plays golf twice a week and works as hard as anyone I've ever met.

'The other night, I looked at the clock and it was 8.15 p.m., there was nothing on the telly so I said to my wife, Kamud, "I'm off to bed." I enjoyed the most excellent ten hours you could imagine.'

And I believe him. I've lost count of how many times I've witnessed this great sleeping guru in action. On the way back from our Boys' Trip to France in April this year, I saw him fall asleep while actually reading the paper. One minute he was studying the *Telegraph* Business Section, the next he was dead to the world, the newspaper slowly slipping through his fingers into the footwell below.

He must have so little on his conscience. Surely this is the key to restful unconsciousness. Or maybe it's because he's an accountant of fifty years' standing and his whole life has been based around order and organization. He looks so peaceful when he's asleep. I remember being so envious of him on the plane that day, a portrait of calm, contentment and tranquillity.

I, on the other hand, have been told on more than one occasion that I sleep with a furrowed brow and a frown. As if I have voluntarily invited the troubles of the world to spend the night with me. That's when I get to sleep at all. For someone whose life revolves around getting up so early, before I encountered Dr Guy, my new sleep mentor, I was a disaster when it came to tryongg to drop off.

Was it my mind that was my enemy? Was it my fat neck and the fact that (apparently) I snore like a grumpy elephant? Was it the hours that I keep? The food that I eat? My drinking habits? My ever-weakening bladder? Our bedroom that's more like a green-house than an igloo? Whatever.

Sleep. Sleep. Sleep.

The thing. The thing. The thing.

Tuesday, 21 April

5 DAYS TO GO

Fuck. Why haven't I done this before now? Obviously that's a rhetorical question to myself. Like everything in life, we never do things until it's time to do them. Frustrating, but true. I remember when I first moved to London, I spent ages procrastinating on whether or not to buy a Kenwood stack system hi-fi. At £600, it was the most money I'd ever considered spending on anything other than the house I owned back in Warrington. Eventually, the evening after I'd closed my eyes and gone for it, back at home, I spent well into the early hours beating myself up for not doing it weeks before. The sound was sublime, the best company I could ever have wished for. I feel the same way today about this running malarkey.

Sure, it's good to know I can now nip out for a leisurely 5- or 10-mile jog without considering much else other than if I have the time, but more than that, it's the feeling currently consuming my very being. I am so looking forward to Sunday. I can barely wait. Every minute of every day is visited by thoughts of the start, or the finish, or whatever lies in between. Of what's going to hurt and what's not, and what it's like to be surrounded by thousands of other people all running in the same direction, trying not to injure each other in the process. Of where Tash and the kids will be and if I'll get to see them. Of the other two-million-plus spectators who will be vying for the best vantage point to spot their loved ones. Of whether or not I take a gel before the race, like my friend Vicki says she does, or whether not to take any gels at all 'because they are the devil's work', as another friend of mine, Jonathan, says.

It's all too much.

In a good way.

Sensory overload of the most stimulating kind for grown-ups but without any illegal substances, alcohol or cigarettes. The ultimate natural high. Christ, even if something happens between now and Sunday that means I can't run at all for some reason, like World War III for example, I've already had as good a time as I can remember. You know that feeling when you are so excited all you want to do is go to sleep and wake up and it's time? That's exactly how I feel. I am bursting at the seams, buzzing like a bee, crazy like a fox. I can only imagine what it must be like for proper athletes the week before a big race.

In the meantime, more protein!

I'm gonna start on the carbs tomorrow or Thursday. There are infinite opinions on when and what you should be eating and drinking. I'm going for carb starve/protein fill Sunday to Wednesday. Carb fill/protein starve Thursday to Sunday.

Oh yes, and I still, really really now, need to tell Tash what I'm up to.

Double gulp.

Thursday, 23 April

3 DAYS TO GO

No more running, decision made. I went to see Phil my chiro last night. He said he's never seen ITBs so tight. 'Mate, they are solid.' He got to work immediately with his acupuncture needles. 'You'll not be able to get very far if they stay like this.' Seconds later, in went the needles, two in each calf, two in each quad and two in my lower back. Sure they hurt, especially when, after leaving me to 'cook' for half a minute, he returns to give them a little 'tweak' deeper, but I don't mind, I don't care. I know they're doing me good. I'll take anything now that helps get me through Sunday.

'Can you come see me again on Friday or Saturday? We need to go again with these.'

'I can't. I'm back to London tonight and then that's me done with Berkshire till next week.'

'Well, you're going to have to do some serious damage to yourself with a foam roller then. Heat your legs up first any way you can – a hot-water bottle is best – and then roll until it hurts. All the best methods are on YouTube.'

Today is my first day of the infamous carb-loading process. There are so many theories about this, the method I have plumped for being protein only for the first half of the week and then carbs only for the second half. Starve, feed, store is the basic theory. As long as I do something it will be more than I've ever done in the past. Being careful most of all not to mistake the 'loading' aspect of the process for an excuse to gorge. All carb-loading should really mean is sub-stituting normal-size meals of one thing for similar normal-size bowls of pasta. It's actually an extremely misleading description of what one needs to do.

Now here's the thing: I love pasta, I mean really love it, but it's fascinating how being told you 'have to' do something changes one's relationship with whatever that something is. After the first mouthful of my official pre-marathon weekend carbfest, pasta had never tasted so viscous and sticky. It was all I could do to chew it enough to swallow.

Bizarre.

I was hungry. Damn I was hungry. I'd been hungry all week. More hungry than I could remember, even though I was eating six (small-to-medium) meals each day. Was this evidence of the power of suggestion? Was I hungry now because I was projecting how hungry I might be during the race on Sunday?

Oh and by the way, don't even think about trying to get a bowl of porridge from any of the healthier takeaway stores in London's West End any time after 10 a.m. in marathon week.

No chance.

Sold out.

Thank heaven for the BBC canteen.

Friday, 24 April

48 HOURS TO GO

Telling Tash

'I knew it! I knew it! I bloody well knew it!' she screamed. Then she was off. And that was only the beginning.

'I knew it all along.'

'Why would you be doing these crazy long runs just for fun?'

'No one does that. No one.'

'Although, when I say I *knew* it, I mean I didn't know it for certain. Because you and the word marathon don't make sense. That was the missing link. But then again, I know when you put your mind to something then you're not going to let it go unless you absolutely have to.'

Pause. Breathe.

'Arrgghh.'

'I'm so angry.'

'I'm pleased for you as well, of course I am, but I'm also so . . . well, more jealous actually. I've ALWAYS wanted to do a marathon. And now, out of nowhere, boom, you've snuck in there before me.'

'Aaaarrrrgggghhhhh.'

'I want to scream.'

She was screaming.

I'm just not quite sure she realized. And it's true she has always wanted to do a marathon. In fact I'm almost certain she could go and run one now if she really wanted to. Naturally super-fit, she doesn't move like a person. Tash's physiology generally is more akin to that of the animal world: long, reaching, smooth, effortless.

'Oh my God, I think I'm going to cry.'

She was still going.

'Not because I'm upset – although I am, a little – but because I cry at the marathon every year anyway on television, I think the whole thing is amazing. To think you're doing it in three days and to think how hard you must have trained to get your head and body around the challenge, it's all too much.'

'I hate you but I'm so proud of you.'

Another pause.

Reload.

And then:

'Can we come and watch?'

And that was about the size of it.

From that moment on it was just a matter of organizing how and where she, Noah and Eli were going to spectate from.

The runner was sorted. The fan club was now the priority.

* * *

HALF AN HOUR LATER

'Will you come with us to buy an inflatable from the fancy-dress shop?'

'What for?' I ask.

'It's far easier for you to see us in the crowd if you know where-abouts we're going to be and we're waving a six-foot banana than it is for us to spot you in amongst fifty thousand other running beans. That's what all the online spectator guides say.'

Tash, already completely on the case.

'Er, well I would honestly love to help you to do that, but I have a very important lunch date I need to keep.'

'Who with?'

'Paula Radcliffe.'

'Whaaaaaaaat?'

Paula is Tash's sporting hero. At this point I can almost sense several saucepans about to come my way.

'She heard I was doing the marathon and I was writing about it in my book and …'

'You've been training for a marathon in secret and it's in your book!'

It was time to make a very swift exit.

• • •

LUNCHTIME

45 HOURS TO GO: 1 P.M.

Paula Radcliffe is a wonderful all-round human being. She is so generous with her time. She has such a gentle way about her. To the extent it's almost impossible to associate the smiling, relaxed mum and wife with the tenacious, gritty and determined running legend she has sacrificed much of her life to become.

The truth of the matter is, when Paula appeared as a guest on my radio show a few weeks before, I had confided in her with regards to what I was up to. She was especially intrigued that I wasn't telling anyone and offered to help in any way she could. One of the greatest marathon runners that's ever lived, offering her services to the shuffle king – what was not to like?

After arriving at the Tower Hotel, the official headquarters for the London Marathon, I'm given the heads-up Paula is outside, stretching after a light training run.

A few moments later, she bounces in, arms outstretched, then gives me a massive hug.

'Hi, Chris, I'll just grab a quick shower and I'll be right back down.'

Paula always has a permanent aura of positive energy emanating from every pore, but here at marathon central, times that by a thousand. She is a living and breathing god.

While I'm waiting, Gary, Paula's husband, introduces himself. Handsome, tough, quite intimidating if I'm honest, the no-nonsense reputation he's renowned for immediately in evidence. By her own admission without Gary, Paula would not have achieved the greatness she has. His protectiveness is the ring of steel she needs to give her the space to focus on being the best of the best.

Five minutes later, Paula's back and Gary is on dad duty, leaving us to have a chat and sit down for lunch in the hotel's bistro overlooking Tower Bridge. With less than two days to go, the atmosphere is already carnival-like. Bands playing, and mobile coffee bars and ice-cream vans enjoying queues spilling out into the road.

My first marathon is to be Paula's last and here we are, having a chinwag about exactly that. I've been ridiculously fortunate to do many extraordinary things in my life but this has to be right up there with the very best of them.

'What do you fancy to eat?' the Champ asks.

'Paula, it's two days before the marathon and I have to get my fuelling right, I'm going to have exactly the same as you.'

'Right, risotto it is, then.'

From then on the conversation just flows. Every two or three minutes someone pauses at our table to wish Paula good luck or tell her what a huge inspiration she's been in their life. All the time she never once fails to smile up at them with a mixture of appreciation and encouragement, not for a moment showing any sign that she's in the slightest inconvenienced, even though she's clearly mid-conversation and in the middle of her meal.

It's only when we get talking that it hits me what a huge weekend this is for her too. All that she's experienced in her running career, all the triumph and the tragedy, the unbelievable highs and the dark and desperate lows, ends in two days, for good.

This is it.

'So how are you going to approach Sunday?'

'Well, I say to myself that my intention is to go out there almost as a fun runner and see what it's like to run a marathon like most normal people do, acknowledging the crowds, talking to other runners, maybe stopping for a few photos and interviews on the way. But then when I really think about it I'm not sure if I can. I suspect that once I'm on the line, my default 'get out there and run as fast as I can' mentality will kick in. I really don't know. What about you?'

Now this is hilarious. The world's best ever, asking me the selfsame question about what she does for a living.

But that's the wonderful thing about marathon running and marathon runners: there is total mutual respect between the lowest and slowest beginners to the quickest and the fittest the sport has ever seen. In fact there is no 'lowest' in marathon running. Everyone out there with a number on their chest on the day knows what everyone else has had to go through to get to the starting line.

I tell Paula I would love to finish in under five hours. That would be dreamsville for me. That's if I finish at all, of course.

'And do you think you can?'

'I've no idea. My last long run was a hit-and-miss French farce with my fastest mile being no quicker than perhaps thirteen minutes.'

'Right, well the best advice I can give you is this: don't start off too quickly. Everyone always does and it almost always comes back to bite them on the bum later on in the race. Even if you think you're not going too fast, look down at your watch and check, because you probably will be. No matter how good you feel, stick to your plan. Adrenaline is so powerful and there'll be lots of it pumping around your body, but it can be very misleading.

'If you feel like you are comfortably cruising, think to yourself, "Could I up my pace for a mile now if I had to and still make it home?" If the answer is no, then you're going too fast, in which case just come off the gas a little. Only ever so slightly – you'll be amazed what a difference it makes.

'Hydration and nutrition are vitally important, much more than a lot of beginners realize. If you're thirsty – or even think you're thirsty – drink. Listen to your body all the way round, it's your best friend. And don't be tempted to miss any energy gels because you think you feel like you're OK. It's just not worth the risk.

'And finally, and most important of all, EXPECT AT LEAST THREE TOUGH PERIODS. At *least* three. Just be ready for them, then when they happen, think calmly about what's going on and what you might be able to do to get through whatever it is that's bothering you. Almost everything will most likely pass, but if you stay relaxed and keep breathing, placing one foot in front of the other, this can only help the situation.'

• • •

This last bit of Paula's advice has stayed with me ever since, not only when it comes to my running but in my everyday life as well. It's so obvious. Of course things are bound to go wrong, from the moment we get up in the morning to the moment we rest our head on the pillow again that night. The last thing we should do is waste energy we might need to fix a potential issue on being constantly surprised that life continues to be imperfect.

My lunch with Paula was one of the most enjoyable and edifying hour and twenty minutes I've ever spent with another human being.

Until she threw in this little curve ball . . .

'And how are your running shoes?'

'Well, they're OK.'

'But they're fresh, yes?'

'They've never run a marathon before, if that's what you mean.'

'No, I know that, but they've got some life left in them, yes?'

'Er, I don't really know.'

'How many pairs have you got through in training?'

'None, my shoes for Sunday are the ones I've had since December.'

'What????'

Oh dear. Clearly this is not good. I can see it in Paula's eyes. At which point none other than serial Olympic gold medallist and former middle-distance world-record holder Steve Cram pitches up.

'Steve, please tell Chris he cannot run on Sunday in trainers that have already seen hundreds of miles' wear unless he has absolutely no choice but to do so. He's just asking for trouble, yes?'

'Eh?' says Steve. 'He's not running the marathon, is he?'

Far from worrying about my footwear it took us the next five minutes to convince Crammy this wasn't a wind-up and that I had honestly been in secret training.

'Well, I'll be . . . Wonders will never cease. In which case, Paula's right. You really could do with a bit more bounce under your heels.'

Now, far be it from me to go against the stellar advice that I was being gifted, but all I could hear was Jim Fixx's words ringing in my head, along with the pain I felt in my calf when I stupidly tried to change my running style a fortnight ago: NEVER change your routine or equipment with less than four weeks to go. MINIMUM two weeks. And certainly not TWO DAYS!!!

But what would you do?

Our greatest-ever marathon runner is telling me I need new trainers. Surely only a complete, 100 per cent idiot would not heed her advice.

'What make do you wear?' asks Paula, now genuinely concerned.

'Nike.'

'In which case we have half a chance – Nike are my sponsors. What model are they? I'll get on to the truck to see if they can send a new pair down for you.'

The fact is I have no idea what model they are. I'd seen a mate of mine wearing them at a Christmas party last year and after commenting on how much I liked them, something I'd never done with regards to trainers before, my wife went online and bought me a pair as a surprise from Santa.

This results in Paula Radcliffe, *the* Paula Radcliffe, going online on her phone and scrolling through hundreds of images of running shoes asking me if any of them look vaguely familiar.

Hilarious.

Twenty minutes later I'm in a Nike shop in Covent Garden.

'You do know that if you're running this Sunday you really shouldn't be changing your shoes this late in the day?' says the friendly and helpful in-store running consultant.

'Yes, but I have a friend who has assured me it's what I need to do.'

'Well, I sincerely hope they know what they're talking about,' he replies, unconvinced.

All around us are massive posters of one Paula Radcliffe.

I haven't the heart to tell him.

ONE SLEEP TO GO

Saturday morning the birds are singing. Although not too loudly. That'll be because it's been raining all night. I can't remember the last time it rained. Not that it was centuries ago or anything like that, it's just that I could barely recall running once in the rain since I embarked upon my shuffling dream.

And there's more rain on the menu, according to the weather folk. All weekend one way or another, particularly forecast for tomorrow morning and the race. I've not been actively avoiding the rain, more like it's been avoiding me. Not to worry, though. Apparently light rain is no bad thing come marathon morning. We shall see.

Lying in bed, the clock ticking ever loudly, I remind myself I must be more excited than nervous and come Monday morning this whole great adventure will be over. After a hundred days, now we're down to just over twenty-four hours.

As the morning goes on, I get calmer if anything. Nothing to do now except enjoy every moment from here on in. Tash and I take the boys for a scooter ride to the running shop, I need to pick up some gels. The guy says for me to take four, three and a spare. 'Any more than that and they'll be causing more harm than good.' Tash buys a new pair of trainers. She already has her running revenge meticulously planned.

After a couple of hours have passed we're still out. I begin to feel my legs starting to ache. Nothing much but I'm hyper-aware of anything. Like when Eli rattled into my right calf from behind ten minutes before on his scooter. We stop off at the fancy-dress shop to buy the giant inflatable banana for Tash and the kids to wave in the crowd so I can see them tomorrow.

After returning home to pack my marathon bag, we set off for the Tower Hotel where I met Paula and Steve the day before. When we arrive it's even busier than yesterday, sunny too. I check in and then go to register. I'm met by two wonderful forces of nature by the name of Jo and Matt. Jo gives me my race number, 25201, and a briefing on what happens tomorrow morning. Matt, who ran the race last year, gives me another take on what to expect. I'm happy to listen to as many marathon accounts as possible, picking up any scrap of useful experience that might come in handy.

Matt then tells me how emotional he was when he crossed the line last year. He ran into the arms of his wife as they both broke down. He was running in honour of his son who was stillborn. He breaks down in front of me, as he's perfectly entitled to. He apologizes, but realizes there's no need as he looks up to see tears rolling down my cheeks. After a few beats we both snap out of it and suddenly we're back in the room talking layers, Vaseline and an early start. He seems like an extremely good guy.

Again the general mantra is:

'Whatever you do, don't start too quickly. It's so tempting with the adrenaline and relatively fresh legs to how your legs have felt for the vast majority of your training.'

I can't hear those words enough.

'And enjoy it. That's the best advice anyone can give you. There's absolutely no point in putting all this work in and then letting your own stupid ego get in the way of a great day. Get around, have fun, get to a pub and talk the hell out of your experience.'

The clock is ticking.

Tash, the kids and I have lunch back in the brasserie. Steve comes over from the terrace, where he's having a relaxed drink with some of Paula's friends and family. We exchange numbers. I tell him I'll see him in the bar later.

'One won't hurt, will it?' I ask.

'Maybe even two,' he replies with a mischievous smile.

It's 5.15 p.m., time for the fan club to leave. The next time I see them will either be thanks to the giant inflatable banana out on the course or after the race somewhere. Tash is dewy-eyed. The kids wish me luck and give me one of their super-special never-let-go hugs. My favourite thing in the world.

Moments later, with the hollow clunk of a London black cab door, they're off and on their way home. The runner is alone. Just as I was when I started this caper, seeing if I could shuffle once around Virginia Water lake without stopping. And now here I am: sixteen hours, a bus ride to the start and 26.2 miles away from accomplishing my goal.

Should something, for whatever reason, between now and the morning stop me from competing in tomorrow's race, what I've already learnt about myself will have made this amazing adventure more than worthwhile.

I really can't recall ever feeling this comfortable and at ease with myself at any point in my life before.

Top Ten Running Bag Contents:

10   Hard rubber dog's ball for trigger-point work.
9   Voltarol cream.
8   Ibuprofen.
7   Energy gels.
6   KT tape.
5   Sunglasses.
4   Hat.
3   Socks.
2   Trainers.
1   Running bottoms, shorts and top.

RACE DAY EVE

OK, I must have a plan. And I do. The dream is to run as many ten-minute miles as possible without stopping and then graduate down from there to try to get inside five hours. If I could pull this off I would be in seventh heaven. Not that I've ever come close to that before. But the thing is, it's not actually that fast, it's just doing twenty-six of them consecutively that's the issue. To run under five hours all I have to do is 26 miles at an average speed of

11.37 minutes a mile, which is really quite slow and in a way a lot more tiring. The longer the plod, the longer the slog, therefore it's in one's interest to try to go about one's marathon in one's optimum time. The less time you're out there, the less time everything has to affect you.

I have also never prepared for any of my previous long runs like I have for the marathon itself. I've had hardly any alcohol for seven days, I've gone about fuelling my body the right way for the first time in my adult life and I've been getting seven hours plus sleep a night. Therefore I have no idea really what I'm capable of.

I need to do a rough gross calculation so I'm not distracted during the race while wondering what to do and whether to rest, maintain, hold back or push. That's if I have a choice, of course. How about I try to maintain a ten-minute-mile pace for the first half and then see how I feel? If I can manage that, it will leave me with 2 hours 49 minutes to get round the second half. Which will mean a gnat's breath under thirteen-minute-mile pace will get me there.

This is all assuming my left knee or right Achilles doesn't go and I can manage 26.2 miles in the first place.

Actually, how about I aim for a ten-minute-mile pace first half but allow myself ten minutes thirty, just in case, and bring my second-half pace down to twelve minutes thirty seconds a mile. That seems to be a lot more sensible.

OK, that's what I'll do. That's the basic plan. Anything more complicated than that and I won't be able to focus when I'm knackered. And if it goes awry early on, then I'll just shuffle, smile and wave and remember to 'enjoy the day'.

Formula is:

10.00 miles in first half gives me 13.00 miles' margin in second half.
10.30 first half gives me 12.30 second half.
11.00 first half gives me 12.00 second half.
11.30 first half gives me flat, i.e. same second, half.

Presuming the second half is going to be slower because that's what all the stats say, 11.30 flat – i.e., all the way through – is a high-risk strategy. If I can rack up thirteen ten-minute miles for the first half, that would be the dream start.

Sunday, 26 April

Waking thoughts:

The human race is so bizarre. We are extraordinary, yet for the most part totally predictable, creatures of habit. It's 5.15 a.m., less than five hours to the start of the race, yet the whole hotel is still in bed and fast asleep. In an hour or two all kinds of mayhem will be going on, but right now, you could be forgiven for thinking it was Boxing Day morning.

I've managed about six hours' sleep, one way or another, which is more than I thought I would get. That's the good news, the not-so-good news is that I over-massaged my right shin with my knuckles last night and it's come up inflamed and painful this morning.

Idiot.

Don't do 'anything' radical last minute the day before, unless it's an emergency. You know the score, yet still you panic.

Right, I'm off for an early breakfast before the rush starts, I'll have a shower and get ready after that. Major priority before I get on the bus: try to have a substantial relationship with the loo.

From the window of the brasserie, the Shard has become the Shroud. Low, dirty rain cloud covers London, the worst day for weeks. It's wet, very wet, and cold. Apparently good news for the quick runners. OK, well good for them, but seeing as I'll be out for more than twice the time they will be, how about it brightens up around midday after that?

Also found out via the Twittersphere that Jenson Button is running number 25202. My number is 25201. For the moment, at least, technically he's behind me.

What to eat for breakfast on race morning is no longer up for debate, I find myself in the queue for the buffet with elite athletes from all over the world: Russians, the Portuguese Paralympic team, the US wheelchair team. It's porridge, watermelon, pineapple, croissant, bagels, scrambled egg, coffee – basically anything you damn well like. It's all energy and everyone's going to need as much as they can get. Although the Russians also have a huge container of POWER PORRIDGE (written exactly like that) on their table. Hilarious, I wonder if there's anything in it or it's just the Ruskies at their breakfast-table intimidating worst.

Back from breakfast, the most important mission of the day, ahead of getting to the finish and spotting Tash and the kids en route, is accomplished. A lavatorial download of monumental proportions and with some considerable gravitational force, I might add. I don't mean to be vulgar but you have no idea what a relief that was. There may be more to come, but I'm not sure there could possibly be anything left.

Time for another quick bath.

My heart is racing.

I am both mega-nervous and hyper-excited. I'm also quite tired but I really don't care. If I can't get myself up for this, then I might as well call it a day where everything's concerned.

I lie on the bed until the absolute last minute before I think I need to get changed. I remember Dr Guy Meadows' words: ten minutes of sleep can enhance a person's performance by 100 per cent over a four-hour period thereafter.

That's what I'll try to do.

At some point between now – 6.48 a.m. and 10.10 a.m. I will try to achieve some brief unconsciousness. Little chance when I'm more excited than an elephant in a bun factory. Right, painkillers, cream, Vaseline, KT tape and it'll be jump-on-the-bus time.

Oh no. I can feel another rumble in the jungle coming on. Maybe my original download wasn't the final article after all.

• • •

The foyer of the hotel is jumping with excitement and anticipation. There are recognizable faces everywhere, some of them I can put names to, some escape me. We are directed towards an old Route-master London bus waiting for us on Tower Bridge. What a perfect way to start our collective day of self-discovery.

I sit on the back seat upstairs with a friend of mine, a far too handsome fifty-year-old Geordie by the name of Graeme Lowdon, who is the extremely affable team principle of Manor F1. We had a sneaky pint of Guinness last night over which to compare notes and calm each other down, during which Graeme informed me most of his training had involved running round various Grand Prix circuits of the world.

'More and more teams go running when we get to the tracks nowadays.'

Is it me or is the whole planet suddenly waking up to the magic and simplicity of pulling on a pair of sweatpants and trainers and going out for a relaxing, feel-good jog?

In front of myself and Graeme on the bus are Helen George, she of *Call the Midwife*, Greg James from Radio 1, Christy Turlington, the ex-supermodel and veteran of no less than four marathons, to her right is Jenson Button and his missus, Jessica, and behind them is the man mountain and all-round superhero that is double Olympic rowing gold medallist James Cracknell.

If I thought the hotel foyer was buzzing, the top deck of this bus is ready to explode. The sheer volume of conversation is deafening. Everyone is totally wired, totally up for it, like a bunch of school kids setting off on the most exciting daytrip ever..

'Sleeping the night before a Grand Prix – not a problem,' says Jenson. 'But last night – not a chance. I barely got four hours.'

That's how much the marathon means, even to someone who's seen as much competition as the man from Frome has.

I try to sleep just for a minute, resting my head against the cold wet glass. Sometimes the kind of ambient hubbub currently coursing through the top deck can be surprisingly comforting. It almost works, I nearly drop off; not quite unconscious, but I definitely cross over into a land less 'present' for a wee while.

As we approach Blackheath the narrow residential streets open up into what is usually a vast and rather magnificent blanket of green. However, not today. It has been replaced temporarily by a makeshift village of marquees, fences, floodlights, portaloos, big screens and food and drink outlets. But the main thing that strikes me is how dank, dark and dreary it is and still freezing cold.

No matter, this is the sight we've been waiting for, we're all just glad to have made it this far. Within an hour and a half, all our prior trepidation, nervousness and anticipation will be forgotten, we will be underway and on our way: each of us one of 53,000 dreams realized.

Wonderful.

Although . . . hang fire a second. No one tells you about the drama of the last hour before the start. I honestly thought I was totally prepped and ready to go, yet it turns out I don't have a second to spare. And it isn't just me: everyone's the same. We're all constantly fiddling with this and checking that and pinning, unpinning and repinning our numbers on to our shirts. Laces are done and undone a hundred times, socks checked and rechecked for stones or grit, Vaseline shared, dropped, lost and found. Not to mention vital last-minute tips for us first-time marathoners.

'What have you taken?' one highly experienced marathon veteran caringly asks me.

'Two Ibuprofen,' I answer.

'Is that it?' He sounds aghast.

'Yeah, but I plan on taking two more after halfway,' I squeak almost apologetically.

'Have you taken any Pro Plus?' he whispers.

'No.'

'You might want to, they make it more difficult for The Wall that comes to find you around mile 18.'

I don't need this explaining twice, I'm in. He takes four, I take two.

'Have you had an energy gel yet?' asks another seasoned elite competitor.

'No, I was going to have one at 10, one at 14, one at 18 and then my fourth one if and when I need it after that.'

'Mate – take one now, immediately, and then take one regardless every forty-five minutes. Don't even think about doing anything else.'

'I've only got four.'

'Here, I've got loads, take as many as you like.'

Now, you see what's going on here? It's actually awesome. These two guys are aiming to finish almost two hours ahead of me, almost twice as fast, but that's not the point. Once again the mutual respect in evidence is on a scale I've never witnessed in anything I've been involved in. That's what's so cool: we are all running our own race against our own demons, insecurities and potential weaknesses. There is zero hierarchy, only ultimate camaraderie. I can't tell you how uplifting that feels.

More tips, more Lucozade Sport, more coffee, more cereal bars, more bananas, more pees. Having deposited our bags back on the bus to be transported to the finish line, intermittently we are ushered in and out like cattle for various pieces to camera, photocalls and interviews. I am the surprise entry. I will talk to anyone and pose for as many snaps as they like. That was the deal, remember? These people have given me the chance to do something I never thought would be within my reach. I am theirs for the day.

Eventually it's time for us to make our way en masse to the start line.

Fuck. Fuckety fuck. With bells on.

I am pumped like never before.

My legs feel perfect, like coiled springs.

As the huge digital clock ticks down to 10.10 hours BST, everyone turns to wish anyone within earshot good luck. I can't see anyone who isn't tense and I can see hundreds of people.

'All right, everyone, here we go,' says the starter. 'Altogether – TEN – NINE – EIGHT . . .'

Seven counts later and finally, after months of wondering and worrying and working out the optimum race pace and nutrition and hydration and target times, we are released, pigeons set free to find our way home.

For the first few seconds I feel physically sick, not so much from nerves – although I am nervous – but more from feeling over-whelmed by the whole situation. I've never fainted in my life but suddenly I begin to understand why people do. When something means so much and it finally arrives, it floods your very being with almost suffocating relief. It's almost all too much.

But then the strangest sensation comes over me, snapping me out of my fug. Here I am, in amongst thousands of people, a giant mass of humankind, a like-minded cross-section of the human race moving forward as one, all there for our own individual rea-sons, all with our own agendas and issues, sharing the single com-mon denominator that we have all made our minds up to don our running gear on this April Sunday morning and get ourselves to south-east London and attempt to run 26.2 miles in what is now 'absolute silence'.

No one has said a word for at least the first half-mile.

And I mean no one.

All I can hear are thousands upon thousands of rubber soles strik-ing the tarmac and pavements all around me. Some heavy, some soft; quick strides, long strides, the odd stumble here and there. It's clear everyone is feeling the same way. The hush speaks volumes. Tense, apprehensive, focused, but most of all euphoric realization that we are finally doing what we have all been training for over the last few weeks, months and, for some I'm sure, even years.

• • •

There are many moments of my marathon experience that I will never forget but this turns out to be the one moment above all others. Totally out of the blue, as eerie as it was magical, but most of all completely unexpected and so special. In fact, writing about it now is bringing big happy tears of joy to my eyes, delayed emotion that I must have subconsciously postponed in order to be able to get on with the job in hand.

• • •

After our collective experience of whatever that special moment was, almost simultaneously we all begin to snap out of it, like individual bubbles bursting, back into life, into the here and now. Realizing that it's all OK, that this is it, that we're doing what we came to do.

The odd comment begins to be exchanged, a giggle here, a laugh there, all more in a tacit sigh of relief than an attempt at meaningful communication. Or perhaps not, perhaps it is the most cerebral interaction, a group 'Relax, we thoroughly deserve this. Let's take a chill pill and breathe in every second of every step.'

With each second that passes, more and more voices begin to be heard as each of us remembers we were born with the ability to speak. We become one huge wave of pacing euphoria. All our senses on high alert, taking in the sight of us all, the sound of us all, the fact that the vast majority of us will be on the road for the next four to six hours. As all these thoughts and anomalies continue to sink in, I feel ever more at home. This is where I'm meant to be. And then suddenly it happens. There you go: I am smiling. That's what this is all about. And I already know I won't stop smiling until I cross the finish line.

But . . .

'Whoa! Wait a minute. What the fuck was that? A bollard, a bloody bollard.'

We all came to, just in the nick of time. I can't say this often enough: there are so many things about running a marathon people don't tell you, things that are not even hinted at on the hundreds of training plan websites. Suddenly we're no longer jogging leisurely towards our first-mile marker, we're smack-bang in the middle of the world's most covert obstacle course.

In all the moving footage I'd ever seen of the London Marathon on television, the shots were always primarily of two throngs of people. Those dressed in bright, gaily coloured running gear bobbing up and down inside the barriers and those cheering, waving and holding encouraging banners on the other side. Never had I seen film of thousands of runners funnelling into residential streets so tight they had to run everywhere and anywhere there was a space, regardless of whether that was on the pavement, on the road or somewhere in between the two. Or the fact that there are bloody bollards, bloody speed humps, bloody pillar boxes, bloody dogs, bloody pedal cars and bloody small children, popping up from nowhere, threatening to take you out at any given moment.

Thank God then for the heroic luminous-jacketed marshals who are on hand to scream, shout and generally frighten us away from all this surprise clear and present danger. And then don't forget the myriad potholes, the varying and rapidly changing road surfaces and the thousands of kerbs. All of which I had encountered in training, but that was when we could see a good twenty feet in front of me as opposed to the few inches in front of me now.

No one tells you any of this shit.

There's more extra-curricular education on the course to follow. Like the way you need to think about positioning yourself at least a quarter of a mile before one of the many and hugely efficient and superbly run drinks-stations. If you're on the opposite side to where they are, there is zero chance of darting over at the last minute; this would cause certain and absolute carnage. As a consequence of which, I miss my first two fuel stops before I manage to figure this out. Necessitating planning for my third and each subsequent hydration station thereafter becomes my main priority for the rest of the race.

Now here's another thing that NO ONE TELLS YOU when it comes to mileage: it's generally accepted that if you have run a relatively survivable 18–20 miles in training, the adrenaline on the day will get you to 26.2. This I find both the most exciting and frightening aspect of my marathon. Because until you've actually completed the course, you just don't know for sure. And it's an experience you'll never get to have twice.

Except!!!

It's not 26.2 miles!

In effect it ends up being at least 26.5 miles, if not closer to 27 miles, depending on which lines you take, how many times you end up zigzagging looking for friends and family in the crowd, the elusive fuel stops and nipping off for a number one or, God forbid, the dreaded number two.

The latest internal tremors of which started again for me at around Mile 7. I know there can't be much left in there, but there's usually enough regardless to cause an issue in most situations if lady luck is not on your side. Anyone who has experienced a pre-endoscopy barium meal will testify to that.

As I daren't risk a follow-through, I decide to take the next available course of evasive action, whatever that might be. However, it's far from obvious what form that might take: there are no portaloos for a good few miles yet and the crowds are too deep to request the benevolence of a marathon-friendly East End resident. But then, as if from nowhere, my prayers are answered.

I see a break in the crowd up ahead on the left-hand side and lo, not only that, the gap is there because it's the entrance to a fire station, which of course has to be kept clear in case the watch on duty receive an emergency call. Now, as I pretty much had an emergency call of my own to attend to, I immediately began to channel all the positive energy I could in the direction of my potential loo haven.

I've always had a very good relationship with firefighters, probably because of the many occasions I've made mention of the fact that becoming a fireman was all I ever wanted to do when I was a kid. Right up until the moment I was told by my careers officer that I couldn't, due to the fact I wore glasses which would preclude me from being able to wear breathing apparatus. I was determined that was going to be my life and was genuinely devastated at the time.

Anyway, realizing this is my only chance to head off impending doom and several potentially embarrassing headlines in tomorrow's papers, I prepare to do whatever is necessary. From a few hundred yards away I can see a group of the East End's finest watching on as this never-ending gigantic snake of sweating, puffing and panting human beings pass by. I immediately go into full-on 'must look like me' mode: head up, so they can see more of my face and signature specs, the widest, friendliest, cheesiest grin I can manage and a little extra bounce in my stride. Fifty, forty, thirty and twenty yards away, and I still haven't caught their attention.

Thankfully, with ten yards to go, just in time, hallelujah, one of the guys nudges his colleague.

'Hey look, it's Chris Evans.'

Thank you, Lord.

I can hear those angels again.

I slow up to give it time for the word to get around the whole group.

'Heeeeeey, Christoff/Chrissybaby/Chris Evaaaans!' comes the most welcome ensuing chorus of collective fire station approval.

'Lads, lads, please may I use your loo?'

'Sure,' says one of the guys, immediately sensing the urgency via my furrowed brow and several tell-tale beads of sweat. This was obviously a number two situation and the fire brigade never knowingly let down a decent, tax-paying member of the showbiz fraternity.

The loo in question is up a brief flight of stairs just on the right-hand side of the garage.

'Ouch!' The steps hurt a bit. 'Careful of your dodgy right hamstring, you Numpty,' I say out loud. Once in the cubicle, I go to crouch into the hover, but more bother – I've double-knotted my shorts so tight in case they came loose and now I can't untie them. All the time, precious seconds are ticking by. I check my watch and my pace reads 00:00:00. Bloody shorts. I will have to rip them off if necessary and complete the rest of the run in just my leggings.

I suddenly realize I am shaking, beginning to panic.

'Calm down, you prick,' a voice in my head rasps.

I just about manage to edge my shorts down around my thighs still intact. I am now a vac pac of my own making. A second later I'm good to go – except, now I'm all set, I don't want to go. Major false alarm. Surely not the first for this fire station. But the most inconvenient phantom poo of my life. Major maranoia. Or is it? I decide to sacrifice a minute of running time 'just in case' there is a boomerang contraction on its way back. I begin to strain, desperate not to get caught between a rock and a hard place, or something much less solid than a soggy place.

To shit or not shit, that's the question. All the while, the panic of 'Oh my God, something as simple as this could completely mess up my sub five-hour target'. Could this be in one of those, meant to nip to the loo for a quickie and end up still in there fifteen minutes later. Even a five-minute mandatory extension could easily see my plans go up in smoke, or steam as the case may be. But then again, if I can't go now and find myself having to go a few miles later, a double stop will have the same effect. What to do?

• • •

NO ONE TELLS YOU:
  Build in major margin for error.
If you want to run under five hours, aim for four hours forty minimum, as you are bound to have at least ten minutes of issues, dilemmas and distractions that will eat into your race pace. Preferably aim for half an hour under what you want to achieve, that's the safest bet. Or perhaps, be ready to expect at least half an hour over what your best race pace might be.

ALL OF THIS WAS NEWS TO ME ON RACE DAY.

Here's a quick top ten to help you see what I mean:

Top Ten Mid-Race Incremental Incidents That Could Derail Your Marathon:

10 Lace coming undone.
 9 Stone in your trainer.
 8 Slipping on a discarded drinks bottle – of which there are tens of thousands, like marbles under your feet.
 7 Run into an invisible immovable object.
 6 Tripping over a pavement.

5 Getting bundled to the ground by fellow runners, looking down at their phones or trying to read their iPod screen instead of looking where they're going.

4 Missing crucial fuel or gel slot and suffering hyperglycaemic meltdown.

3 Blisters.

2 Cramp.

1 Poo Gate.

• • •

I made a sensible decision and I'm happy. More importantly, I no longer have the distraction of whether I need to go putting me off everything else I need to concentrate on. The only thing I get wrong is my failure to notice the name of the fire station so I can thank the lads for their benevolence the next day on the radio. I have since rectified that oversight and would like to thank them via this missive in black and white.

Gentlemen, I thank you greatly for taking pity upon my internal gastric rumblings during my 2015 Virgin London Marathon experience. Please allow me to buy you an evening's worth of beers, with or without my company, whichever you would prefer.

Peace and Love,
Chris Evans
Radio 2/Channel 4

Ex Boy Scouts – well, cubs, actually, I left when I was dropped from the lead in *The Gang Show* to the rear end of the Little White Bull or Diddy Man. I chose Diddy Man but was privately an emotional wreck as a result. In fact, this may have been the reason for a life of debilitating insecurity that drove me on to crave public approval ever since. I just want to be loved, that's all.

• • •

My next challenge is to spot my wife and kids in between Mile 8 and Mile 9. There had been much discussion, debate and planning concerning where best we might get a chance to exchange a kiss or a wave, who knows, perhaps even a group hug.

What NO ONE EVER TELLS YOU is when it comes to marathon spotting, it's much easier for the runners to spot people in the crowd than for the people in the crowd to spot the runners. Looking for a pal or loved one in amongst 47,000 people for up to an hour can send your eyes crazy. I know because I experienced just that when I went with my friend Kev to watch his wife Jen complete her first-ever marathon in a stunning 3 hours 47 minutes at a grand old age. The best tip is the novelty inflatable tip: make sure your 'fans' have something that makes them stand out from the rest of the crowd. Becuase, at over two million people, that really is some crowd.

We nearly didn't bother with the now infamous inflatable banana, but I'm so glad we did. Perhaps the best £4.95 I've spent this side of the millennium as it enabled me to spot my clan from a good sixty yards away. As I draw ever closer to my waiting brood, my heart begins to sing like I never knew it could. Ecstasy on top of euphoria with a whole dose of unconditional love thrown in, enough to make a guy feel half decent about himself.

'I don't expect you to stop,' Tash had mentioned the day before. 'We just want to see you, Noah can't wait.'

But it's not as if I'm in the middle of a world-record attempt here where every second counts. I can't wait to hug them all although when it comes to it, little Eli is dead to the world, snuggled up in his pushchair. Tash on the other hand is in bits, tears streaming down her face.

'We're so proud of you,' she just about manages to blub, Noah beaming down at me from atop her shoulders.

It's all over in a flash, there were two kisses in there somewhere I'm sure, as I wasn't crying then but I am now. What tears are these? They really should prescribe whatever's going on here via the NHS, it really is astonishingly life affirming.

Our next scheduled rendezvous is at Mile 11. The intervening two miles of which disappear in a rainbow of cerebral other-worldliness, I'm running on air. In what seems like no time at all I am looking out for the mighty banana once again. And there it is, left side of the road, as planned, a bright yellow beacon to my little band of three. This time as I approach I can see there are more smiles than tears. We've had the big 'Wow, moment – it's time now to whoop it up and generally go crazy at puffing Daddy.

'BA – NA – NAA,' I scream pointing with both hands as I run up to them. We've lost our collective marathon virginity and the tensions that go with it; all-round pottiness is now the order of the day. Another group hug, Eli as well this time, more priceless kisses and another ultra-high to super-fuel miles eleven to thirteen.

I've never loved my family more.

Their presence has almost rendered any palpable physical exertion non-existent over the last hour, and look here what's next to help me on my way. It's Tower Bridge's turn to work her magic. My oh my, what an honour to be able to run west down Jamaica Road, past Shad Thames and my old flat in Cinnamon Wharf, the only place south of the river I've ever lived, flanked by crowds on either side so deep now, they begin to merge with the buildings behind them. Then turn right to behold the magnificence that is Tower Bridge on London Marathon Sunday.

This really is one of 'the' moments of my life. I will never ever forget how bloody amazing it was to see that sight. If you ever have even so much as half a chance to bag a place in the happiest marathon on the planet, you must do whatever is within your power to make it happen. The wall of noise that greets all the runners as they edge step by step from the south side of the Thames over to the north with the Tower of London on the left and St Katharine Docks on the right is absolutely immense. The crowd just keeps on cheering, the noise not so much following us as pulling us along. A grade-one listed wall of sound. Screaming, cheering, laughing, shouting, more screaming, more cheering. I now sense this is how it's going to be right to the finish.

First half done and dusted:
Duration: 2 hours, 25 minutes.
Distance: 13.1 miles.
One very happy Duracell bunny.

• • •

As the road opens up heading east and out towards Canary Wharf I begin my first mental check list for Part II. Calmly I assess my body, how is each of my various vital components faring? Shoulders fine, actually a little tense, so I drop my hands down lower by my sides, which simultaneously reminds me to give my legs a few hundred yards' shake-down. These procedures immediately make me feel more relaxed. I even remember to breathe a little more deeply for a while. That feels good too.

Next my thighs and quads. Thighs are fine but my quads are definitely letting me know they need a bit of TLC from now on. Could mean it's time for another gel, take one just in case, more isotonic hydration required and nearly forgot, my halfway point second dose of Ibuprofen – crucial. This may all sound a little over-elaborate for someone only trying to break five hours, but around me much younger and clearly much fitter bodies are breaking down in chronic pain. They have either not planned or trained properly, or haven't listened to their bodies until it's too late.

It's very difficult for anyone to blag any distance over a half-marathon without encountering serious consequences.

When it comes to long-distance running, if you can feel anything that's not quite right, you are potentially only moments away from it developing exponentially into a chronic, race-threatening issue. Ignore any red flags at your peril.

I get to work consuming what I need to in order to put my mind at rest. Next I give some thought as to how my fragile left knee is holding up. This is unquestionably my biggest concern. But so far, so good, it seems fine. I even try to imagine some pain. Nothing. Although I know it will come. It has to.

Left: With my wonderful assistant Hiten, the Frothy Coffee Man. (Hiten Vora)

Bottom: Fiat 500 – the New Way Forward. (Hiten Vora)

Above: Last night at *The One Show*, ten minutes after coming off the air. With Alex, Hiten and Gareth Collett. (Hiten Vora)

Left: There's the silver screen, the small screen and then there's the green screen. (Hiten Vora)

Above: The morning before the *TFI Friday* that night. The beginning of a 24-hour shift. On my Radio 2 breakfast show, Boris Becker, Joss Stone, Stephen Merchant and Gary Barlow were that morning's guests. (BBC)

Left: The man with the blue guitar. (BBC)

The return to Channel 4 of *TFI Friday* after 15 years. Total disbelief. 'Is this really happening?' (Jeff Spicer / Alpha Press)

Moo-ve over, Tom Daley. (Jeff Spicer / Alpha Press)

Mum steals another scene. Today's victim is F1 world champion Lewis Hamilton. (Jeff Spicer / Alpha Press)

Above: Adam Waddell, Mr *Top Gear* Worldwide, obviously thrilled at my appointment. (Rowan Horncastle)

Left: Jay Hunt, the no-nonsense straight-talking head of Channel 4. (Channel 4 / Adam Lawrence)

Below: Me and Clarkson, two weeks before I was offered his old job – the last time we spoke. (BBC)

Above: Soup and toast for lunch.

Left: First day at Big School equals Big Everything.

Below: Children in Need golf day. Nine years and counting . . . (Dusan Bozic)

A serious side to the little one. I like it.

All that matters.

No matter, for now, I couldn't be more grateful. My forty-nine-year-old bag o'bones is doing me proud.

Paula's advice whispers in my ear, there to protect me all the way.

'You will almost certainly have three dips. Be prepared, always.'

And Paula would know. Of course she would. Better than anyone else in the world.

And so I must wait, ready for something to go wrong, something to break down.

I keep on running. I keep on giving thanks. I am praying. To God. Archbishop Sentamu, I have made my decision. I'm in.

'One foot in front of the other, that's all you need to do.'

'A quiet run is a good run.'

Each mantra doing the trick, helping me notch up another ten, twenty, few hundred yards, then half-mile and then mile.

Each celebratory offical mile marker a huge fifteen-metre-high arch of balloons festooned with cascading ribbons snaking in the wind, a huge digital clock next to each one to let the marathon parade know how it's getting on.

● ● ●

My growing list of NO ONE TELLS YOU now includes the giant screens and pulsating music that sucks the runners into the underpass sections and spits them out the other side. I heard subsequently this came about because in past marathons such sections had become mass latrines.

NO ONE TELLS YOU either about how sticky the road surface gets around the energy gel stations with each subsequent discarded sachet. Tens of thousands of them necessitating a major jet-washing operation in the wake of the back markers. Later, as we make our way back west up Commercial Road, we see exactly that taking place. In less than twelve hours this, one of the world's busiest arterial routes, will be back open for business servicing the nation's capital.

As I enter at the Canary Wharf area still no major issues except for a few helpful twinges here and there to keep me on my toes. But by and large I am almost running in shock, like it's a dream. I know I have at least another five miles in me for sure. The training is paying off. I am enjoying every second of my marathon.

And I'm so glad I'm having to write this down because it's making me retrace every moment and realize just how special it all was. I've heard people claim not to have been able to remember whole swathes of their marathon experience, something I never really understood until now. Canary Wharf, though, I will never forget. The crowds there were absolutely huge, even compared to the mighty Embankment, which was yet to come.

Not only were the endless weaving throngs either side of the route ten, twenty, even thirty people deep in parts but they were elevated as well, tiered in some places. Bloody huge. Bloody loud. Bloody brilliant.

After the general breathlessness of the Isle of Dogs and all that wonderful crowd had to offer it's back out into the relative openness of the couple of miles that followed. I vaguely recall going up a long graduated slope leading to a maze of traffic lights and a roundabout I'm not sure exactly where but I think it may well have been the flyover section above the tunnel where a fantastically loud drum-troop had provided our live soundtrack half an hour before. Another gel station and then it was time to turn north towards Bow.

We were now no more than a mile away from the old lock keeper's cottage from where we used to broadcast Channel 4's *Big Breakfast*. Another fond memory, another five hundred yards of super-fuel. Smiling works when it comes to marathon running. And if not, there was still the crowd, still hundreds of thousands of them.

● ● ●

After Bow, time to turn left and embark upon the home stretch back into London and the cacophony of noise that I have read so much about. As we runners have clocked up what is now over four marathon hours, it becomes more and more evident our army of support has been doing similar when it comes to their own partying. Everyone is still entirely good humoured but there is a certain amount of bawdiness creeping into the proceedings. Like a well-attended Test match building to a thrilling climax.

Having hit the 20-mile marker, I am now in double unknown territory. Not only have I never run this far before, I have also never run as far as this without stopping. This is all new to me, I'd always stopped in training for one reason or another. But not today, not for a step; my legs have now been doing whatever it was for longer than I could be sure they were able.

Again, Paula's words flash into my psyche:

'Three dips, be prepared for three dips. They will almost certainly come. It could happen at any time. Be ready for them. Especially when you're feeling particularly strong. That's when your race is most likely to take control of you as opposed to you controlling it. Over-confidence is a killer. Quiet, mindful confidence is the key.'

And something is beginning to happen in my weak left knee. I'm almost relieved. At least I know now. There's no way a knee so vulnerable only a fortnight ago could make it round 26-odd miles and not break down. As usual it begins with a twinge, a warning. I chance a few steps running differently to see if I can nip whatever's about to happen in the bud. A few seconds later, pow, there it is – the debilitating stab I've come to know so well and been waiting for. If this were a training run I would pull up immediately at this point. But it isn't, it's the marathon, and I need to see how much pain I can take without stopping.

I recall Kilian Jornet's tales of running with freshly chipped bones rattling around in his skin, blood curdling at the back of his throat, I know it sounds silly but this is it for me. I may never get the chance to run this far as part of such a wonderful occasion ever again in my life. I am willing to do anything I can to get to the end. And I'm so close, I can almost smell Tower Hill and the Tower of London.

Before I can summon up anymore helpful distractions, however, a second much more intense stab of pain stops me dead in my tracks. In fact I pull up so abruptly there's an audible gasp from the crowd.

'Right, I know what this is,' I tell myself, or at least I have an idea what it is. The IT band located down the side of my upper left leg is so tight it feels as if it might snap at any moment. It feels more like bone or a metal rod than a tendon, pulling on my knee – torture. Somehow I must get enough life or elasticity back into there to ease the tension just enough for my brain to give my body permission to run again. Furiously, I massage the general area of my left quad and thigh with the knuckles of both my right and left hands. After twenty seconds I try to run again. And I manage, but only for a few hundred yards. Then I am forced to pull up again, more welcome sympathy from the folks behind the barriers. This time I ask a lady in the crowd if I can lean on her shoulder while I do some emergency stretching of the whole of my left leg. She's happy to help.

A moment later I'm back on the road, the pain has abated, I have no idea why nor any time to care. I can see the 22-mile marker. I look down at my watch. Sub-5 hours won't be possible if I have to walk for any substantial distance hereon in. But I realize also that I have far more fuel in my tank than I anticipated I would by this point. I decide therefore the most useful course of action is to increase my pace dramatically with immediate effect. As I do so my Garmin begins to register sub-10-minute-mile pace for the first time today.

'Who knows what's going to happen?' I tell myself. 'I might as well just go for it.'

The next half-mile is fantastic. Truly fantastic. But I know I'm running on borrowed time. As I approach St Katharine Docks it happens again: pow, again I jump to a stop, again more gasps from the crowd and another willing shoulder for me to lean on. I dig my knuckles in as deep as they'll go to the skin above my left kneecap. The idyllic rhythm of the first 20 miles a distant memory.

I am now in full crisis mode.

The only strategy available, to finish, any way, any how, it really doesn't matter any more.

Paula was right, of course she was. 'Expect at least three dips.'

Christ, I've had all three of mine in the last mile and a half! Not so much a case of 'hitting the wall' as the wall collapsing right on top of me. For the first time I begin to panic. Doubt explodes within me. I question everything. I can no longer think straight.

I need help.

Please.

And then it comes.

Boom.

Most clichés are true, which is how they became clichés in the first place. Ergo, allow me to confirm everything you may have heard with regard to the last 3 miles of the London Marathon. The crowd literally picks every runner up and carries them home. I am in tears as I recall the sensation. It is incredible. A wave of human spirit for us to ride on, all we have to do is try to stay upright. Even though I know my knee is not working any more, my brain has no choice but to 'not feel it'. The crowd won't allow that to happen.

My levels of adrenaline and endorphins have reached a new high. The like of which I had no idea existed. I cannot stop smiling. This is simply extraordinary. Beyond comprehension. Beyond belief. Total Nirvana.

'The crowd will carry you.'

I start to run as fast as I can while being able to sustain it. As the clock ticks slowly by, I am now passing more people than are passing me. Not that any such thing matters per se, but this observation tells me two things:

1. People are pulling up and having to walk all around me, so who's to say I won't be next?

2. I am at my limit, this is definitely a calculated gamble.

Less than 2 miles to go and though my watch is telling me I'm doing fine for pace, each second seems to take longer, therefore it feels longer. My legs start to feel heavy for the first time. Way markers take an age to arrive. I scale them down to consecutive lampposts. But they remain in slow motion.

Then as we dip down again to negotiate the final underpass on the Embankment, the crowds disappear up as we stream by.

My knee goes again, with no one there to lean on this time, I slump against one of the huge concrete slabs. I can hear people screaming encouragement from above as they realize I'm in trouble. I just grab hold of my left ankle with my left hand, pull it up behind me and snap my knee back as hard as I can. I don't know particularily why, it just seems like the right thing to do. I have to get home.

Having not dared to look at my watch for a mile or so I have little or no idea where I am with regard to my dream of a sub-5-hour time. Now, with the chance of having to stop running altogether back on the agenda, I have to look to plan for the worst-case scenario. Feeling slightly nauseous, I glance down. My watch reads 4:41:17.

Yeeeeees!

That means I have NINETEEN minutes left to cross the finish line in a time beginning with 4 hours something. That's all I want. That's what all this has been about. The shuffling at Christmas. The running to Kensington to buy my first proper running kit. The clandestine hours away from my family. The countless visits to Phil the chiropracting genius. The hyper-glycaemic tablets that it took me ages to find online. The life-changing decisions to do with diet, sleep, smoking. The marathon paranoia, i.e. the maranoia, for the fortnight leading up to the race, about not pulling a muscle or stubbing your toe going for a pee in the middle of the night. My new love affair with drinking water and discovering the nuances of the city where I've lived, worked, laughed and cried for the last quarter of a century. The weight loss. The new-found energy. The realization that a pair of trainers and a spare hour or two out in the fresh air will forever give me more joy than a thousand exotic sports cars and a hundred Monaco Grands Prix put together. The list goes on.

And here I stand in the absolute knowledge that, unless I pass out or die on the spot, I can literally crawl to the line from where I am and still record something within the magical 5-hour window.

'It's not a proper marathon unless it's under 5 hours.'

Harsh, but ten words that have stayed with me from the moment I heard them.

This was the moment not to fuck it up. This was the moment not to get greedy. This was the moment to slow the fuck down. This was the moment to give thanks by doing what all amateur runners of any level must always remember to do:

ENJOY, ENJOY, ENJOY.

• • •

And I promise you, that's exactly what I did. I'm almost certain I could have come in a minute or two quicker, but that really wasn't the point. The point was that to run at all is a wonderful thing but to run and complete the greatest fun run in the world was a total and utter honour and a privilege. To have sacrificed soaking up the last ten minutes of such a magical experience for anything, least of all a meaningless quicker time, would have been to render the whole learning process of self-discovery redundant.

A good life is about the journey. A marathon is the perfect metaphor for such a life. Life is not about how much you do or how fast you do it, but how well you do it and how much fun you can have along the way.

From now on whenever I sense any phase or major event in my life coming to an end, I shall remember that last mile of 26 April 2015 when I slowed up, looked around at tens of thousands of smiling faces and waving arms, and remembered to remember.

Once over the line I was grabbed by Matt, the nice man who I cried with and who checked me in on Saturday morning back at the Tower Hotel.

'Chris, we need you for a quick pic.'

'Sure, Matt, but I just need to keep moving for a few minutes otherwise my legs will turn to concrete and I won't be able to walk for the rest of the week.'

Photos done, it was time to track down Tash and the boys who were waiting in the gardens of St James's Palace. More tears, this time of joy, were cascading down Tash's cheeks, the kids not entirely sure what all the fuss was about. They were vaguely aware that Dad had finally done something that Mum was mildly impressed by. Perhaps it was never having experienced this before that was confusing them. This was Tash's kind of challenge, I was speaking her language.

My feet were a mess. I didn't care.

I felt weird generally. I didn't care.

There was barely anyone else around. I didn't care.

There was a man in a giant emu costume lying on the ground next to me. I didn't care.

I was so happy.

Like I had never been happy before.

• • •

The thing about post-London Marathon is there's nothing really to do afterwards. As you wander/hobble back out into reality, you are surrounded by tens of thousands of people, all now going their own separate ways. Some go alone, smiling euphorically to themselves, others in groups quietly reflecting on what a wonderful few hours it's been. I wondered why there's not a party or a free music concert, say in Hyde Park, for everyone to go to afterwards and enjoy a few hours of group closure. Maybe the powers-that-be consider the marathon is the party, and the sooner everyone goes back to where they came from the better. Perhaps they have a point.

And so what do you do after running your first marathon?

The question I had asked everyone I'd met who'd run a marathon in the last six months.

Here's what I did.

I took a cab with the fam until we were a mile from home, where I asked to be dropped off so I could try to walk off some of the stiffness that felt like it was trying to immobilize me for the rest of my life. Noah came with me on his scooter for company.

'Haven't you just run the marathon?' commented a lady walking her dog who must have seen me on the telly.

'Yes, I have,' I beamed.

'Wow, and now you're out playing with your son, that's impressive.'

'Thank you.'

Well, I wasn't going to tell her I was in fact in the park for entirely selfish reasons, was I?

Ten minutes later Noah and I had rendezvoused with wife and son number two in the pub where the kids ordered pizzas, I ordered a Guinness, and Tash a Bloody Mary. After which Tash informed me she'd booked a babysitter and that the grown ups were going out to celebrate.

'The kids can finish their dinner, then you stay here while I take them home and I'll be back in ten minutes.'

All of a sudden I could hear those angels again.

Half an hour later, Tash and I were in Odette's restaurant on Regent's Park Road. After three starters I tucked into a huge steak with a bowl of the most buttery salted new potatoes I've ever tasted, all washed down with a bottle of white wine, a bottle of red and several glasses of house champagne. At no point did I feel full or tipsy, let alone drunk.

And the next day:

Ping!

I was up at 4.30 a.m. as bright as a button, ready for work and a morning of post-marathon glow. Apparently the post-marathon glow is a recognized condition. It's the closest I've ever felt to becoming enlightened other than the time I went down to the business end to see Eli pop out of his mummy's tummy.

The glow lasts between thirty-six and forty-eight hours, after which it disappears, poof, into thin air, as mysteriously as it arrived.

And that was basically that.

My marathon story, from shuffling start to achy breaky finish.

Will I do it again? Yes, absolutely.

Did I wear the new trainers?

Actually, no, I didn't.

They are still in the box.

Whereas my old faithfuls, their glass case is being measured up as I speak.

I want to be buried in them, or cremated in them, or whatever happens to me.

They changed my life.

Forever.

For better.

PART 3

Planning for 'Life Part II'

Ten Things That Make My Life Easier, Simpler and More Relaxed:

10 Wear the same coat every day. No need for constant transfers of stuff from one to the other means almost zero cases of lost keys, forgotten wallets and general all-round wasting of precious minutes, hours, days you'll never see again.

9 Only handle any paperwork once. It either goes where it needs to or straight in the bin, no more piles pending.

8 Only think about a decision once. No more 'Can I let you know tomorrow?' The next time you think about it will be then anyway, so make a decision now.

7 Only use cash wherever possible. It's quicker, it makes us more accountable and it won't be around for much longer – so let's enjoy it before it becomes a museum piece.

6 Don't buy any non-essential non-consumables for a year. Save presents for special occasions. Buying stuff is a habit that can be broken much more easily than one might imagine.

5 Embark on a constant purge of all the stuff you already own. Especially clothes, coats, socks, T-shirts and kitchen spatulas.

4 Have a serious word with yourself about how come you still hang out with certain people from whom you gain nothing. Cut them loose, sooner rather than later.

3 Check out the weather forecast and look forward to bad weather days giving you back time to sort your shit out.

2 Drink more water.

1 Sleep more.

So how do we go about estimating how many heartbeats we have left?

I decided to look around at various people I know who are older than me. Friends and family, work colleagues who I admire, and observe their general level of fitness, awareness and mental sharpness compared to their age. The conclusion I came to was that, with the minimum of self-preservation, everyone from all the above categories was generally very OK till at least their mid sixties, and still OK-ish until their mid-seventies.

It looks like we really are ageing more slowly than our parents, grandparents, aunts, uncles and cousins. Not surprising really, considering they had to survive a terrible and bloody war just so we could lie on the sofa scratching our gonads.

In fact it increasingly looks like we may be the first generation in two thousand years of regular massacres that has managed to slip through the net and not had to endure very much at all.

That doesn't mean we can take life for granted.

I am very good friends with a chap who has been hugely successful in a particular sport. A gentleman who is also widely and fondly regarded as being the life and soul of any party he chooses to grace and lace with his presence.

'What would you change if you could do it all again?' I once asked him.

'That's simple,' he smiled ruefully. 'A couple of years ago at Christmas, I said to one of my kids, who's now grown up, "Come here, give your old dad a hug." At which point, he looked at me and broke down into floods of tears right there and then. "What on earth's the matter, son?" I asked. "You just don't get it, Dad, do you?" He could barely speak, so upset was he, all of a sudden. "You were never there."'

Wow.

'And you know, he was right.'

As you can imagine, this was a real wake-up call for my pal. The moment which crystallized for him the fact that he now has more money left then time, an issue he has since seriously acknowledged and done something about.

How many of us have made that call: 'Don't wait up, I have to work late.' Or, 'You eat with the children, I'll pick something up on the way home.' Or, even more pathetically, sent a text.

These are not just hours we're missing, these are golden nuggets of everything that's important in life – and we are wilfully throwing them away.

These are *super-minutes*, our most valuable time. The time that, if time were a commodity, would be the best-performing stock. Time with loved ones, lost for ever, is totally irreplaceable. No matter how many millions you throw at it, it's not coming back.

Therefore we have a duty to ourselves, and to those dear to us, to identify our own individual super-minutes and guard them with our lives. Bedtimes and bathtimes with the kids, the time when they're at their most reflective and receptive. The most important time to seed their subconscious with sunny, stimulating, positive and loving thoughts before they drift off to sleep.

I'll never forget a particularly joyous session of splish-splashing with my eldest son Noah when, without realizing, I slid down on the bathroom floor, having floated off into a happy cloud of contentment.

'Daddy?' he said.

'Yes, son,' I replied, immediately snapping out of my trance.

'Why have you gone all quiet?' And then he looked at me for an answer, as if his whole world was on hold while he figured out what was going on.

A beautiful moment in time, a moment I will never forget. A moment we would have never experienced had I not put time aside for my super-minutes.

Equally as important are super-minutes with the older members of our family. Those for whom time with those they love is now all that matters. Every day more valuable than the last. Every second, ever more priceless.

Super-minutes in the gym. Super-minutes preparing a special meal for our friends and family. Super-minutes sitting by a stream, or listening to the birds, or lying under a tree in the dappled light of our life-giving sun.

Yet we waste these precious minutes.

Why, I've no idea. All I know is that we need to stop.

Sleep is the land bank of super-minutes, yet how often do we wake up groggy from not giving ourselves enough?

We need to make quality time and then protect that quality time for all it's worth.

A minute late picking the boys up from school may not seem like such a big deal, but they go to sleep at seven. Why would I want to put any of those minutes up to tender?

We can buy time but we can't buy time back. We can't grab the pay-cheque, and then having missed out on a precious family afternoon at Nanna's as a result, ask to swap it back again.

We say 'time is money' when what we should be saying is TIME IS EVERYTHING.

When I think about my radio show and how to fill it every morning, it's not as daunting as you might imagine. Sure, it's three hours long, but it's already scheduled to be full of records, news, sport and travel, before I even begin to get a look in. If I break the issue down, it's much less of a worry bomb – and it's exactly the same when it comes to planning the rest of our lives.

Getting whatever time I have left organized to work for me, as opposed to me working for it, has become a huge priority over the last year. During which I think I've reached a eureka moment.

My biggest enemy isn't time itself but the voice in my head that keeps screaming for me to get on with it because the best is no longer yet to come. When surely the opposite must be true.

When we enter the second half or final third of our lives – mental, physical, social conditions notwithstanding – we will in fact be in a much better place to enjoy our lives as never before.

Guilt over opportunities missed or mistakes made is time's favourite weapon to attempt to knock us off balance and bring on a withering paranoia full of wrong decision-making.

All we have to do is to remember not to fall for such a transparent and unsophisticatated tactic. The greatest thinkers become wiser the nearer they get to their own mortality; great conductors are revered ever more as they enter their ultimate decades; surgeons, doctors and pioneers continue to hold the key to their professions' futures as each day goes by and each new lesson teaches them something they thought they already knew but didn't.

Modern marketing is stupidly against us but it will have no choice but to change when we show it that we have declared that the game has changed.

Time can be looked at as an arrow, pointing either forwards or backwards, or simply as the universe's version of a Post-it note, to let us know when things happened. Can we slow time down? Does time actually matter?

Yes to the first question, and no to the second. Time is like football, overhyped and over-egged.

We are surrounded by clocks telling us time is important just as we can't move for adverts, newspapers and sports channels bleating on about a game, the playing of which makes up barely ten per cent of the content it drives.

Well enough is enough.

I'm calling time on time.

But the future, now that's something else.

The future is nothing to do with time. The future is a direction of travel.

The one unique and brilliant advantage it has over the past is …
WE CAN STILL GO THERE!!!

So come on, buckle up. Let's get on with it.

Top Ten Most Irritating Phrases:

10 Yes, no, I know.
 9 Are you *sure* you're all right?
 8 I'm so old.
 7 You look tired.
 6 To be completely honest with you . . .
 5 Literally.
 4 Fine, fine, really – I'm fine.
 3 Well there it is, you see.
 2 I'm a vegetarian but I eat fish.
 1 Those were the days.

If someone says out loud, like really, in real life, the words, THOSE WERE THE DAYS, do yourself a favour and either slug them in the mouth or run for the hills. Because whatever the heck it is they're talking about, they don't actually mean it.

THOSE WERE THE DAYS are the most nonsensical, annoying, brainless, pointless, worthless, needless, groundless four words of the modern age. The people that employ them are just speaking out loud because they think that's all one has to do to be listened to. They truly believe it's far better to fill a potentially useful void of silent thinking space with mindless detritus rather than risk a moment of slight unease waiting for something actually worth saying to come along.

DON'T EVER WASTE SILENCE.

People who do should be gifted their own special circle of hell. Sandwiched somewhere between pay-day lending barons and online gambling tycoons.

For Christ's sake:

THESE ARE THE BLOODY DAYS.

These, get it? Present tense.

Muppets.

The past is for Happy Snaps, Facebook, graveyards and crematoriums. Days long gone, dead and buried, don't hold a candle to the here and now and what's still to come.

The future is the freedom of not knowing. The future is about to go live in 5, 4, 3, 2, 1 – Blast-off Land! They say we can't time travel. They're wrong, we bloody well can. And we do, all the time. 'To infinity and beyond!' Buzz was right.

'Still to come . . . !' That's what we want. And never before have we been in a better position to make the most of what that's going to be and everything it encompasses.

If you are in or approaching your forties, fifties, sixties, seventies, or who knows even way beyond, you should be throwing your hands up in the air to give thanks.

We have never had more strings to our bow, more knives in our drawer, more rabbits up our sleeve than we have right now: more wit, more wisdom, more experience, more patience, more tolerance, more knowledge, more vision, more of everything of what we need to have the roller-coaster ride of our lives.

All of it effortlessly and unconsciously being prepared for our disposal via the various legs of each of our journeys thus far. The grand culmination of where we came from, where we've been and who and what has influenced us on the way.

At the age of forty-nine, I couldn't be further away from dreading reaching my own half century. I cannot wait for the big Five-O. Bring it on. What downsides could there possibly be?

I can't remember my eighteenth or my twenty-first, and now I know why. Because they were so unimportant compared to where I am, what I'm doing and how I'm feeling now. They didn't mean anything because there was nothing for them to mean.

My belief is beggared when I talk to people of a similar age to me who seem to have honed a whole act out of claiming to feel the opposite of how I do. Why pretend to be like this? What's the point? What good is it going to do them?

Since becoming aware of their legion I have become more adept at avoiding their natural habitats: bars, reunions, late-night chats, the 'Can I have a word?' chats. 'Can I have a word?' is almost always code for 'I have a whole heap of negativity and

I would just love to dump it all over your happy head, if you don't mind.'

Well, I do mind. No thank you. Not any more. People who really need a chat will most likely already be on our 'concern radar'. That's how it is between friends real friends.

This faux 'chat' condition bizarrely can befall even the most intelligent people. I met an erstwhile friend recently who came across as if he was ready for the nursing home even though he's only slightly older than me. I've got to tell you, I have absolutely no idea what door he thought he was knocking on. Most annoying of all, there was no sign of any rational, cognitive process of contemplation, deduction, deliberation or resolution to any part of his conclusion.

As far as he's concerned, all that remains is to annoy our GPs and threaten to burst anyone's bubble who dares smile in our direction.

What the heck is that all about?

And we're talking about an attractive, intelligent, fit, healthy, once extremely prolific ladykiller here. I couldn't believe what I was hearing and I grew yet more incredulous with each weary word of his unremitting woe and general despondency.

Stupidly, I began to reason with him. An hour later, I swore to myself never to see him again. And I haven't.

In much of today's developed world there is a growing pandemic of inaction and excuses perpetrated by a lazy media low on resources, low on confidence and lowest of all on ideas. They are befuddled by what to do save send their paranoid yet still precious days peddling their 'worry more' and 'enjoy less' dogma. This bunch of deathly desperadoes represent the vanguard of the official midlife crisis; no can do, no thank you, collective. They are the doom-mongers whose disciples' main achievement is to have collectively and stupendously given up on themselves and everyone else.

Broken Dreams Inc has just moved in.

Right next to the 'Those were the days' scrapyard.

But they are wrong, my friends.

They are just so bloody wrong.

THESE ARE THE DAYS.

They always have been and they always will be.

Never Go Back: Bollocks to That

The most fun I never had on the television was hosting my Nineties cult music and guest show *TFI Friday*. It looked like a blast from the outside, but for those of us who worked on it, it was a permanent treadmill set to panic, flying by the seat of our pants week in week out, until it eventually came crashing down around our ears. My hubris and all-round mental and emotional fragility being the final fatal nails in its rock 'n' roll coffin.

I always said I'd never bring *TFI Friday* back, despite constant calls to do so, until last year when Channel 4 requested not a series but a one-off anniversary special. 'Now, that could be interesting,' I thought. No pressure, all the fun we forgot to have back in the day, and ultimate closure. (Bearing in mind I walked away from the original series with ten shows to go – never a fan of goodbyes.)

Fuck it, I'm going to be fifty in a minute.

It's all our yesterdays once more.

It's time we gave ourselves permission to party again.

Making Programmes: What I Love

TFI – 10 DAYS TO GO AND COUNTING

Shit, fuck, I mean really. I am so bloody excited about this now. Christ, I hope Channel 4 like what we've come up with enough to order a series or perhaps even two. I mean, I know they must secretly want to. The airtime they're giving our trails is unprecedented. This can't all be for just a one-off.

The thing is, ninety minutes, which is what they've given us for this special, half an hour longer than *TFI* used to run for, just isn't long enough. The huge advantage of having done hundreds of hours of live entertainment television is that we can imagine one draft running order after another. This means we can save both time and money without having to go to a rehearsal, but after some intense deliberation we decide almost everything we have prepared for broadcast is too good to leave out.

What to do then?

As opposed to the original show, which consisted of three or four parts depending on the ad quota, this one-off will be made up of no fewer than six parts. All but one consisting of a live music performance, all of which have now been confirmed: Years & Years and Rudimental representing the here and now, Blur bridging the past and present, and the sizzling combination of Liam Gallagher collaborating with Roger Daltrey for a unique version of 'My Generation' featuring a band consisting of the Stone Roses, Ian Broudie and Zak Starkey just to ensure people are truly blown away.

As the industry stands at the moment, merely by being back on the air we will instantly become the UK's biggest live music show.

It's more than I deserve to be reunited with Will MacDonald, my old producer, *TFI* on-screen sidekick and one of my best pals. The two of us really do work well together. It's like we've never been apart. The truth is we are two television nerds who take great joy in intricately piecing together a TV running order, item after item, second by second, changing the odd word here, the odd camera shot there, whatever it takes to build to a moment or disguise what might be coming up to wrong-foot the viewers.

Guest-wise, we're looking at lots of members of the public who originally appeared as young adults, teenagers, kids and even babies returning for a well-deserved curtain call and a chat about what they've been up to since. We are particularly looking forward to meeting the six-month-old baby with exceedingly big hair; he's sixteen now, still with an amazing barnet apparently.

Celeb-wise, it looks like we have confirmed Lewis Hamilton, who was top of our list. We wanted a big Brit who had never really been seen in a *TFI*-type situation having some fun and being able to relax. Also looking good is Amanda Seyfried, the sassy and super-cool female lead in *TED 2* – big rude toy bear comedy sequel, bound to be huge. Peter Kay has agreed to be our in-house DJ, Jeremy Clarkson has recorded a wee *Top Gear* skit for us and we have walk-ons booked for Olly Murs, Mark Carney – the Bank of England Governor, my old friend John Sentamu – the Archbishop of York, and the *TFI* legend that is Shaun Ryder.

Also in the mix are a gorgeous old couple who've been married for seventy years and a wheelbarrow full of puppies in our all-new-for-2015 'What's Cutest?' slot.

Have to be careful, though. Getting far too enthusiastic on social media. I tweeted the Liam/Roger collaboration, whereupon we were inundated with calls of – How? Where? Really? You sure? Followed by a few calls from Liam's camp asking us to be a bit more 'low key' where his appearing was concerned. Not the exact phrase they used, but I'm sure you get my drift.

Interesting development on the publicity front. After suddenly feeling the need to kick up a storm from next Monday right up to transmission on the Friday, I call my old friend Matthew Freud to toss around a few ideas. He educates me as to the 'new way' publicity works nowadays.

'PR is as much about what happens post an event today as it is pre an event. For example, Comic Relief USA, which recently took place, may only have been watched by 3.5 million people but the sketch where Chris Martin sings with the *Game of Thrones* cast was rewatched over 10 million times on YouTube within twenty-four hours of originally being broadcast. Based on viewing figures on the night alone therefore, there's a good chance Comic Relief USA would not have been recommissioned, but thanks to the post-broadcast social media traffic, it almost certainly will.'

Obvious when someone points such things out. Apparently the same goes for lots of television events – James Corden and his hit late-night US chat-show, for example. Millions more people watch his 'bits' online the day after than watch the 'donor broadcast'. Kids really do watch what they want, when they want, where they want. They neither know nor care where anything was originally broadcast.

'How many bits do you have in your current draft running order that you think might immediately be uploaded to YouTube the moment they're broadcast? That's so so important nowadays, absolutely key.'

My response goes something like this:

'Er . . .'

Quickly, Will and I scrabble through what we have.

'Well, there's potentially the La Ferrari lap round the *Top Gear* track. Every car fan in the world will want to watch that.'

'Good, what else?'

Er, can we get back to you?

Fuck, shit and fuck again. He's bang on the money. Identifiable moments as opposed to a monologue-esque narrative are the modern way and therefore what we need to do. But, thank God, Will and I gradually realize that's what *TFI Friday* has always been anyway: signature bubbles of bonkers hit-and-miss tomfoolery underwritten by an overall and half-grown-up proscenium arch of mega-musical talent and A-list superstar heat. Once we stop hyper-ventilating and count our chicks, we figure we have at least fifteen instantly YouTube-able bits.

Phew, we might yet get to be 'down with the kids'.

Wednesday, 3 June

9 DAYS TO GO

Sneak home to Ascot to see Tash and the kids. So worth it. We watch the rough cut of the TV ad for the first-ever *TFI Friday* compilation album I filmed against a green screen last week. It's come out well. Except I look more lardy than I want to. Don't know how, I'm still weighing in at 12 stone 6 pounds. Do I starve myself next week? With all the old footage we're planning to play in, there will be constant comparisons to then and now. It's not so much a vanity thing (I'm lying), more a case of not wanting to look too ancient in case Channel 4 do consider moving forward with a series.

Also clothes-wise – because I don't really care about, or have many clothes – I am in danger of falling into that age-old TV trap of trying too hard to look like me. I remember bumping into Hugh Fearnley-Whittingstall one day, out shopping with his stylist.

'I need to look more like telly Hugh than real-life Hugh apparently!' he shouted while being dragged up yet another escalator.

Television is certifiably bonkers.

Thursday, 4 June

8 DAYS TO GO

Overnight I receive confirmation we have definitely secured access to the old *Top Gear* track in five days' time – next Tuesday, three days before *TFI* goes out. This is brilliant news.

Following the shock departure of Clarkson from his legendary car show after an alleged drunken fracas with a producer, there has been much speculation about who might take over. My name has been the bookies' favourite from the off, so we thought it might be fun to stir it up a bit by doing some filming down at Dunsfold where they make the show.

One of the things they never got to do in the end was put the Stig in the new super-car La Ferrari to see if he could break the lap record. This is what we planned to do.

Waking up to this news at 4.30 a.m., I ping an email off to Ferrari in Italy:

Finally, a La Ferrari is going to get to do a flying lap around the *Top Gear* track. It's bound to be the fastest yet, which can only be good news. Is there any chance of secretly getting Sebastian Vettel or Kimi Räikkönen to be the driver of the car on their way back from the Canadian Grand Prix? The lap will be shown on a cult UK TV show that makes its return after a nineteen-year sabbatical three days later. Once we post the film up on the Internet during the show, it's bound to be a sensation.

One of two emails I send before getting out of bed, the other to the absolutely bloody marvellous Sam Smith. After picking up FOUR Grammy awards and embarking upon his first-ever world tour, Sam has experienced a voice issue serious enough to require surgery. As a result he's not been able to speak – at all – for almost a month now. I get the feeling he might need a little pick-me-up.

Dearest Sam,

Hope your recovery is going as well as it possibly can. Meanwhile, how about some light relief?

Our crazy TV show is back on the air a week on Friday, live on Channel 4 – the one you did that brilliant 'I like to juggle' trail for. Booked to play live, we have: Blur, Liam Gallagher, Roger Daltrey, Rudimental and Years & Years plus we have Lewis Hamilton, Amanda Seyfried, Jeremy Clarkson, Peter Kay, Samuel L. Jackson, Olly Murs, Kirstie Allsopp, the Archbishop of York, Sir Kenneth Branagh and Mark Carney, the Governor of the Bank of England. Now, I know you can't talk, but would you like to be there? We can write a little funny, silent sketch for you – which would be hilarious. People would go bananas if you turned up unexpectedly. And so would I!!!!

Plus, it will be a right laugh. Double promise.

Sam had already recorded our first-ever *TFI* viral trail entitled '100 days to go'. He has both fantastic timing and fastastic karma. I woke up this morning with a feeling in my tummy telling me to get him involved. We shall see. I just want this special to be bursting at the seams with unpredictable possibility.

I head off to meet Paul, George and Ringo – my new nicknames for Claire, Will and Suzi. (Claire and Suzi made up the original gang of four along with Will and I who produced *TFI*.) We'd arranged to meet in a Swedish café round the corner from Radio 2; questionable food but again, excellent karma. We're there from 10 a.m. till 1 p.m., another highy productive session with regards to the running order. Every day we're just turning the screw. Refining and tightening. With over a week to go, we've already paid more attention to it this *TFI* than all the previous scripts put together.

Spend the rest of the day reviewing archive footage – my God there's so many bits I'd forgotten about. Helen Mirren and me falling in love in the rain, a whole black-and-white Sixties title sequence filmed in central London, the precursor to an interview with Michael Caine at his Chelsea penthouse, Noel Gallagher in my living room on the show we did live from my flat, losing a toss and then welshing on a bet, a whole *Lock Stock* parody directed by Guy Ritchie. All absolute gold.

Also have a text exchange with Lewis Hamilton – still sweating on a confirmation from him, he was on his plane flying to the Canadian Grand Prix – desperately wants to do the show but may have a timing issue with an event he's committed to for Samuel L. Jackson and his charity on the same night. Fingers crossed.

Review the Clarkson skit we filmed last week when he popped in to my radio show to give his first interview post alleged punch-up. He was very open and honest. After we came off the air we took a ride around London in La Ferrari during which I asked him for a *Top Gear* presenting lesson. He was a great sport, very funny, as usual.

'You haven't even been offered my old job have you?' he says during our exchange on camera.

'No,' I answer, crestfallen.

'I knew it. No one has.'

And it was true. Lots of zealous agents were making out their various clients had been approached by the BBC but not a single phone call had been made. The truth was that the BBC was hoping James May and Richard Hammond would carry on as a duo. This is what we all wanted to happen.

Also confirmed to drive the La Ferrari was super-quick top bloke BTCC Champion driver Jason Plato. He would be our 'Stink' to *Top Gear's* Stig for our La Ferrari flying lap.

All good. Still getting far too excited.

Receive a message from Jay Hunt, boss of Channel 4: she's excited too, has heard we've been working hard. Expectations are high. Excellent, so they should be. Keeps the pressure on.

Friday, 5 June: 4.45 a.m.

ONE WEEK TO GO

Close to finalizing the running order once and for all. There comes a point in televison when you have to say, that's it, so that everyone has a chance to get to grips with what we're going to try to achieve.

Radio show in a bit with guests including motorbike guru Charlie Boorman, TV hottie Emma Willis, he of the big phone – Dom Joly, broadcasting legend Johnnie Walker and Mika singing four songs live. After that it's straight up to Glasgow for a *One Show* live music special and hopefully back in time for *Saturday Kitchen* tomorrow morning to kick off a week of *TFI Friday* publicity and promotion.

Saturday, 6 June

6 DAYS TO GO

Air travel's interesting nowadays, don't you think? Getting slower instead of quicker. I was bumped off my original flight yesterday after it was over-booked and the return flight to Heathrow was delayed due to being late in-bound and then, get this: 200-km headwinds. All of which conspired to make us the last plane to dock back at Heathrow before the end of business. I got home at 1 a.m. this morning: twenty-one-hour day. Mmm, lovely.

The folks at *Saturday Kitchen* have very kindly squeezed me in to what is already a packed show. For the first time they are going to have a celeb kitchen porter nipping in and out. The idea being at some point this will give me the chance to mention *TFI Friday* is back in six days' time. As it turns out, the front man of one of *TFI*'s fave bands, Supergrass, is also booked to appear. Gaz Coombes and I fire up the retro Nineties chat at every given opportunity: Blur vs Oasis, Jarvis Cocker mooning Michaeael l Jackson at The Brits and then being hauled off by the police.

Thank you Amanda Ross, James Winter and James Martin for freeing up some precious *SK* minutes. I owe you – big time.

Before the show, not such good news, however.

Fifteen minutes prior to transmission Peter Kay emails me. He can't make the show in six days' time. I call him, he picks up immediately. I'm still talking to him as I hear the SK theme tune being played in. We're on the air. 'Got to go, Peter.'

'I'm so sorry.'

These things happen.

Onwards.

Sunday, 7 June

5 DAYS TO GO

Up early again for more promo, this time on Channel 4's *Sunday Brunch*, a show that began life on BBC2 as *Something for the Week-*

end and is now in its tenth year, having evolved into a three-hour Sunday-morning extravaganza. Today featuring the radiant British actress Samantha Bond, a new up-and-coming girl/boy music combo from the US by the name of Lion Babe, Mary McCartney talking veggie cooking, the acting guru that is Sir Ian McKellen, and myself.

Again, *SB* have done us a huge favour by having me on – Tim Lovejoy being an old pal and Suzi our exec having been one of the original founding mamas of the *Sunday Brunch* production team. The only thing you have to be careful of is that on a show that's three hours long it's easy to forget you're on telly at all and end up a little too relaxed. Good for the viewers but dangerous if you let something slip by accident. As an antidote to this I write on the back of my left wrist *DFFSFYOLT* – a little mantra I adopted a few years ago: Don't For Fuck's Sake Forget You're On Live Television.

One of the themes of the show is bucket lists, following up on a news report that only one in five Brits feel they are living life to the full. There is a list of 37 things that one ought to have done by a certain age. They ask all the guests to estimate how many they could tick off. I'm way ahead with over twenty: one of the panelists claims not to have done any. I don't believe him.

When it comes to the interview, Tim and Simon ask some pretty pertinent questions. Or do I just think that because they allow me some pretty decent answers? Like the old adage, 'You think your wife has a great sense of humour? All she's doing is laughing at all your godawful jokes.'

They ask if I'm doing *Top Gear*, I tell them, 'Some *Top Gear* filming has taken place.' Keep stirring the pot.

Meet up with Will, Suzi and Claire for a rare Sunday meeting, the first in our careers, in my local pub in the afternoon to talk about the running order prior to our meeting with my pal and co-writer, Danny Baker, on Monday.

It's a beautiful day. We all hit the rosé, I don't even like rosé – the devil's work: headache guaranteed and only ever tastes bearable at best, usually 'cos it's ice-cold and therefore doesn't really taste of anything. Does anyone actually like the taste of rosé? Except for English rosé which I later discover is the best in the world, the sparkling rosé best of all.

This is the first time I have sensed our 'special' is in danger of being over-thought. But I like that, it's reassuring. Means we've been putting the work in. Claire leaves first, then Suzi, Will and I go on a restaurant crawl – a starter in one place, a main course in another. We part company circa 21:00 hours. I'm done. I go home and treat myself to a small brandy and a couple of squares of dark chocolate. It's been a good day.

I phone my wife. 'You sound chirpy,' she remarks. Marriage-speak for drunk.

I am.

Monday, 8 June

4 DAYS TO GO

Awake at 3 a.m. – and the weird thing? Not tired at all. I know I really need more sleep but I feel good anyway, one more hour would get me to my minimum required six. I get there somehow and by the time I set off for work at 5.45 a.m. I am totally recharged. Comfortable in my own skin, looking up at a bonus California clear blue sky, I fairly skip through Regent's Park and into the West End. My Radio 2 show, the key to everything, a loyal wife as opposed to a fly-by-her-nightie mistress.

After which, it's all about the *TFI* script. Our first meeting with Danny Baker at the new studios. Not only do I want him to see the new layout ahead of show day, but I haven't been there in a while and you never know.

Good job too. The team is unsure about the orientation of the main interview area. We decide to flip the whole bar round, far better energy and less restricted views for our audience. People need to be able to see the show to enjoy the show. Amazing how often this isn't the case in a television studio.

Danny takes everything we pitch him in that 100-mph way of

his, declares he's across it and disappears off after a couple of hours, deep into the heaving human mass that is Central London at lunchtime. He really is a wonder of nature, like a volcano. Don't know where he gets his energy from. He never does a tap of exercise and eats almost exclusively white-bread door-stopper sandwiches, red meat and giant wedges of Cheddar cheese. Usually washed down with a bottle or two of Chablis.

Return home, well almost. Bump into the fragrant Sharleen Spiteri walking her dog in the local park. We stop to chat and while doing so are bibbed by Loz – Laurence Fox, my ex Billie's husband. I only catch his gaze for a millisecond but instantly I recognize the look.

'Fancy a quick pint?', that's what it says.

After Shar and I finish up, I text Loz straightaway.

ME: PINT?

LOZ: BE THERE IN 5

Hurrah! Karma decrees I drop Shar a text too in case she fancies a swifty. She does. Ten minutes later the three of us are in the pub.

Bed soon after.

Hit the mattress like a felled oak.

Thud.

Out for the count.

Tuesday, 9 June

3 DAYS TO GO

Meet Will after the radio show. Drive to Dunsfold Aerodrome to film *Top Gear* sequence. We take off in a Ferrari 458 Spyder loaned to us from my pals at Maranello in Egham, Surrey, just off the A30. Lovely way to get there, but more importantly an excellent car for surveillance laps so we can save the La Ferrari for the flying, record-breaking-attempt laps.

A full-on multi-camera film crew is there to meet us, all ex *Top Gear*. They have shot countless of these signature flying laps for the actual show. Jason has been there for half an hour or so, everyone is raring to go.

Several paparazzi have been spotted clicking away in the bushes. I don't mind, good luck to them, we've all got to make a living somehow. We're only a bunch of blokes playing with super-cars, it's not as if we are harbouring the second coming. Besides, when you are launching a new show, any publicity helps. Within minutes, photos of what we're doing begin to appear all over the Internet.

The spotter laps go well, Jason is cool as a cucumber and confident we can post the world's fastest time around what has become one of the most famous bits of tarmac and concrete in the universe.

He goes to change into his cover-alls while we set up the cameras in one of four positions we will need to shoot from in order to be able to screen a whole lap on *TFI Friday* in three days' time. This is properly cool. I begin to mischievously wonder what it might be like to hang out here once a week for a few weeks a year, ppututting together a new version of whatever the new *Top Gear* might end up becoming.

Little did I know.

And I REALLY DIDN'T know.

Problem, though!

Big, big, big problem. Our beautiful million-pound Fezza has got the hump and decided her computer needs to talk to the mother ship back in Italy before she can bring herself to whizz round the track at anything like the speed we would like her to. Several very clever Ferrari technicians get on the case, but the mission is cast in serious doubt. At which point the new me kicks into action.

The me who used to see red and freak out in situations like this has been dispatched, replaced by nice, helpful me, who realizes we're a long time dead and nothing's more important than doing what you're doing with a smile on your face, if you're doing what you're doing purely out of choice. Why else would you bother?

That's not to say a wee bit of squeeky bum doesn't go amiss, in this instance just enough for me to call my mum who, bizarrely, only lives two miles away from Dunsfold, and ask her to perhaps save the day.

'Mum, how do you fancy being perhaps the last person to record a timed lap around the *Top Gear* circuit?'

Despite being just about to leave for an afternoon trip down to Worthing with my sister, she agrees to come to the rescue. What ensues is a full-scale film shoot starring 89-year-old Minnie beginning in her garage as she emerges determined and steely-eyed, back-lit on her ten-year-old mobility scooter, and ending with her kicking Jason and the La Ferrari's butt. Not exactly we planned, but much funnier and, who knows, may actually end up being better telly on the night.

We run out of track time without the Ferrari turning another wheel. Good decision, well made. Or at least *a* decision, well made. We arrange to try to attempt to break the lap record on Friday morning. It will still be a coup if we can manage to make it happen. For now, though, Minnie is the 'star, thrashing a million-pound car.'

Head back for Ascot and a late dinner with Tash and the kids. Again a long day but not particularly tired. Feeling blessed with energy all this week.

Once the kids are in bed, Tash and I watch a docu-film on Netflix: *Bobby Fischer Against the World*. All about when chess was bigger than the World Cup back in the Seventies, as the Cold War was in full swing. Russia and the United States considered chess to be the ultimate metaphor for war, the perfect propaganda if your man could beat their's.

The gripping film chronicles how the uber-eccentric Fischer beats Boris Spassky in what became the most infamous coming together of two Grand Masters a comedy of errors that took place in Iceland of all places. Fischer went on to win after Spassky pulled out, unable to cope with the precocious 29-year-old's genius and antics. After which Fischer himself, unable to deal with what he had become, gradually grew more and more of reclusive, eventually going insane and denouncing his Jewish upbringing. A brilliant movie about a brilliant but tragically tortured soul.

Afterwards I sleep like a deed man.

---

2 DAYS TO GO

Bizarrely, nothing scheduled after the radio show today, but I'm working back in big-time telly, that's just not how it is. Within ten minutes of me arriving home, Will's on the phone. He wants another run at the script.

Sure, no probs. 'I'm loving being back in the *TFI* groove, bring it on.'

We begin with the opening titles and pre-titles sketch and plod on from there. Five hours later we are in the pub, Guinness having now replaced the endless bottles of water but Will's laptop still a-glowing. We have to get to the end of the show. Eventually we do, in a restaurant over steak frites and a half-decent bottle of Bordeaux.

We're happy with our days work, feeling we've captured the essence of old and new with the right balance of each. The guest quota is hotting up. Lewis Hamilton has now confirmed but has requested to remain unannounced until the night – he will be coming straight from that prior Samuel L. Jackson engagement, but doesn't want anyone to know he's in town beforehand. Fair enough, as long as he arrives at 9.56 p.m. or earlier, which is when he's due to be introduced. Please God.

Sir Kenneth Branagh, Ewan McGregor, Noel Fielding, Kirstie Allsopp, U2 and Nick Grimshaw have all now also agreed to appear one way or another. More good news, my favourite booking the wonderful Archbishop of York, John Sentamu, has purchased his train ticket. I love the bones of that guy.

I arrive home circa 10 p.m., pour myself a modest brandy and break off a couple more squares of chocolate from the never-ending bar in the fridge. What a taste combo chocolate and brandy is. But two of the worst things you can possibly consume the night before you have to speak on the radio the next day. Chocolate gives you phlegm and brandy dries your throat out. Hey ho, too late now.

I slide into bed, call Tash for our touch-base goodnight chat and by the time my head hits the pillow the script is but a fond and fading memory. No point in even beginning to go over what we've written so far. It's bound to change at least five more times before it settles down and tells 'us' what 'it' wants to be.

I fall asleep knowing tomorrow is going to be another big day. They all are at the moment.

But little did I have any idea just how big.

When I closed my eyes I was eighteen hours away from receiving 'that text' about 'that job'.

Thursday, 11 June

1 DAY TO GO

After the radio show I go to the *TFI* studio for a rehearsal of Parts 1 to 3. We call it a block through. It goes well. We're all surprised just how well, and it gets big laughs from the crew. All-important, those crew laughs – they tell you where the script is flying and where it needs some urgent attention. After Part 3 we realize we are already way over time and need to start cutting immediately. This always feels disappointing at first, but it's key to making a good, tight show. When entertainment shows start to spread they become leaden very quickly, and once that happens viewers begin to lose interest at an exponential rate.

We drop the opening sketch and any parts of the first half of the show that are just gags, as opposed to items with gags attached. When we're done with Part 3, that's it for today, we'll pick up where we left off tomorrow ahead of the dress rehearsal.

Will and I walk home to my house. I need a quick ten minutes' power nap before we revise what should be the final draft of the running order and script. Refreshed, I'm back downstairs with Will in my living-room. We take up our usual positions of Will sitting with his laptop perched precariously on his knees – which is always guaranteed to take several tumbles during a writing session. While he does that I lie on the sofa opposite, spouting out whatever nonsense comes into my mind like a ginger Barbara Cartland minus the make-up and pink chiffon négligée.

I've never known what it is that makes Will and I work so well as a 'two' but all I know is that I am much better with him than without him. Even when he's not around but I know he's back at the office, I still come up with much better ideas than when he's not involved.

We begin by going through the words, concentrating on the rhythm. It's good, but everything is playing longer than we first thought. This means even more stuff has to go. We carry on squeezing and cutting until Will declares he needs some food and nips out for twenty minutes to the café around the corner while I check my emails and texts. The last of which is a text from Andy Wilman, the former exec producer of *Top Gear* who, along with his old school pal Clarkson, resurrected the show back in 2002. They tore up the rule-book and transformed it from a safe little parochial half-hour magazine show in the Seventies, Eighties and Nineties into the worldwide Car-mageddon television phenomenon it is today.

Andy, along with Jeremy, has often cited *TFI Friday* as part of the inspiration for their reinvention, the industrial warehouse-looking vibe, the general deconstruction of what a television show is usually like. That's what his very welcome text alluded to:

> Hello mischief maker. Just wanted to wish you best of luck for *TFI* – can't wait and really excited about showing my Noah what we pillaged. Also, do you want me to send you a copy of the final *Top Gear*?

Love that he opens with 'Hello mischief maker'. Pot/kettle or what? But lovely of him nonetheless. I see this message as a very good omen, perfectly timed. But just how ironically perfectly timed? I was about to find out.

Will returns from his food run and we resume our cutting-and-pasting collaboration. Half an hour later my text alert goes off again.

This time it's Mark Linsey, Controller of Entertainment Commissioning for BBC Television. His text reads:

> Are you still up for a conversation re: *Top Gear*? If so please call me.

That was it, two sentences, fifteen simple words.
An explosion went off in my head.
Air raid sirens.
A volley of klaxons.

> Are you still up for a conversation re: *Top Gear?* If so, please call me.

Whaaaaaaat?
Of course I am up for a conversation re: *Top Gear*.
I will always be up for a conversation re: *Top Gear*, even after I become worm food.
Will is busy rearranging, he is the cutting-and-pasting king. I excuse myself. I try to remain calm. I want to scream but I can't. Besides, I don't know exactly what 'Are you still up for a conversation re: *Top Gear*' means precisely yet. It could mean anything. I go downstairs to the ground floor, out of earshot.
Once on the phone, Mark informs me that the BBC have now ruled out a return to *Top Gear* for James and Richard as well as the already erstwhile Jeremy. He explains that the BBC had left the door open for them to return but that door could not be left ajar indefinitely. Since, as of twenty-four hours ago, they had chosen not to walk through it, it was time for everyone to move on.
I'm blown away. I can't quite get my head round the fact that James and Richard don't want to carry on Jeremy-less. The brand is so hot and as long as they both agree to stay, not just one of them, the *TG* global audience really wouldn't mind. I know I certainly wouldn't. Regardless of what they might potentially be offered elsewhere as a threesome, I think in their shoes I would have at least given it a go.
But now, that's suddenly not the point. Mark said: 'We want to

give the show to you. You can do anything with it you see fit. Complete creative control. You pick the production team, the presentation team, everything. We want you, your vision, your production experience, as well as being the face of the whole shooting match, of course.'

Oh my good God.

You never know what's around the corner.

I can't believe I'm now being asked if I would like to take over my favourite television show. I mean, it's true when all the shit hit the fan back in March I did receive a message asking me to keep an open mind about what might happen with the programme in the future, but I genuinely presumed this was out of courtesy rather than any real intent.

Fuck. Fuck. Fuck.

Shit. Shit. Shit.

● ● ●

'You all right?' asks Will as I walk back into the living room.

'No, not really,' I reply.

'What's the matter?'

I have to tell him. We've shared so many things over the years, this will just be the latest in a long and mercurial line. Besides, I'm obviously in shock, it's clear something major has just happened.

I take him through the conversation I've just had.

'Fuck,' he says.

'That's what I said.'

'That's mental, did you know they had you in mind?'

'No fucking way. We all thought James and Richard were going to come back. They still were until last night.' Which is 100 per cent true.

When it was first announced that Jeremy had 'left' I'd been playing with the idea of stepping in for him on the radio but only as a bit of fun. When the bookies then put me down as favourite to get the job, I very quickly, clearly and loudly ruled myself out. This was partly because I didn't want to become a pawn in what could easily become a very ugly game, but primarily because *Top Gear* is the Holy Grail of factual entertainment and one of the best-produced television shows of all time. The manner in which some people were glibly and shamelessly touting themselves to take over was to my mind insane. The perfect way of telling the world they didn't have the first clue of what a monumental task that might be.

Not only were the vast majority of these names being mentioned nowhere near experienced enough in telly, none of them had any real conversations with the car world. *Top Gear* is one of the toughest gigs out there. That's why it's so bloody good.

'So what do you think?'

'I think I have to say yes. It's what I do for a living and it is as big as it gets. If I say no, I might as well pack up and go home.'

'But you are home . . .'

• • •

After calling Mark back to scream, 'YEEESS PLEEEASE, YOU BET YOUR GRANNY I WOULD LIKE TO TAKE ON *TOP GEAR*,' this bolt out of the blue instantly had a positive effect on *TFI Friday*. From that moment on a mist lifted, Will and I began to relax. Tomorrow night we really were going to party like it's 1999.

In fact within an hour, Will and I were back in the pub, still tinkering with the running order on Will's laptop, but becoming happier by the minute with where we were at. The combination of *TFI Friday*, three pints and the *Top Gear* news was just what the muse ordered.

As Will carried on tap-tapping at his keyboard, my attention wandered to the crowd of enthusiastic drinkers on the pavement outside, bathed in the golden sun of a gorgeous summer evening. Looking closer I recognized one tall guy in the French-style black -and-white stripy top. It's the lovely Nick Grimshaw, my BBC colleague and host of my old programme, the Radio 1 *Breakfast Show*. Gradually Nick and I have become good friends, and now often exchange views and chat about a whole host of subjects.

He looks so cool, relaxing outside with his Ray-Bans on, his long legs that seem to go on for ever and that signature sparkling white smile of his. I have no idea who the girl beside him is, but she looks even cooler: gold-rimmed shades, flip-flops, dark skin, blonde bobbed hair, gorgeous. Wow to both of them.

They're doing their thing and we're doing ours, so we leave them to it for now. A few minutes later, however, the girl comes inside to get another round of drinks. Will and I are sitting next to the bar by the door on two old, battered, wicker chairs – my favourite spot in my favourite North London pub.

'Hi,' she purrs 'Nick's out there, he says hi but doesn't want to disturb you as he can see you're obviously working.'

And he knows what we're working on. Coincidentally, only yesterday I'd asked Nick to be part of the show, a bit where we were going to do the speed-dating version of a chat-show, at which point several well-known faces would run out one by one to answer a question each and take a bow: Noel Fielding, Kirstie Allsopp, Olly Murs, Stephen Merchant and Ricky Wilson had all agreed to join in.

'Hey, no, tell him it's fine if he wants to come and join us, we're actually done for the day. We just didn't want to bother you because you both looked so happy out there.'

'Oh, OK, we will then, if you're sure that's all right.'

The more this woman talks and smiles, the more beguiling I realize she is.

After she leaves, 'Do you know who that was?' Will whispers under his breath.

'No idea.'

'Only Rita bloody Ora.'

Bloody hell! I really didn't have a clue. I'm not up with the current pop scene and when I do watch television, other than sport, the news and *Top Gear*, it's almost exclusively via Catch Up or Netflix. But even I've heard of Rita Ora and caught her on *The Voice* a couple of times. I also remember the whole Brits thing that she was nominated for earlier this year. But she looks so different in the flesh.

A few minutes later, in come the two beautiful young things and plonk themselves down with youthful aplomb next to us two crusties. Their energy immediately turbo-charges the conversation and volume to a different level. They are excited, and for good reason.

Turns out he and Rita have both been signed up as the new judges on the forthcoming series of *X Factor*. The world has not yet been told officially, this is classified information. Cool. They are obviously great friends, thrilled to bits and looking forward to every minute of it.

Eventually, after more *X Factor* gossip and why Kate Moss recently had a fracas with an air stewardess on an EasyJet flight, resulting in her being thrown off the plane (Nick knows everyone!), talk turned to *TFI Friday* and Nick's cameo role.

'Ah, that sounds well fun,' says Rita.

'Well, you can do similar if you like,' suggests Will. The more celebs we can get on and the less time they appear for, the funnier the 'bit' will be. Seconds later we've confirmed another guest. Rita is in.

Marvellous.

Will and I stayed for one more beer before bidding our young friends night-night and heading for our regular steak frites *avec vin rouge*.

Friday, 12 June: 3.06 a.m.

Ding! Bolt upright, wide awake as awake can be. Not the best news ever, with a radio show to do in three hours and then the most important television show of my career twelve hours later. But with the prospect of *Top Gear* on the horizon, sleeping for longer than absolutely necessary would be impossible.

Try for half an hour to nod off again. It's a lost cause. Turn instead to going through Part 1 of what is now 'tonight's' running order in my head. It feels good, concise and most importantly a comfortable watch, which is usually a good watch.

I send a 140-character tweet:

Aaaaaaaaaaaaaaaaaaaaaaaaaaaaaaaaaaaaaaarrrrrrrrrrrrrrrrrrrrrrrrrr-
rrrrrrrrgggggggggggggggggggggggggggggggggggggggghhhhhhhhhh-
hhhhhhhhhhhhhhhhhhhhhhhhhh!

Immediately people begin to reply:

@PeterGraydon: @achrisevans Can't sleep? Too excited?
expect u r dressed, sitting and waiting on the edge of bed.
#Busyday
@BenWinston [James Corden's US TV producer]: @achris-
evans enjoy every min. It was greatest show of all time without
even looking like it was trying. We can't wait to relive it with you.
@BattagliaAlan: @achrisevans what have you done now??

Barely any abuse, another first and another good omen. Not
that I get much abuse anyway – yet, that is. I'm bound to get loads
next week when it's announced I'm the new face of the show whose
owners received a petition signed by a million Clarkson fans
demanding he not be sacked. Not that abuse of any kind bothers
me, especially from people I've never met.

I really don't understand why some famous people declare they
are suddenly 'leaving Twitter' in a hissy fit of exaggerated outrage
after someone publishes a post slagging them off. Trolls, yes, I agree
they are nasty, rotten and spineless individuals who should be
banned life forever, let alone from social media. But as far as being
on the receiving end of their bile is concerned, I have found they
get bored of themselves way more quickly than we could possibly
be offended by whatever they've written. From a Twitter following over two million I generally have a relatively abuse-free time.
Twitter for me is a useful source gauging what people are thinking,
as well as a constant source of fresh ideas, observation, reflection,
humour and information.

No chance of me getting back to sleep. I surrender. I'll have to
catch up this afternoon.

Make a quick cup of tea before going through interview's for Friday's radio show, guest and live music day. Today: Gary Barlow,

Boris Becker, Stephen Merchant, Rod Stewart and live music from Joss Stone. It's 4.30 a.m. That should be just enough to take my mind of *TFI* for a while.

9.30, radio show over. Never seen Messrs Barlow and Becker so up for a laugh; Stephen Merchant was his usual delightful self, so funny and always with such great warmth. Can't wait to see the West End play he's appearing in. As for Joss Stone, she fairly tore the roof off the studio with the four stunning live numbers she treated us to.

All good.

By 10.05 I'm back out in the London sunshine. Nooo! Really don't want it to be such a nice day; 'the hottest this year' the papers are saying. Hot weather and balmy, sunny Friday nights are TERRIBLE for viewing figures.

We shall see.

Go to the gym for a steam, my throat and voice are on the brink of waving the white flag. Please God not that, not today. Today is a good day to go to church. I seriously consider it; if I have time, I will. In the steam room, a guy asks me if am I going to take the *Top Gear* job, the question I've been asked every five minutes since 'Punchgate'.

But this is the first time I have genuinely had to lie, because I have taken the *Top Gear* job. A good lesson – I need to get this story out there as soon as poss. It's OK to fib to a bloke in the steam room, but if a heavyweight journalist comes at me with the same question and I deny it, well, that's how wars start and careers go up in smoke.

After showering I go for a quiet five-minute relax by the pool. In between sips of water I lie back and close my eyes to contemplate what the rest of the day might have in store.

Most important of all, though, like the last mile of the marathon, I drill myself on how I mustn't forget to enjoy what's about to unfold. I am content beyond words, to the extent I feel myself unexpectedly drifting off into a bonus power-nap. I must need it.

But no.

No way.

Not so fast, sonny.

Suddenly I am wide awake.

As alert as I have ever been. Ice-cold with realization.

A realization that has just hit me smack-bang between the eyes.

'Fuuuuuuuuuuuuuuuck!' I yell out loud.

'What the fuck are we doing, dropping the kids who lost out on the speedboat and the car?'

Where this thought has spontaneously sprung from, I have no idea. I wasn't even thinking about it. Bloody subconscious up to its tricks again.

The reason we were bringing them back in the first place was because we'd originally made them cry in front of millions of people for no good reason whatsoever. A much-deserved apology was more than a decade overdue, and now what had we gone and done?

The show that had made two gorgeous innocent little souls cry proper upset tears, live in front of the nation as small, vulnerable, children, had booked them, got them all excited, and bloody well CANCELLED them!

Had we learnt nothing?

There was no way I could let this happen. It would be such bad karma. 'Hey, kids we made you cry then and look! Nothing's changed. We're still lost in showbiz having lost all sense of what's right and what's wrong.'

But the fact remained, as the show stood at the moment, we still didn't have enough time.

All this week, however, I've been in a really good place in my heart and head. It's been as if every time I've needed an idea, it was there, almost like it was on tap. And – ping! It happens again: I decide there's only one thing for it. I will call the boss of Channel 4 and request more time. Actually, I send a text.

Dear Jay, curve ball, any chance we could have more time
tonight, we're having to drop loads of good stuff that we might
never be able to do again.

No more than ten seconds later Jay Hunt, the no-nonsense shoot-from-the-hip, straight-talking Channel 4 controller calls me back.

'How much time do you need and how good is this material you're going to have to leave out?'

Of course, we're already scheduled for ninety minutes, sixty minutes more than ever before.

'Ooh, I don't know, fifteen mins, twenty-five max. The stuff is as good as everything we've ever done. All potential television gold.'

'All right, if you're sure, let me see if I can make it work. Stand by.'

Five minutes later she's back on the phone and the kids are back in the show.

'Yes!'

That feels like such the right decision.

At 11.30 I go to record two radio interviews for *TFI Friday* – the first with Matt Wells from 6 Music. Matt co-hosts their Breakfast Show and actually performed on *TFI Friday* five times as a bassist in a band called Headlight. He couldn't have been more positive about the show and the 6 Music crowd is an audience we need to reach out to. After Matt it's Steve Wright, one of my broadcasting heroes.

Steve pre-records all his interviews and, like Matt, is very enthusiastic about *TFI Friday*'s return. There is a lot of love and goodwill out there for the show, much more than I dared hoped for. That said, there's going to need to be for a new show to work, even a new old show with a proven track record; all the stars will have to be aligned, come nine o'clock tonight.

After Steve it's back to New Broadcasting House for a face-to-face sit down with Mark Linsey re: *Top Gear*.

This may well be the maddest day of my life so far.

I've met Mark many times before. His demeanour towards me having warmed gradually over the years. Let's face it, I wasn't exactly the safest pair of hands for a good while. Serious telly people weren't going to just welcome me back, give me a whole bunch of shows and forget about the train crash that happended last time I had a hit run.

But today, when I walk into the room and hold out my hand to shake his, he doesn't even bother, just coming in for the full-on man hug. Fine by me, I'm comfortable with that. It also bodes very well for our meeting. A full-on man hug is not a sign that the person giving it does not want you in their lives.

He may actually be more excited than me.

I tell Mark what I think could and should be done with the biggest brand the BBC has ever had. The more I talk, the more his smile broadens to threaten the perimeter of his face. I'm obviously saying the right things. He becomes more and more animated. Heat meeting heat, energy meeting energy, two positives coming together and sparking off each other like flailing electric cables. Our combined heart-rate easily over 300 bpm.

'Days like this are what it's all about,' he enthuses.

I couldn't agree more.

'Let's just do a deal and make the show.'

'I need to contact your agent.'

'I thought you might say that. He's downstairs waiting to get in the lift and come up.'

'Perfect. Have agent – will deal. Let's get on with it then. Off you go, good luck with tonight, we'll all be watching.'

'You're on, Michael,' I whisper to my partner-in-crime of the last thirty years back down in the foyer.

I really have no idea what happens next, I never have. I leave it to Michael and whoever is on the other end of whatever it is we're doing, and wait for the next stage. Usually this comes in the form of draft contracts followed by the first round of to-and-fro, give-and-take negotiations.

When negotiating there are conditions and objections. It's vital to know the difference, with an objection being something you would 'like' changing whereas a condition is something that you 'need' changing.

In other words, a deal breaker.

I have only two conditions where *Top Gear* is concerned: full creative control – a single vision for anything in entertainment is key to its success. My second condition being a minimum of three years' commitment. This will tell me the BBC is completely behind me, come what may.

It's 1.30 p.m. Finally, I'm at the studio, I'm in *TFI Friday* land, this is it nothing else matters now.

We begin by rehearsing Parts 3, 4, 5 and 6. Basically where we left off last night. The plan is to do that, then for me to go and have a sleep for an hour before coming back for the dress rehearsal, wardrobe and make-up before show time.

The weather people were right, it is the hottest day of the year so far – fact. Our studio is temporary, fashioned inside a derelict theatre that is soon going to be redeveloped; consequently there is no air conditioning whatsoever and hardly any windows or doors.

It's like we're in a giant oven. By the time we get our audience in here tonight, after a day of natural incubation as well as the added heat our massive studio-lights produce, it will be more like a furnace. I mean sizzling.

Massive cooling fans have been ordered and are on their way over.

Otherwise, the atmosphere is extremely relaxed and carefree, no tension whatsoever. Like it should have been back in the day but never was.

The new script is getting new laughs from the crew.

I am on the verge of feeling too confident. I have never felt like this in a television studio before. We're either about to get it very right, or fall horrendously flat on our overly smug faces.

Be humble.

Be calm.

Be in the moment.

These are my mantras for the day.

At 5.00 p.m. the crew break for tea and we set about rewriting parts of the script and rejigging the running order. Yet again Danny has written a really funny opening but it's quite wordy and a big ask in my head for the top of the show, when all I want to do is get on with it. Danny agrees if it's playing on my mind we should cut it. I feel a huge sense of relief.

Another last-minute glitch (not to say there won't be others). The sack of feathers we want to cover the audience in the bar with, right at the top, has been deemed unsafe. We've used the same feathers tens of times in the past, but now Health and Safety tell us Brussels has declared them 'potentially fatal'. There's a heated discussion – hilarious – over the killer feathers. Later it transpires that if we can get them sprayed with the right coating then we can go ahead.

Dress rehearsal is scheduled for 7 p.m., we are way behind. I've not seen my dressing-room let alone a bed and a sleep. I can feel my eyes going red around the rims, beginning to sting. But the window's passed, time for Dr Footlights to do his stuff. Dr Footlights – the mythical medical man who gets live performers through whatever it is they need to get out there and do. I believe the technical term for it is adrenaline.

The dress goes well except for one thing. It doesn't finish until . . .

. . . 8.42 p.m.

Eighteen minutes before we go live on air.

This is so not ideal, but worrying about it will only use up more valuable time, energy and emotional capacity I simply don't have. I sit in the make-up chair, my face now bright red – a combination of internal overheating and sky-high blood pressure. I ask for the time, there's now only twelve minutes to go before *TFI Friday* hits the screens again for the first time since 2000. Allowing for the fact I need to be back down for 8.57 so I can say hello to the audience and walk through the first few camera positions one more time, I now have all of nine minutes to wash my hair, get it cut, coloured and dried, get all my war-paint on and change into my show clothes.

Obviously that's not going to happen. What was planned as a nice, relaxed, organized pre-show half-an-hour routine turns into a full-on Formula One pit stop. I have three hair and make-up artists

277

working on me all at the same time. It is no longer a question of how good they can make me look, just how 'not that bad'.

At 8.51 p.m. Suzi bursts into the make-up room with Will, Danny and Barty in tow. The A Team, something big must be going down.

What now?

'There's something you need to know.'

'Go on,' I reply.

'Damon Albarn has lost his voice and can't sing!'

'What?'

'Are you serious?'

What the fuck!

Blur have been our big coup since weeks ago when we revealed to the nation *TFI Friday* was indeed coming back. Not only that, they're due to play not one but two songs for us: a big opener and the finale at the end of the show, the big finish.

Shit, fuck, bollocks.

All of the above and more. None of which I say out loud.

At this point fifteen years ago I would have gone ABSOLUTELY BALLISTIC. Of course, that would have not been in the least bit helpful. But such logic never entered my head in those days. I was permanently in the 'no one understands, poor me' wilderness.

Tosser.

'So what are we going to do?' I ask calmly, while quietly shitting my pants.

'It's OK. We've changed Parts Three, Four and Five around. We can tell you what we've done now or in the break after Part One, and then in each subsequent break after that,' Suzi replies in a flash, her lieutenants standing steadfastly behind her. I like what I'm seeing, and even more impressively I like the confidence and defiance with which Suzi has delivered their solution.

'Yes. Yes. Yes. Hallelujah. God, tell me what you want of me and I'm yours!'

In that instant, in that moment of make-or-break decision time I finally realize THIS is why we do what we do. This is us in battle: kill or be killed, big decisions call for big kahunas, we were on the precipice of being outflanked by the 'shit happens' machine but we had sent it off yelping with its tail between its legs.

What a team.

What a ring of steel.

'OK, do whatever you have to and tell me each new part as the last one ends, during the commercial break.'

The show that Will and I have lived with over the last four weeks no longer exists.

So what? No point in worrying about that now. Only Part One will remain as it was, but at least I can focus on getting that right.

Four minutes later, I'm down in the bar. It's heaving with people, expectation and perspiration. A massive cheer goes up when I enter. I couldn't be any happier. Life doesn't get better than this. Sure, I look like crap, having ended up with a 1970s snooker player's vampire quiff, tired eyes and the same jeans and T-shirt I've had on all day, but again, so what? I'm not exactly Robert Redford to start with.

In many ways it makes me even more relaxed. This is it – time to say goodbye to the television show that has given me so much, but nearly killed me in the process.

Toby the floor manager: '. . . and five, four, three, two, one – we're on titles.'

CUE *TFI Friday*.

Fuuuuuuuuuuuuuuuuck.

Friday, 12 June: 9 p.m.

The show begins as always, with me walking in from the main auditorium where the bands play. When the theme tune strikes up, the noise from the audience is louder than I have ever heard in a television studio. It reminds me of Super Saturday at London 2012 in the Queen Elizabeth stadium. Sometimes, if only for a few brief seconds, the sound cheering humans can make is extraordinary. Not that they're cheering just for me: they're cheering for themselves, their own past, life itself, and some of the younger ones because they're at a show they'd only ever heard about almost as if it were the stuff of legend. Now they are here witnessing it for real.

I see the red cue light sweeping towards me on the techno-crane camera whilst spinning above the audience's heads – we're back in the game. Time to march into the bar and be on the telly for a bit. I fairly gallop along the gantry and up the final steps, gesture to the camera and before I know it, I'm back behind that famous old desk.

The opening sequence is now much simpler to run through in my head, a natural procession of moments linked to each other, as opposed to a list of jokes, that I have to get word-perfect in order for them to work. I don't get on with jokes, never have done, they frighten the life out of me. I much prefer pictures I can imagine, that can be brought to life with colourful delivery as opposed to precise articulation.

Will makes his entrance, again to huge applause. We fire the now 'asthma-friendly' feathers all over the crowd in the bar with a movie special-effects giant fan. Immediately it's chaos, like we've never been away, fifteen years wiped out in the opening two minutes. We're back in the groove, only this time it really does feel like fun. Knowing the show inside out helps, even though it's all about to change.

This approach is far more *Toothbrush* than *TFI Friday*, definitely the way forward, I'm so relaxed. You have no idea how important that is when you're on live television. If you're not relaxed, it's all you can do just to remember your name. And *remembering* is a million light years away from *knowing*. When you know something, you have the spare capacity to deliver whatever it is you're doing with warmth and a smile, or whatever the situation requires.

So many people on TV forget to smile when they are supposed to be having a good time, even if they really are. Whereas the old pros can look like they're having a blast, even though their minds are already in the car on the way home.

I recall what Stephen Merchant said to me when I commented on the fact that he was about to go into rehearsals for his debut play in the West End yet he seemed so cool about the whole thing. He told me he'd already learnt the lines back home in Los Angeles where he lives. All that remained for him to do therefore was get started and see what magic dust he could sprinkle over them. So obvious when you hear it put like that.

That's exactly what's going on with me and *TFI Friday* tonight. My goodness, I cannot tell you the difference it makes. The show flies by and everything we do works. This never happens. Some things end up stronger than others, but literally nothing fails to hit the mark. It's a unique experience, a new one on me. I know things are going well when I notice that, as the rest of the audience continue to shrivel up under the now almost unbearable heat, I'm actually not sweating at all. If you watch the show back you can clearly see there's not a drop of perspiration anywhere near me.

Bizarre.

By far the biggest hit of the night is my mum in the emergency mobility scooter *Top Gear* skit. She absolutely brings the house down. When she trundles on to the set to be presented with her winning driver's laurel wreath by none other than F1 World Champion Lewis Hamilton, she receives what is easily the most triumphant ovation of the whole time we're on air.

Lewis himself is the best I've ever seen him on a chat show. Twice during his interview I need him to change tack and lead the conversation by asking me two predetermined questions to get us to the next film. I tap his foot twice under the table to let him know when. He delivers perfectly, both times, right on cue.

In the end the show runs over by almost half an hour, but we could have easily gone on for longer. Maybe this is the way forward for a series. *TFI Friday – The Show That Doesn't Know When to End.* Sounds good to me. You want unpredictable television, it doesn't get more unpredictable than that.

As the end credits finally roll, I feel an immense sense of calm and satisfaction, like nothing I've ever felt before in or around a live television event. This has to happen again surely, it has been the best night of my career. *TFI Friday*, the best it has ever been, warmer than it's ever been and, most importantly, more sustainable than it's ever been. Surely we can come up with at least a couple more years of this new, more survivable incarnation.

• • •

With the end credits still rolling:

I quietly slip off the set unnoticed and slowly walk, head lowered, down two flights of stairs and out the side entrance to the underground car park. I swear if there'd been a doctor there to take my pulse it wouldn't have been much above normal. I was ice cool. Do you know what? It may have been even lower. I've only ever felt like this once before, and that was, guess when? The day after the London Marathon when all felt right with the world.

That sense of being at one with the world was back with me for only the second time in my life, just a few weeks after I first encountered it. Is this what they refer to as enlightenment?

If so, it's encouraging that it can be achieved in a scuzzy concrete car park after two hours of relative madness, not solely in a remote Himalayan hermitage over a twenty-five-year period of solitary meditation.

The return of the kids we made cry to receive their long overdue apology plus a free Caribbean holiday each – we had to give them something – was sensational. The second-best moment of the show for me after my mum's show-stopping appearance. I can't imagine I'd have felt enlightened at all if we'd left them at home.

Karma in need. Karma indeed.

'Do you work on the show?' asks the driver of a black peoplecarrier waiting to take someone home. He's foreign with a friendly smile, very polite.

'Yes, I do.'

'You're the first out, they say there's going to be a big party now, could go on very late.'

'Really? Well, I suppose that is usually the case. There's a lot of very excited people in there.'

We chat for a few more minutes. It's clear he has no idea that

I even work on the show, let alone present, produce and own it. Perfect.

Turns out he's Serbian and has been in the UK for six years. Just the grounding, unaffected conversation I need as an antidote the preceding mayhem. It will be hyper back inside: 'How great was that? How hot was it in there! How many more *TFI Fridays* do you think there'll be now?' I can hear the hysteria and repetition from here. Nothing wrong with this, nothing at all, and far better than everyone awkwardly trying to avoid the elephant in the room when a show has tanked. But by and large, collective adrendine kills individually, and when you're the star of the show, its's usually the best idea to make a quick getaway.

A few moments later, Will appears.

'Ah, you're here. You OK?'

'Fantastic, best night ever.'

'Wow, really?'

'Yeah. You?'

'Don't know, haven't had time to think about it. Yeah, I guess.'

I love Will. He can be so intense one moment and so entirely lost the next. As we continue to chat, Tash, escorts my sister and my mum outside to find their taxi. One of my best pals, Noel Fitzpatrick, the Supervet, is cadging a lift home with them. Noel's a genius who has achieved a worldwide hit with his bionic vet-themed TV shows. I've known him for fifteen years, ever since he fixed Enzo our German Shepherd's back legs. He also happens to live around the corner from Mrs Evans, Senior.

Midnight: Tash and I are back home leaning against the kitchen island, enjoying a glass of champagne with my daughter Jade, her husband Callum, her mum Alison, Al's husband Wardy, Alex Jones – my colleague from *The One Show*, her fiancé Charlie, and my faithful assistant The Frothy Coffee Man. Everyone's dog-tired but still smiling.

3 a.m: Talking of dogs, my wife is currently running up and down the streets of Primrose Hill chasing one. After Jade's lot went to bed, the rest of us nipped out to a party Matthew Freud had

spontaneously announced he was throwing. I've known Matthew for years, ever since he came down to a dark and dingy basement studio one Saturday morning back in 1989 where I was training his sister Emma how to operate a radio studio. He'd just started his PR business and was always bursting with excitement and weird ideas.

His house is so cool. Situated behind a grand Georgian terrace of approximately twenty houses, you access it via a metal door which fills an odd gap between two gable ends. After stepping through the mesh gateway, the space immediately opens up to reveal a courtyard and the front of what is a monument to contemporary design.

'Have nothing in your house except that which is beautiful or useful,' said William Morris. Matthew's place is the quintessence of the great man's ethos.

The dog wasn't found until the next day but found nevertheless. The party on the other hand rendered most attendant humans lost until well into Saturday afternoon.

Saturday, 13 June

TFI FRIDAY + ONE DAY

I wake up exhausted but couldn't be happier.

We've made a ten o'clock booking at a fantastic New York-style diner for brunch. A table for eight and a half, as little Teddy, our five-and-a-bit-month-old grandson will be hanging out with us officially for the first time. Hungover, weary, drowsy but with seven (and a half) of the most important people in my life around me, I feel like a very lucky man.

After brunch we go for a walk and a play on the swings in the local park. I check the time, it's already past one and with Jade and the northern gang having to make tracks soon, we give the kids their final five-minute call.

While all this has been going on, I notice an unopened email symbol on my home page. It's from Jay, at Channel 4, entitled simply – RATINGS.

Ah, ratings, the death knell to any ensuing euphoria the day after the celebration of a potentially hit TV show the night before. The odds are always against you, you see. In as much as there are far fewer successful television shows than not. Chances are, you are going to have a turkey on your hands. One of my early career problems was ironically the fact all three of my first three big TV shows were hits, which meant I was almost ten years into the business before being woken up to the reality check of habitual failure.

As I was in my family bubble of everything that really mattered, I decided to postpone finding out how many of the Great British Public had or had not watched our show last night until they had left.

At 3 p.m., having waved off the northerners, Tash declares she is pooped, as are the kids, who enjoyed their own mini late-night yesterday while we were in telly land. She's desperate to watch the show, as are Noah and Eli, but she knows I won't want to. It's not that I mind watching myself on screen, I just don't want to do it for a day or two days afterwards in case the show didn't 'play' as well as I imagined. I tell her to go ahead, I nip out for a walk and to open the dreaded email.

I decide to go for a coffee in my favourite Italian deli. I sit at a quiet table in the corner.

OK, this is the moment of truth.

'Be prepared to be taken down a peg or two, Christopher,' I say to myself. 'You know the routine.'

The truth is I am hoping for the late one-point-something million; 1.9 million would be brilliant. Anything beginning with a two and it will be party time all over again.

Matthew!!!

I scroll to Jay's email with her little yellow sealed envelope icon staring back at me. I click on open. Ping. And there it is. The number.

The dreaded bloody number.

The number that can make or break lives and careers.

But I find myself having to blink. One of those comedy blinks like in a cartoon.

A double take with a slight shake of the head to nudge your brain back online.

Did it really say:

3.8 MILLION!!!

Shut the front door.

3.8 MILLION. What???

That was the average figure throughout the broadcast.

Unbelievable.

No, really bloody unbelievable.

But then what was this on the next line.

Surely more fiction.

How about, in addition to 3.8 million – a peak audience of . . .

4.3 MILLION!!!

That's even more insane! I am in total shock. This is not possible. Both figures are more than double what the original *TFI Friday* ever managed to score. And I mean ever.

Fuck, fuck, fuck.

A day now to celebrate more than ever.

I down my coffee and run back to the house to tell Tash. As I fling open the front door, almost off its hinges, I can hear the muted shouts and screams coming from the television downstairs.

'Babe, the ratings have come through. Look.'

Tash is cuddled up with the boys on the sofa. I pass her the phone, waiting for the information to register. She burst into tears. Another marathon moment.

'OH – MY – GOD. This is amazing.'

She is so pleased for me.

Surely this means Channel 4 will simply have to pick up their option for a series – who knows, maybe more? *TFI Friday* has also won its slot against all other channels, including the mighty BBC1 and 2 and ITV1.

This is dreamsville.

That said, I take a moment to remind myself this is showbusiness. The business that sent Benny Hill packing when he was still being watched and loved somewhere in the world by 300 million people every week. Similarly, let's not forget the moment when Metro GOLDWYN Mayer (the clue's in capitals for you) thought it perfectly reasonable to dispense with the services of SAM GOLDWYN from the company. Not only was he the man who founded the legendary studio that had just sacked him, in the first place, but he was one of the founding fathers of Hollywood itself.

No, I have learnt to expect the unexpected, even to be ready for the ludicrous. That said, I have to admit to feeling the most optimistic I've ever felt while awaiting a call from a channel head.

But you never know.

You just never know.

Sunday, 14 June

It's 11.30 a.m. and I'm at my mum's with Tash and the kids. Minnie wasn't expecting us as we'd seen her for most of Friday at *TFI* but we love hanging out at my mum's little bungalow, the world is much simpler from her point of view. Especially when the preceding forty-eight hours have been a little crazy. Which they had.

After seeing the northerners off yesterday Tash and I had treated ourselves to a night out at the O2 Arena to watch Take That. So good we've decided to go again next weekend and take Noah to his first big concert.

Gary, Mark and Howard have really nailed this threesome thing.

'Much more symmetrical with three,' said Gary to me backstage. 'There's always one of us in the middle which means the other two can go a bit more freestyle if they want to.'

Though Tash and I are a little more bleary-eyed than a half-ten finish Take That gig can lay claim to.

We went on a bar crawl afterwards, just the two of us having our own private little celebration in honour of how well *TFI* had gone.

Actually I say bar crawl, the truth is we enjoyed our first post-

Take That cold beverage at Danny Baker's house in Blackheath. We'd been given four tickets for the gig but when at the last minute the two pals we were supposed to be going with pulled out, and it was so close to show time, I remembered, 'Danny lives five minutes from the O2,' so I called to ask him if anyone in his family might want to drop everything to come with.

Danny's wonderful and long-suffering wife Wendy, along with their ever-smiling daughter Bonnie, both did exactly that, and we all had a whale of a time. Especially Bonnie, who I've known most of her life. She is a delight to be around and has been a Take That fan since the very beginning, twenty-five years ago next year. In fact, when they originally split up back in 1996 she took a week off school in protest. Maths and English can wait, real life will come soon enough. A kid grieving for their first pin-ups is a heartbreaking business.

She also wrote a letter to each one of them every day until admitting defeat and reluctantly returning to her studies.

Almost as soon as Wendy put the key in the door upon our return, Danny was waiting in the hallway with that big beaming cartoon grin of his, wielding one of his signature bottles of ice-cold white wine.

'Wa-hey, let's hear it for The Thatters, the Thatters That Matter, three cheers for you four – hurrah!'

Yet another bizarre twist of fate.

Having spent countless days over at the Bakers' in the Nineties, I hadn't been over to theirs at all for a couple of years and suddenly here we were again, the day after I'd been working with Danny all week.

All meant to be. All written in the stars.

• • •

But back at Mum's.

Still no word from Channel 4 about a series, or Michael my agent re: how the *Top Gear* deal is progressing. I decide to email him. He replies that the *TG* deal is ongoing and has been all weekend as all sides want to announce sooner rather than later, before it leaks out. Which it will; things like this always do. He further informs me that he has heard from Jay at Channel 4, who spookily said that she would like to pick up the option for a *TFI Friday* series forthwith but pending 'what might be happening with Chris and *Top Gear*'.

'Do you think she knows?' Michael asks a minute later when I call him.

'How could she? At least not yet anyway.'

'I don't think she can either. Maybe it's just the obvious question to ask at the moment where you're concerned.'

We decide it'll be best if I call Jay. Straight is the only way to be.

'All right,' she began calmly down the line, while apparently huddled outdoors under a blanket somewhere near Manchester. She was thre to watch one of her best pals, *BBC Breakfast*'s Louise Minchin, compete in a triathlon as part of her quest to represent Team GB at the Rio Olympics.

'Let me put it like this: if you were a betting man, would you say you are more, or less, likely to be doing *Top Gear* next year? Just so I have some idea of what I'm dealing with here.'

It was as covert as we were going to manage.

'I would say more.'

'OK, well – not ideal, to be honest, but as long as the two don't run concurrently and there's at least a couple of months' separation I would still say yes, we'd like to do an initial series of eight more *TFI Friday*s this side of 2015. I'm talking about a run up to Christmas after the Rugby World Cup at the end of October/beginning of November.'

An excellent offer for which I'm very grateful, but as it's cards-on-the-table time I have to ask her about something that's been preying on my mind since the crazy ratings had come through. After catch-up and repeat figures were rolled into the original 3.8 million viewers, we were now talking about an overall viewer rating of well over 5 million – on the way to 6 million, even. This was verging on ridiculous. Far beyond any of our wildest predictions and aspirations.

'May I ask you, Jay, if – since the figures are stratospherically higher than any of us ever expected – if it has crossed your mind to offer me a substantially bigger contract?'

'No, not at all. If you weren't such a high-profile BBC face, then yes, I probably would, but you are and so I'm not going to do that, that's not how I run the channel.'

So that was that then.

A straight answer to a straight question.

All very un-showbiz. That's not usually how it works.

Not that I fully understand her logic. Actually I don't understand it at all. When we originally did *TFI Friday* I was hosting the Radio 1 *Breakfast Show* and much more high profile than I am now. A dual radio and TV career for me have always been separate entities that can coexist on different networks via the same persona, especially if both programmes feed off similar material. But no matter, Channel 4 is Jay's channel, she's the controller and it's up to her to control it as she sees fit.

All right then, so a miniseries of *TFI* it is. More bonus for a few Friday nights at the tail end of this year. What's not to like about the prospect of that?

Time to refocus.

Time to get the *Top Gear* deal done, signed and announced.

Monday, 15 June

I'm called in straight after my radio show goes off the air to BBC New Broadcasting House to meet Kim Shillinglaw, the Controller of BBC2, Adam Waddell who runs *Top Gear* BBC Worldwide, and Mark Linsey. They need to see the whites of my eyes just to make sure once and for all I'm the man for the job and I mean business.

By the end of the meeting it's pretty obvious I have never been more serious about anything in my life. My initial overview is simple. There are two ways of looking at the situation *Top Gear* is in now:

A: Fragile and vulnerable because of the shock departure of the the Three Amigos plus their genius producer Andy Wilman.
B: An unexploded bomb perfectly primed over the last decade by the aforementioned, ready to be detonated like never before.

Of course, I'm looking at it from the point of view of scenario B. And I absolutely bloody believe it. In my opinion *Top Gear* right now is like the old League Division One before it became the Premiership and very quickly became a stellar multibillion-pound franchise. Yes, Jeremy and Wilman had dragged a dreary old motoring show kicking and screaming into the twenty-first century and brought it to life like never before. Only a fool would argue otherwise, with it now achieving a global audience in the hundreds of millions. But somewhere along the line its evolution had come to a grinding halt.

Where most other people could only see paralysis by analysis and comparison for whoever 'dared' take over next, I could see only potential for the show to be even bigger than it ever has been.

For a start, where is Top Gear World, the theme park? People would come from the four corners of the planet to stay there for a few days, even if it were located in grey old England. We live three miles from Legoland, and it's packed all year round. I mean, Legoland is OK but it's no Universal Studios. And of course *Top Gear* the television show would be filmed at Top Gear World, and were it to exist, fans could visit on show day and win tickets to be in the audience.

Then there is *Top Gear*'s current format and content, as was. How come the show had basically morphed into little more than three films and four links, with only the celeb interview and the news to break up the running order?

And the big one for me:

Why hasn't it ever been live?

Imagine that: 'And now, ladies and gentleman, boys and girls, it's eight o'clock and live on BBC2 – it's time for *Top Gear*.'

That would give it the kick up the backside for sure. The great thing about a live television show is that it only takes as long to do as it lasts. Sure, you lose the ability to edit and put in 'the funny', but you gain so much more. The script has to be tighter because it simply can't afford to spread as much and everyone has to recalibrate their focus as a result.

As for what it does for the show itself, there's no way the viewers can be sure of what's going to happen, because it's obvious no one is sure. What will be will be on live TV.

It's impossible to second-guess something that's yet to take place. That's the joy of it all.

The other key to sustainable and acceptable edginess is in the writing of each sequence. Take the Farrelly brothers, who have written some of the most popular movies of the modern era. They openly concede to deliberately writing themselves into a corner, so they then have to spend hours, days or even weeks getting themselves out of it again. The genius of this approach being that if it takes them a week to figure out a thirty-second twist, what chance does the audience have of doing the same in just thirty seconds?

The twist on the twist – love it.

I've come to today's meeting with a list as long as my arm of issues I think we need to and can overcome, the emphasis at all times being on evolution, not revolution. After our scheduled meeting time of one hour and fifteen minutes, the meeting comes to a close and the message goes out to close the deal so we can all sign as soon as possible.

This will be a game changer for all concerned and we need heads of agreement printed, checked by legals and signed by 5 p.m. this afternoon so we can announce 7.15 p.m., two and a bit hours later. Again, avoiding any leaks is key, we must try to keep control of the story. If it starts tidy and unanimous, it has the best chance of staying that way.

• • •

Now, let me tell you, IT IS IMPOSSIBLE TO DO A DEAL OF SUCH MAGNITUDE within a week, let alone six hours.

As proved to be the case here, despite everyone pulling out all the stops to get the deal over the line. The Monday 5 p.m. deadline came and went, with contract negotiations and writes and rewrites continuing through the night and into Tuesday. But it was one of those rare processes where we were all moving forward as one, no one side trying to trip up the other to gain an advantage. Few deals in my business take place amid such unified bonhomie.

There was no doubt this was going to happen – the moment we could announce, we would.

Patience Christopher, patience.

Tuesday, 16 June

Today is the day. It has to be. Usual routine for me: jog to work, drink as much water as I can bear, grab papers and coffee, read overnight brief from my producer Paul, go to loo, start show and see what happens.

My daily radio show is like a working screenplay that begins at 6.30 every morning: we take our time at the beginning to grow things we can harvest later on. It's all about priming little grenades of content that we can explode as the show unfolds.

A few years ago I learnt not to panic in the first hour of the show. If things are quiet, relax, play a few more records. The key is to let the narrative come to you instead of chasing it. And it always works. It's been a complete revelation.

Something will always happen sooner or later, it's how the universe works; the only thing we can get wrong is to get in the way or presume we can out-world our world. Of which there's no chance, no chance at all. Of course we've all tried to do it, but life has taught me that, barring childbirth, a broken down car or a troublesome door, it's usually for better to wait than push. Other than on these rare occasions, nine times out of ten, if you do push in the first place you'll end up having to push back at some point in the future. More often than not a lot further back from where you originally started.

After the show finishes I have to attend the screening of the new Jake Gyllenhaal film, *Southpaw*, which, as well as serving as a welcome distraction to 'the wait' for the deal, also turns out to be the best new film I've seen in ages. Some of the films I have to watch as a proviso to securing an interview with one/some/all of the stars are absolute tosh. This, though was something truly special. And a boxing film, to boot. I thought all the boxing films we'll ever need had been made. But no, do yourself a favour: make sure you see *Southpaw*, it's dynamite.

With my eyes red and my nose still snotty from all the repressed snivelling and sobbing I'd been doing during the flick – I'm such sucker for a weepy movie – I stumble back out into the blinding sunlight of a scorching hot central Soho.

Sunglasses on.

Head down.

March.

I turn on my phone expecting to see a 'DEAL IS DONE. PLEASE COME SIGN' text from my agent, Michael, but nothing. The cogs of corporate legal departments and interdepartmental alliance are still whirring away somewhere in north-west London.

I am cleared to go home, as my signature on a contract will not be required anytime this side of late afternoon. The plan still being to announce to the world that *Top Gear* will be a bit more ginger from now on – at 7.15 p.m.

'I'll write a car review,' I decide upon arriving home, a good omen. I've had my car review column for the *Mail on Sunday* since 2013 (April 13th – Subaru BRZ, I'll never forget it) and I always look forward to scribbling down my thoughts each week.

Some weeks, admittedly, the car in question is less inspiring than others, but those are the weeks I have to dig deeper and therefore learn more about how to write and what to write to sustain the reader's interest. This week's car is the perfect case in point. The Nissan Nismo – as unappealing a 'thing' as I have ever laid eyes on – forces me to go for my first ever split five-star review. I give it one star out of five for design –because it's hideous – but five stars out of five for its hugely unexpected half-decent performance when it comes to handling.

Later this afternoon, a friend of mine who I haven't seen in a while has arranged to come round for a catch-up. We're supposed to be meeting at mine, but a text pings in on my phone. It's from my agent.

DEAL DONE. VERY COMPLICATED.
GOING FOR 7.15 p.m. ANNOUNCEMENT.
GET READY. THIS IS IT.

I call my pal and ask him if we can meet in the pub as something big is going down. 'I can't tell you what right now, but all will become clear if you stick around.'

Cut to 5 p.m. – we're sitting outside my local on one of the creaky wooden tables, the glorious sunshine still with us, two ice-cold pints of Guinness the icing on the cake.

We place our phones on the table and began to chat about life, love and all things good. We're giggling a lot – my pal is an extremely funny guy, funnier than any stand-up I've ever seen. We've all told him he could sell out arenas if he could be bothered to write himself a ninety-minute set.

'So what's going on with you?' he asks after about forty-five minutes of hilarious impromptu monologue.

It is now only just over an hour until the moment when a simply worded BBC2 tweet will be posted, very calmly and quietly breaking the 'Evans is New *TG* Host' news, but I still can't tell him. I have to leave it just a wee bit longer. Obviously he wouldn't tell anyone and I'm not even particularly paranoid, but for the first time in my life I find myself in a 'don't want to jinx it' frame of mind.

I've never felt this way before, not even close, but this is different. This is the biggest deal I have ever been involved in. Bigger even than when I bought and sold my media group back in 2000 for hundreds of millions of pounds. Why? Because it's not about the money this time, it's about the opportunity and the faith the BBC, the most revered and respected broadcasting company on the planet, have put in me. This is the business I have wanted to work in ever since I was a little boy. It doesn't get any bigger than what's about to happen.

Just writing that gives me goosebumps.

And then my friend makes my mind up for me:

'Right, I'm going to shoot off,' he says. 'Good to catch up. Whatever it is that's going down, good luck, tell me about it when you feel like you can.'

'Oh no. You can't go. I need someone here. With me. Now. Well, soon anyway.'

Suddenly he's worried. Not my intention at all.

'Is everything OK?'

'Oh God no, nothing's wrong, nothing at all. Far from it. Couldn't be further from the case.'

'So what, then? What's happening?'

'Er . . .'

'Are you sure you're all right? You're being a bit weird?'

I decided to tell him.

'What's up is . . . the Beeb have asked me to do *Top Gear*.'

'What??'

'The BBC. They've asked me to take over *Top Gear*. I said yes and they're going to announce it at quarter past seven tonight.'

'Shiiiiiit! That's in fifteen minutes.'

'I know, please will you stay till they do.'

'Fuck, yes of course. This is massive!'

'Massive is one word.'

'Right, fuck, hang on, I'll go and move my car. Hold that thought. You get us another drink and I'll be back in a second. *Top Gear*, what? Christ. This is mental!'

Moments later, our glasses recharged, my pal is back and the questions start coming thick and fast.

Top Ten Questions He Fired off within the First Five Minutes:

10 How?

9 When?

8 How come?

7 But really when?

6 But really how?

5 How long for?

4 When from?

3 Who else knows?

2 What did Tash say?

1 Do 'The Boys' know?

'Do The Boys know?'

By The Boys, he meant Jeremy, James, Richard and Andy.

'No, not yet but I'll tell them just before it goes public.'

'OK, good, yes, that's good. That's the right thing to do. Excellent, yes, you should – definitely.'

7.05 p.m.: I did precisely that.

I have discovered over the years that it always – and I mean ALWAYS – pays off to just keep doing the right thing, no matter how much it might make you feel sick or fill you with dread at the time.

I send the same text to each them:

BEEN OFFERED TOP GEAR. HAVE SAID YES.
HOPE THAT'S COOL.

Within moments Wilman and Clarkson respond, wishing me luck. As I'm reading their texts, my phone rings, I look at the screen, it's James May.

All good.

No hard feelings.

Not easy for any of us.

I can only imagine how surreal this must seem to them.

Almost as much as it does for me.

I look down at my BlackBerry. It reads 7.14.

All still quiet on the Western Front.

Seconds later and – click: the clock on my phone changes to 7.15.

A beat.

And then . . .

It begins to buzz and doesn't stop.

Each subsequent text crashing into the last.

The first of which reads:

What?

Is this a wind up?

The BBC have just announced you're doing *Top Gear*.

By 7.16 my phone has gone into total and utter meltdown. And it has pretty much stayed that way ever since.

• • •

There's fame and then there's *Top Gear* fame. The two almost entirely unrelated. What started off as a monthly, regional half-hour motoring magazine programme in the Midlands back in 1977 had somehow in the last thirty-eight years mushroomed into the most popular, notorious and controversial television programme the BBC has ever broadcast.

Now it's up to me to take that very same show in whichever direction I believe its destiny lies next.

The latest and greatest challenge of my career to date is well and truly under way.

I've been here before, but I've never been this *me* here before. I am healthier, happier, more content and more stable than I have been for as long as I can remember.

If what I said in the opening pages of this book is true, about fifty not being the beginning of the end but rather the end of the beginning and the start of whatever comes next, then it's going to be OK.

In fact it's going to be more than OK.

Moments like these are what we train for all our lives, we just don't know it until they happen.

And that's the best bit.
Stay in the game, always.
It's the only game there is.
And remember:
If you're doing something you don't have to and you're not enjoy-
ing doing it, you're doing the wrong thing.
And on that bombshell . . .

Doubts and Certainties

Top Ten Doubts:

10 Have I already killed half my liver and half my brain?
 9 Should I have read more?
 8 Do I spend too much time thinking about cars?
 7 Am I fit enough?
 6 Am I getting enough sleep?
 5 Do my kids know how much I love them?
 4 Do I love me?
 3 Do I know what love is?
 2 Am I any good at anything?
 1 Do my wife and children love me as much as
    I love them?

Twins from the same womb. Yin and yang, night and day, the sun and the moon. If you average them out over a lifetime, I wonder whether we all have equal amounts of both. Something tells me we probably should and that we probably do. Or at least it feels that way, which in the end is all that matters.

How was your childhood? Forget that, I don't care. How did your childhood *feel*? Now you're talking, a far more relevant and useful question. Mine felt pretty good, as it happens, but I'm sure from the outside looking in it may often have appeared pretty darn shifty. But if the facts never come to light, perception is all that matters, perception is all there is.

The midterm/midlife half-time period is an excellent breeding ground for doubts. This period is to doubts what the Pill was to the Sixties: a promise of unbridled promiscuous possibilities, more often than not running off in all the wrong directions.

Doubts can send you crazy.
Doubts can send you mad.
Doubts can give sleepless nights,
On a scale you've never had.

Who hasn't doubted themselves? No one worth their salt, in my book. I've doubted everything I've ever been or done. From my sexuality to what I currently do for a living. But what of doubts *per se*? What are they there for? Where do they come from? More spookily, where do they go? Or do they just get fed up and move on?

I suspect this may very much be the case.

When it comes to doubts I have decided it's far better to adopt the Warren Buffett buy/sell philosophy. Buffett famously buys when everyone else is selling and sells when everyone else is buying. Run with the herd and you'll only ever be one in a thousand. Instead of focusing on my doubts when things are not going as swimmingly as I hope they might be, like I used to, I cut myself some slack and regroup all my energy and ideas to charge in the direction most likely to help change the situation for the better. Almost as if I'm on the front line with no time or headspace to concern myself with anything other than survival or progress.

Conversely, when things are going well, whereas in the past I may have gone out and partied for a week or so, now I step back, have a cup of tea and check for bullet holes. Wow! Is this verging on sensible? Well, gee, I guess it is. And since sensible is verging on organized, my God we might even be within sight of the path of righteousness and all that other Mother Jazz.

I've also come to realize that eureka moments are not what I previously had them down to be. For the last twenty-five years I have interpreted eureka moments as incendiary explosive instances of spontaneous revelation that come from the gods.

Well, that's obviously not true, is it? I now recognize them to be what they truly are: the answers that have been staring us in the face all along, that we fail to hear or see because we are too busy trying to be the hero of a moment that will never come.

If we are meant to know things, we will know those things already. Because we will already have done all the hard work to give us the information and experience our subconscious needs to arrive at a useful solution.

The more I recognize this fact every day, the more I benefit from its wisdom. It's like my wise old Indian accountant when it comes to money. He has saved steadily and regularly all his life so he *never* has to worry about money in the autumn and winter of his days.

Not only that, he has enough money not just to survive but to do all the things he's ever dreamed of. That was the dangling carrot that kept him going throughout his working life. He had a clear goal, applied a precise strategy and then rolled up his sleeves and went to work every day for forty-two years, hour by hour inching ever closer to his own private Elysium.

The same is true when it comes to cashing in your eureka chips. Many of the answers to our most profound questions are already answered and just waiting to be dialled up within our psyche. Again, it's not unlike training for the marathon. Come the day, if you've put in the right amount of hours doing the right thing, everything you need should be there for you when you need it.

After spending so much precious time trying to persuade people to buy into my ideas, or me, or whatever I was peddling at the time, now I realize something so obvious it makes me want to scream.

If they don't want to buy in the first place and it isn't going to change my life one way or the other, then my only course of action should be to move on straightaway.

Let Go. Let Go. Let Go.

The Dalai Lama was once asked about the single most influential slice of wisdom he'd ever heard. He responded by telling of a fellow lama of his who spoke only two words of English, yet they were enough to ease the deepest woes of most human beings.

Those words were:

Let go
Let go
Let go

The monk in question would sit quietly at the front of gatherings, attending to each person in turn who had queued for hours, sometimes days, to seek his wisdom. After they had finished speaking, he would smile, take their hand and place in their palm a small piece of paper on which were written these six simple words.

A phrase that, ever since I read it, has never left me. I think about it many times every single day. But even so I still sometimes forget that they are available to me. How crazy is that?

Sometimes it's only the following day that I remember:

Let go
Let go
Let go

This is why we all need to practise some sort of meditation at least once a day. A moment to remind ourselves who we are, where we came from, what's important in life, what unwelcome surprises might come along to trip us in the next few hours and what we have available in our arsenal to deal with such issues.

Let go
Let go
Let go

And watch what happens when people do the opposite, when they:

Hold on
Hold on
Hold on

Problems need to be dealt with of course, if they can be, but it's the problems out of our control that we need to let go of. Someone's attitude towards us, someone who's done wrong by us, someone who's spread false rumours about us. Other peoples' general slander and lethargy will wither and die in our mind's eye if we cut off their energy supply.

I used to be the world's worst when it came to reigniting situations, when I perceived myself to be the victim of an injustice. I can't tell you the effort I wasted and the misery I shepherded, making sure everyone knew how aggrieved I felt.

But now when I see people doing the same thing I quietly shake my head in a mixture of empathy, frustration and embarrassment on their behalf. If they could only see themselves, if they could only hear themselves, if they could only grasp the concept that it's they who are perpetuating whatever it is that's driving them to distraction.

Letting go lances the boil instantaneously.

This inner impasse that we previously steadfastly refused to get over disappears into thin air. Inner peace restored. The visceral spanner in the works that stops our natural flow and brings our common sense grinding to a halt removed.

When we become angry, we immediately become more stupid. We also become massively less attractive. And lose our ability to be funny. Three major factors that could otherwise be enhanced to win someone over or get them to see our point of view. Which ironically is what we're usually trying to achieve when caught up in these situations.

No one has ever cracked a really good joke when they're angry. No one has ever seduced the focus of their desires when they're angry. No one has ever made a small child laugh when they're angry. Our memory, our ability to reason, our vocabulary, our voice, our complexion, our humanity, our grace, our modesty, even our ability to hear, speak and see are all diminished when we allow ourselves to be taken over by the deathly red mist.

And how bad does getting angry make us feel afterwards?

I used to feel a prick for hours, sometimes days.

For a while we kid ourselves that this ugly and confused state will convey to even our most resilient adversaries that our passion runs deeper than they realized: 'You're messing with the wrong guy here!' – things like that. The type of twisted logic I clung to for years when possessed by such madness.

But, of course, that's not what they think at all. They merely see someone self-destructing in front of them, generally losing the plot and making them feel a whole lot better about themselves in the process.

Becoming angry in otherwise entirely civil situations only confirms one thing:

'I am an angry person anyway because of stuff I've not figured out yet. And right now I'm blaming ALL THAT STUFF ON YOU AND THE REST OF THE WORLD.'

Three other traits frequently on display in these situations are:

1. The aggressor tends to be in a superior role to the people he/she is shouting at, i.e. their boss or their employer.

2. He/she is shouting at someone whom they have paid to perform a service.

3. He/she is screaming at and going blue in the face over a lover, partner, loved one or best friend.

All three of these scenarios have one thing in common. They are all situations where the aggressor has a reason to suspect that he/she can get away with such unreasonable and unacceptable behaviour.

There is no doubt in my mind that a direct correlation exists between power, intimacy and aggression.

But when we cease to be aggressive, our overall sense of perspective immediately begins to return. Slowly peaking up from behind the sofa where it's been hiding till the tsunami has passed. People, if they love us, will begin to forgive us and edge a little closer to see if the fire is truly out.

We will once again be able to ascertain and differentiate between surmountable objections and insurmountable conditions.

Either way the situation will move on, if not completely resolve itself.

Anger, ninety-nine times out of a hundred, is entirely useless.

Let go
Let go
Let go

And as you exhale that breath you've been holding the first thing you will experience is a surge of relief. You can't help feeling more relaxed when you repeat those two little words.

If we really want to pick up our worries, insecurities, our frustrations, our sadness, our paranoia and run with them, screaming out to the world what a terrible time we're having, then they'll always be there for us to do so.

But letting go can become a habit that will change your life for the better.

When I'm really on my game, even before I step out of the house – or how about even before I've swung one leg out of bed – I will have put myself on emotional red-alert. I wake up with all my little checks and balances already flashing away in my stay-calm-stay-positive routine. If I show signs of snapping early on, I know I'm fragile and need to be careful that day.

I remind myself the world is exactly as I left it the night before, when I was fine, so if it's not changed something inside me must have.

Sometimes I think about Gandhi's view of negotiation, the fact that only a fool would not first consider the wishes of the opposing party: 'Why would he want to give me anything I want, while giving up anything he wants?' he used to say, making the brilliant and obvious point that there has to be conciliation for things to move on. In Gandhi's eyes, negotiation was conciliation.

And so we must negotiate with ourselves before even contemplating engaging with anyone else or the universe.

If we can take the sting out of any potential conflict right at the outset, everyone in the room will feel they have a chance. And that attitude has to begin within ourselves. What begins as a pleasurable and reasonable experience has a better chance of developing in the same vein. Everyone will be happier, everyone will be more willing to open up, everything will be more positive and more productive.

'He doesn't want to do this. She doesn't want to do that.'

Fine. Then what *do* they want to do? There's no other sustainable way.

Peoples' eyes, their minds, their views, their balance sheets, their secrets, their misgivings, their humanity and desire to get a deal done all need to be accepted and taken into account.

The ears have it, always.

Stay cool, stay relaxed.

• • •

My most extreme and testing 'let go, let go, let go' moments happen either between my mum and me, or when I'm at work.

Both are exaggerated versions of normality for different reasons.

Mum has just turned ninety. She's been an amazing mother and a tower of strength to myself and my elder brother and sister. She deserves to have the best time possible for every second of whatever she has left. So, why would I do anything to stop that from happening?

If she says things that might hurt or upset me, so what? That's not her intention. I know this because of all the love, protection, advice and support she has given me over the years.

So why is she saying them? Well, here's the thing: it doesn't actually matter. She's allowed to say whatever the hell she likes as far as I'm concerned. Because that's where 'let go, let go, let go' comes in – I've learned to apply it to almost everything she says and does. Nothing I say in reaction is ever going to change the way she thinks now. On *any* subject.

If she wants to have a sly dig at me, or tear me off a strip in front of people to show them that she's still the boss, then . . . honestly, good for her.

Is she saying these things because she's overwhelmed by a sense of unfinished business, disapproval, or just needing to impose her authority – or is that all in my head, and the reality is that Mum's just sitting there being old and tired. And yes, a bit grumpy.

Top Ten Grumpy Film Titles:

10 Braveheart Dodgy Hip
 9 Sideways and Pear-Shaped
 8 Raging Bullshit
 7 Lying King
 6 Dr No I Want a Second Opinion
 5 Shitty Shitty Bang Bang
 4 Good Riddance, Vietnam
 3 Les Really Miserables
 2 Forrest Grump
 1 Embrace the Grump

Embrace the Grump.
For the Grump is coming,
Make no mistake about it.
Fee fi fo fum,
I smell the Grump
Of a middle-aged man
But first he has to smell it himself.

Grumpiness definitely has a sell-by date but as long as we see it for the good it can do, catch it, embrace it and learn to love it before it begins to go off, it can be one of our most valuable midlife friends.

The Grump can get you to where you want to go. Sometimes the Grump is the best way forward. The Grump does not want to move in. The Grump is merely a peddler passing through town. Only a fool would not lend an ear to the lessons the Grump has to give.

Grumpy Old Man Syndrome should never be confused with Miserable Old Sod Syndrome, from which there is seldom salvation. Miserable Old Sods are the twisted, creaking creatures who scurry out snarling and snorting, wielding a carving knife to stab into kiddies' treasured footballs when they land in their garden by accident.

When I was a small child I spent hours and hours trying to correlate how any ex-kid could grow up to become a fully qualified Miserable Old Sod. How does this happen? Or maybe they're an as-yet-undiscovered subspecies that were never kids. That would explain things.

When it comes to grumpiness, however, we are talking more weedlike, i.e. just a flower in the wrong place.

Grumpiness begins to kick in when other things begin to check out. It's purgatory on earth. But also the dawn of acceptance, true contentment, not taking ourselves seriously any more and finally seeing the world and everything in it for what it really is. A vast ongoing display of entropy affected by every single micro-action of every single movement, thought, word, raindrop, breath of wind . . . that takes place here on Earth and consequently in the universe.

The Grump lets us know we haven't quite realized this yet by desperately clinging to the driftwood of our past. The songs we spent the first half of our lives listening to are songs that the second half of our lives can't possibly live up to.

'Why are we here?' Becomes 'Why should I bother being here?' But only for a while.

The Grump does not want us to get old. And the more the Grump dwells on this, the grumpier the Grump gets. Until one day the Grump realizes that we are not getting old, we are merely getting older. *There is no old if we don't want there to be.*

We need to embrace the Grump, thank it for for the heads-up and assure it we're going to be OK. Whereupon it will mellow, relax, lie back and hopefully drift off into a deep, smiling, dreamless sleep. From which it will then awake like a reformed Grim Reaper minus the cloak and scythe.

Once our Grump has moved on, we can then fling open the doors to welcome in that lovable old duo ECCENTRIC and BATTY.

Eccentric and Batty are never more entertaining than when happening around kids. They love adults who no longer see the point in behaving like grown-ups.

Grown up. Urgh!

'What the hell is that supposed to mean?'

Just one of the many useful reality checks and balances kids naturally impart to us.

Parenthood

The madness of having kids in the first place keeps all other madness at bay. We may have been constructed BK (Before Kids) but there's very little space or time for frothy self-regard and posturing once the ankle-biters arrive.

Each kid is his or her own mini Big Bang, the beginning of a whole new universe. Another brilliant ball of expanding nonsense we stupidly try to make sense of first, before realizing they are just there to remind us what life's really about.

A new benchmark for life is set when you have and accept that you have kids. You suddenly just 'get it' where before you might be scared to even chance a look. Our relationship with our own parents also changes dramatically. From not having a clue what the hell all the fuss was about, we're suddenly fledgling members of the same club, singing from the same hymn-sheet as they were.

And now you stand together, shoulder to shoulder, looking fondly down at the next generation of confusion being primed to have a go.

It's around this point we're also allowed into the secret of the knowing smile. The one we've seen countless times on the faces of kindly nurses, Mother Teresa, Trevor McDonald, you know the one.

Suddenly we realize it comes from the ability to feel unconditional, unrequited and selfless love. It's a smile of pure joy, of freedom, of being released from the burden of 'what is it all about and why am I here?' More than anything, it is a smile of abject relief.

Grandmas and granddads that get to dote over their grandchildren live with such smiles, constant smiles beaming from ear to ear, with loving eyes to match, permanently on the brink of tears. Could a human being be any more content?

Of course not.

One of the advantages of having a child when you're young is becoming a young grandparent, which now, thanks to my daughter Jade, is a realm I have entered. The opposite of where I sit chronologically with my two young sons. Like my own dad, I was well into my forties when Noah and Eli came into the world.

My father is now deceased, God rest his soul, and there's little we can do about that, just as it would seem there is little death can do to thwart my mum at the other end of the mortality scale. She continues to defy all bad luck that comes her way by refusing to be brought down by anything death cares to throw at her. Even though she's been beaten and battered, torn and bruised more than any other living person I know, she's simply not interested in giving up the ghost of life anytime soon.

She was ninety on 17 September this year, the last but two to turn in after a night of revelry.

So there you have my immediate family. My most treasured possession in the world. And like homeland security to any chief of staff, my number one priority at all times.

The meaning of 'life' is to protect the lives of those who deserve it, along with those of the people we love.

There, I've said it. Problem solved. The philosophers can relax and go home now. Job done. We're sorted.

Life is not only what happens *when* we get here. It's also *how* we get here. That is the gift we are born to look after. Everything else should and must come second.

Because of the way my dad died when I was thirteen, perhaps, without being aware of it, I went on to associate parenthood automatically with being old and dying. No one thinks to tell a kid who loses a parent early that it's precisely that.

Premature.

Not supposed to happen.

Not fair.

Not usually like this.

A serious bit of bad luck.

But – boy, should they.

A few tender and carefully chosen words would save millions of people from decades, sometimes whole lives, of misunderstanding, confusion and needless heartache.

To borrow a line from the movie *Fight Club*: the first rule about parenthood is, don't talk about parenthood – except when a kid needs to know why one, or heaven forbid, both of them are no longer there anymore. And so we finish where we started.

How do we stick around for as long as we can for our own sake, as well as everyone else's?

Dr Ed's Top Ten Annual MOT Recommendations:

10 **Annual blood tests for anything you may be worried about.**
9. **Liver.**
8. **Kidney.**
7. **Cancer.**
6. **Diabetes.**
5. **Sugar.**
4. **Blood pressure.**
3. **Weight.**
2. **Lifestyle.**
1. **Stool issues.**

Ed says we should also always carry out an in-the-shower bumps and lumps look-out. And consider colonoscopy and endoscopy where high-risk/family history issues are concerned.

'All the usual, but within reason and never to the extent of wasting anyone's time unnecessarily. Not that this is an excuse for inaction, should there be genuine reason to suspect something may be wrong.

'To recap, though, please tell your readers to remember the best things we can do to manage our well-being as we approach middle age also happen to be the least expensive. Again, they are: stretch, walk, breathing exercises – and when it comes to what you stuff in your mouth, imagine you live in Italy and try to eat what they might.'

But, Doc – red meat? You said that was OK earlier, an advantage nonetheless!

'Red meat's not the end of the world and does give us protein and energy. But as a more general rule, if you stick to what grows out of the ground or on a tree and combine it with things that move quickly or swim in the sea, this time next year you might even feel like Superman.'

So that's it, then.

'Pretty much.'

● ● ●

The meaning of midlife is getting midlife to what we want it to mean. It is here to help us realize that everything will only begin to make sense when we stop trying to make sense of everything. The gloriousness of being, finally ours for the taking.

It's been a long lesson but now it's jackpot time.

'Those were the days!' cry the living dead.

WELL, FUCK THEM!

'These *are* the days!'

And they're the best days we're ever going to get.

Main engine start.

I ain't hanging around for anyone.

Thus it transpired, after almost two years of reflection, projection, cogitation and discussion, that learning is never permanent, only temporary.

What I thought I knew about life I had forgotten, what I had yet to find out about life I was about to discover by looking in the wrong pools. Most importantly, what I really wanted from life had no room to breathe and therefore no capacity with which to shout out in my direction and halt my wandering focus.

The period before I met Natasha had become a sustained period of simplicity with regards to how I lived day to day. Sure, I owned a relatively substantial house in North London, but there was barely anything in it. Often there were more people than objects in it. A far preferable state of affairs to surrounding oneself with dust-collecting, inanimate 'stuff' of zero consequence, use or value. Books and glasses for wine and curtains to keep too-early morning light at bay – all perfectly permissible but little else surely. Yes, I'll allow a few beds and a table and sofa and a quartet of upright chairs, but other than the basics what more does a single man need? I mean really. I didn't even have a car at my disposal, something I almost completely forgot until the last gasps of writing this book.

Was I happy though? You bet. Delirious, no less. Over the moon. Ecstatic. Top of the world, or rather top of my world. Because, for the first time in a long time, my world was small enough for me to be on top of.

Since then, though, I had splurged again, more than ever before. Middle-aged spread of the worst kind. Materialistic. Like a fading old empire, ever more desperate to prove its worth by expanding further and further away from its centre. The very thing that made it what it is in the first place and held it together ever since. The more of everything else we have, the less of ourselves we are left with. Which is fine, if we're referring to other human beings, but when we are merely referring to stuff and nonsense, how can this ever be a good thing?

In a heartbeat, I'd forgotten everything I had read, breathed in, slept on, considered, been conflicted by and inspired by. And the most alarming factor of all? Not once had I remembered how much I had forgotten, in SEVEN YEARS. It was as if the part of my brain responsible had been lobotomized one night while I was asleep. What a thoroughly bizarre thing to happen, even though I'm sure it happens to most of us, most of the time.

This is why it helps, why it's essential to have a daily mantra of one type or another, to go back to, to make sure life isn't running away with us any more than we want it to. Whether it's a regular walk by the river, a gym session, running, meditation, prayer, a nightly conversation with our loved ones over dinner, a diary, a checklist – it really doesn't matter. As long as we have a daily Post-it note to remind ourselves of where we've come from, where we are and where we want to be and, most importantly of all, why we're doing any of it in the first place.

I suppose what I have been missing is not so much a mission statement but more of a 'mission accomplished' statement. Along with a 'maintain this mission' statement.

That's what this book and all the words within it and all the people I've met and learnt from and all the angst, revelation and resolution I've been confronted by on the way, has all been about. I knew there was something awry but I had no idea what it was. I was aware there was an itch but I didn't know where to scratch.

Phew. Thank goodness for fifty, otherwise I would have been flailing about until the end of my days.

Why some people dread their birthdays I find very difficult to understand. Apart from the transparent nonsense to do with vanity or the fact our passport says we're a year older. For me, from now on, I will use the passing of each of my own calendar years as an opportunity to take stock of how far I have travelled and developed in the last twelve months. I shall use that information as a guide to how I can be a better person for myself, and therefore everyone I am involved with and who has to put up with me, every day until I die.

As things stand right now, what I need to do is simple. I need to get back to the idyll where I was before I met Tash and introduce it to the idyll since I met Tash. The Recent Past + The Past = The Now.

• • •